Professional Care for the Elderly Mentally Ill

Edited by

Liz Matthew

Directorate Manager, Services to Older People with
Mental Health Problems,
Department of Psychiatry, Tameside and Glossop
Community and Priority Services NHS Trust

CHAPMAN & HALL

London · Glasgow · Weinheim · New York · Tokyo · Melbourne · Madras

Published by Chapman & Hall, 2–6 Boundary Row, London SE1 8HN, UK

Chapman & Hall, 2–6 Boundary Row, London SE1 8HN, UK

Blackie Academic & Professional, Wester Cleddens Road, Bishopbriggs, Glasgow G64 2NZ, UK

Chapman & Hall GmbH, Pappelallee 3, 69469 Weinheim, Germany

Chapman & Hall USA, 115 Fifth Avenue, New York NY 10003, USA

Chapman & Hall Japan, ITP-Japan, Kyowa Building, 3F, 2-2-1 Hirakawacho, Chiyoda-ku, Tokyo 102, Japan

Chapman & Hall Australia, 102 Dodds Street, South Melbourne, Victoria 3205, Australia

Chapman & Hall India, R. Seshadri, 32 Second Main Road, CIT East, Madras 600 035, India

Distributed in the USA and Canada by Singular Publishing Group Inc., 4284 41st Street, San Diego, California 92105

First edition 1996

© 1996 Chapman & Hall

Typeset in Times 10/12pt by Saxon Graphics Ltd, Derby
Printed in Great Britain by Clays Ltd, St Ives plc

ISBN 0 412 58990 7   1 56593 3273 (USA)

A catalogue record for this book is available from the British Library

Library of Congress Catalog Card Number: 95-074637

Professional Care for the Elderly Mentally Ill

Contents

Contributors

Carol Ainsworth DipCot, SROT
Carol is interested in exploring the benefits of using activities in therapy and is currently involved in designing balanced activity programmes in hospital settings. She has spent the last ten years working with older people who have mental health difficulties.

John Casson MA, RDth
A UKCP psychotherapist, John has worked as an NHS therapist in adult psychiatry since 1984. In his capacity as Arts Therapist Coordinator for Tameside and Glossop Community and Priority Services NHS Trust, he founded the Guide Bridge Theatre Project for people with long-term mental illness. He established Dramatherapy North West and is a founder member of the Institute of Dramatherapy. John is responsible for many innovations and developments in good practice, and has run training workshops in the UK, in former Yugoslavia and in India.

Deborah Cavanagh DipN, RMN
Deborah is at present a Discharge Coordinator with Tameside and Glossop Community and Priority Services NHS Trust, a role which involves the planning and coordination of discharge arrangements for patients with complex needs on general and psychiatric wards. The previous six years were spent working in acute psychiatry with patients under and over 65 years.

Laraine Chaisty RMN, RGN, BSc (Hons)
At present Laraine is a clinical nurse specialist. After qualifying she was employed as a social and recreational nurse for older people with long-term mental health problems. Her work with older people as a community psychiatric nurse gave Laraine a different perspective on care issues.

Anupreeta Kumar BA (Sociology)
Anupreeta is a postgraduate student in the Department of Community Studies, Manchester Metropolitan University. As a result of action-research experience gained while working on a development project for MIND, she helped to set up the Asian Community Mental Health Team for Tameside Social Services. She

has trained in counselling, psychodramatic approaches to practice and group psychotherapy, worked in a specialist mental health team, conducted training programmes, workshops and seminars, and has been advocate for ethnic issues at mental health conferences.

Liz Matthew MA, RMN, RGN, CPN Cert
Liz is Directorate Manager for Services to Older People with Mental Health Problems for Tameside and Glossop Community and Priority Services NHS Trust. She has trained in general and psychiatric nursing, maintains client contact by retaining a small community caseload and has experience in both in-patient and community clinical settings.

Bonnie Meekums MPhil
A leading dance movement therapist, Bonnie manages the arts therapies team for Tameside and Glossop Community and Priority Services NHS Trust. She has lectured in the UK and the USA, published widely, sits on the advisory board for 'The Arts in Psychotherapy' and maintains a varied clinical caseload. Bonnie is at present engaged in research into women's perceptions of arts therapy groups for adult survivors of child sexual abuse.

Carol Dawn Noble RMN
Carol is a manager in a day hospital. Most of her experience has been with older people, and mainly in continual care in a large psychiatric hospital, a district general hospital and in a community purpose-built modern unit.

Steve Pugh MA, BSocSc, CQSW
Steve is a team leader with Tameside, following post-qualifying experience with Trafford Social Services. He has worked primarily with older people and adheres firmly to anti-oppressive practice and the rights of service users. In common with all the contributors, Steve continues to learn and contribute to the learning of others, the major influences which have brought about these chapters.

Hazel Smith RDth
A registered dramatherapist and founder member of the Institute of Dramatherapy, Hazel has worked in the NHS at Tameside General Hospital for over ten years. She has carried out groupwork with the elderly and training sessions in assertiveness, reality orientation, grief transition, dramatherapy and introducing dramatherapy to nurses.

Bob Spall BSc (Psychology), MSc (Clinical Psychology)
Bob is a consultant clinical psychologist with the North Staffordshire Combined Healthcare NHS Trust and a member of the management committee and the personnel and professional purposes sub-committee of the Bereavement Care Centre, Hanley, Stoke-on-Trent. He is a recognized teacher in the Clinical

Psychology Department, Liverpool University, and has recently taught a mental health option for the MA course in Gerontology, University of Keele. His initial experience in the field of adult mental health led to specializing in work with older people. Bob gained experience of running grief therapy and transition groups with Hazel Smith, has conducted individual therapy for various forms of loss and has extensive experience in running workshops on coping with loss.

Elaine Stott DipCot, SROT
Elaine is a senior occupational therapist and a member of the Forest House team working with older persons with mental problems at the Royal Oldham Hospital. She is at present studying part-time for an MSc in applied psychology. At the time of writing, Elaine was working at Tameside General Hospital with older persons suffering from organic and functional disorders.

Andrew Yates BA (Hons), RMN, DipN (London), RNT
Andrew is a lecturer/practitioner at Tameside General Hospital and Manchester College of Midwifery and Nursing. His specialist area of practice is in the mental health/psychiatry of older age. Prior to taking up his present post, Andrew was a community psychiatric nurse with elderly services.

Introduction

Services to older people with mental health problems have gone through radical change in recent years. Legislation has had a profound effect by dictating how care to older people is delivered both within hospital and within the community.

The recent government agenda emphasizes cost effectiveness, value for money and accountability. This, too, is an important driving force in re-evaluating the service, although not everyone would agree with many of the proposed strategies and there are clearly different views as to the appropriateness of many of the services. One thing is certain, however – the move towards interdisciplinary working is here to stay.

Not all change has been led by legislation, and many innovations have been founded in the day-to-day practices in the care of older people with mental health problems.

A service, of course, does not become integrated merely by imposing joint-working on a number of professionally based disciplines, and in many ways this may not be desirable. At its worst it produces duplication, where people from different background are all doing the same job. This is not the intention of joint-working, instead it should attempt to improve the quality of service by a rich mix of skills and experience from a number of related disciplines.

Each discipline brings with it a uniqueness and philosophy based on particular experiences, which at its most effective provides a synergy which results in a value greater than the individual contributions. The key to effective management of such work is to harness these positive aspects and develop their potential. The intention of this book is to support this progress.

In looking at my own area of work, it soon became clear that there were a number of initiatives worth sharing with others. These were illustrations of good practice which could be applied in other areas. It is not my intention that the reader should slavishly accept these premises; they should view them critically and apply them when appropriate. I have tried to include examples from a variety of disciplines, which I think illustrate these points.

It is also common practice to work in isolated pockets where the quality and value of what is being done are not recognized by those involved until they read of a similar project elsewhere and exclaim, 'But we're doing that!'.

There can also be an adversarial aspect to working across different areas of professional work which engenders a culture of defensiveness. We can no longer afford to take this attitude. As health care workers we have a multiplicity of creative and valuable skills and these need to be used to their greatest effect.

We need to ensure the resources we already have are used in the most efficient, effective and economic way. Because we have come from different organizations we still tend to use our resources departmentally. We can no longer afford to do this. As joint-working increases the need for commonality, we will no longer able to expect an increase in resources.

In this book we have tried to recognize these problems and the challenge they provide.

The contributors have been selected because they are practitioners. They talk about the practical aspects of their work. They talk from their own background and experience. It is not their intention to provide theories of integration, but rather to illustrate how a particular individual has handled the situation, sometimes alone and sometimes in the context of joint-working.

An overview of the present scene shows a variety of good and bad practice. It shows the need for a new and more social perception of older people with mental health problems as well as a clear understanding of the processes involved in caring for them.

Laraine Chaisty begins by challenging the stereotypical view of being old and being mentally ill, and how we label individuals to fit our own perceptions and previously defined systems – how we try to fit square pegs in round holes. Although Laraine is a nurse, her views are of value to all people in this area of work, and this is demonstrated in the case studies she uses, which highlight the fact that by imposing our own standards and expectations we can deny individuals their basic rights.

This theme is pursued in the next chapter by Deborah Cavanagh who suggests a more positive approach to giving people a voice and the opportunity to be a partner in their own care. The recent changes to empower the user of the service force that responsibility on health care planners. Deborah stresses the need for a more proactive approach which puts emphasis on developing advocacy and empowerment as part of a more equitable partnership. She challenges the defensiveness of the 'professionals' and suggests a change in culture to meet the new challenges of genuine accountability, and highlights the particular implications of this for older people with mental health problems.

The implications for ensuring the ethical use of power are continued in Elaine Stott's discussion of the implications for assessment. The ethical issues surrounding decision making and the level to which it is informed are considered. The importance of a wide-ranging context is examined which takes on board the physical, social and mental as well as degenerative effects of ageing, and the importance of monitoring therapy as a guide to the appropriateness of assessment decisions. Elaine uses her experience as an occupational therapist to demonstrate a wealth of practical detail in this area.

Steve Pugh examines the process of risk and decision making. He looks first at the theoretical models of risk and risk assessment and then applies them to nursing practice, particularly those risks which affect older people with mental health problems. If risks are seen to be significant then decisions will have to be made, and Steve identifies models of decision making and links these to the more important issue of judgement.

The need for accuracy and accountability is examined, and a move towards flexibility rather than autonomy is advocated. The importance of these processes when linked to abuse is related, and its implications for working with other disciplines are examined, including the rights of individuals and their relationship to litigation.

Finally, Carol Noble looks at working practices rather than the clients directly. Carol uses an extended case study from her own experience as a nurse, but her experiences of working through a process of change have broader applications. The title of her chapter, 'From factory to free range', encapsulates the change in attitude to the care of older people with mental health problems from a task-based process to, hopefully, a more people-centred approach.

Having considered the context of care the next series of chapters looks at particular activities which are extending this role in areas that could be described as good practice.

Carol Ainsworth considers the factors which influence choice in deciding on activities to promote competence in the function and performance of life roles. Occupation, she argues, is a key function of human activity, and when there is a loss of such activity positive and appropriate therapy may be necessary. A close understanding of the client plus an understanding of the process of normal ageing will increase the effectiveness of such an intervention, as will an analysis of activities.

A particular model of therapeutic activity is the use of dance movement described by Bonnie Meekums. Bonnie describes the context and background with particular reference to older people with mental illness. Specific case studies illustrate particular themes, so that practical description is also put into a theoretical context.

Bob Spall and Hazel Smith take a particular situation, that of bereavement, and share some of their practical experiences with a group of older people. The selection process, group dynamics and their impact on individuals are examined in some detail, and consideration is given to the effectiveness of such groups and the value of examining issues together, in a particular mental health context.

Andrew Yates tackles the often ignored element of sexuality. He is particularly concerned about the rights of individuals to their own sexuality, particularly in institutionalized settings. He examines the myths around age and sexuality and the added stigma of mental illness, and suggests practical and positive ways of helping individuals understand their own sexuality and the sexuality of others.

The disadvantages of old age and mental illnesses are particularly disabling, but ignorance and misunderstanding are even more prevalent when the individual comes from a different cultural background. Anupreeta Kumar discusses this issue, with particular reference to the Asian community, covering problems such as lack of communication about treatment and its effects, the perception of health services by the community and reasons for their underuse. She also suggests that racism is a major factor in poor quality service delivery for Asian families, resulting from stereotypical views of Asian culture. Anupreeta suggests how older people should be targeted and highlights projects which have been successful as a source of good practice.

The future of the service depends on the creativity of the present service and what potential there is for translating vision into action. The final three chapters of the book take three distinct areas of development.

John Casson's view of the older person trapped in the constraints of mental illness takes a sensitive view of developing communication and understanding. His plea to listen sensitively rather than literally to the communication of those with mental illness is based on his view of a hidden, childlike quality within all of us that can be utilized through a variety of skills.

Steve Pugh's study of abuse highlights this problem. This area is now recognized as a growing challenge for all those involved with older people, particularly those with mental health problems. Steve concentrates on those living outside formal institutions but his observations can easily be applied to most caring situations. The definition of abuse can be far reaching, and include both mental and physical abuse. As well as examining the research, Steve considers some practical steps in preventing abuse which are capable of being used by others.

The final chapter is a consideration of the need for clear service planning. In this chapter I recognize from my own experience the lack of planning models in what has often been a neglected service. By using one model based on strategic planning, I have attempted to illustrate how the theory can be implemented in everyday management situations.

Finally, it is worth pointing out that all these studies are a 'snapshot' of some services delivered by people in different disciplines, sometimes working together, sometimes working alone, but all having a common theme of developing services which are trying to respond to need rather than professional considerations.

It is not my intention to promote good practice in my own authority as a definitive working model, but merely to give an insight into some of the work being attempted. If it inspires the reader to implement some of these suggestions, or even make public similar work carried on throughout the country, it will have achieved its objectives.

Square pegs in round holes: the social context of the lives of older people

Laraine Chaisty

Your birthday tells you when you were born not how old you are.

(Spokes Symonds, 1987)

One of the biggest myths about growing older is the assumption that everyone miraculously becomes old at the age of 65. When this time arrives we are made aware of it, by no longer paying full price for entry to cinemas (as long as we go when others do not). Our hair is cut on 'pensioner days', we are allowed cheaper bus travel if we go out when 'workers' have left for work and, if we are unfortunate enough to become ill, we are nursed in areas known as 'geriatric', 'long-stay' or 'rehab' units.

Within health care, this stereotyping may lead to the creation of services which are inappropriate, narrow or misdirected, so that sometimes older people are slotted like 'square pegs in round holes' into services which do not meet their needs.

There are many practical examples of such miscalculations. On one occasion a referral was made to the mental health team for assessment of an 80-year-old woman whose only 'mental health' problem, it transpired, was the fact that she could not meet an 81-year-old man! The thought of going to any of the local old people's clubs filled her with dread because, 'My dear, they are full of old people who have let themselves go!'. Her carers on the other hand could not understand this attitude in 'one so old' and, therefore, presumed that she must have some mental illness, hence the referral.

In contrast, another lady visited was more fortunate in that she lived near to an Education Centre which suited her requirements. At 75 years old she had been 'bullied' by her friend of 83 to go along for singing lessons. The reason for this was purely selfish on the part of her friend who had recently also taken up a new venture at the Centre, that of guitar playing, and she required a singer to accompany her!

Most older people visited by the mental health team report that they still feel like a 25-year-old inside an older person's body. In actuality this is not so, because they can provide us with the knowledge and experience that a 25-year-old cannot (that is if we allow them to).

> Once formed, the adult personality is unlikely to change radically, even in such pressing circumstances as retirement and impending death. In fact, personality is one of the prime determinants of how someone will react to such pressures. ...People with well-integrated personalities may have little difficulty 'mellowing out' in what they perceive to be the final stage of a successful life cycle. People with poorly integrated personalities may encounter the same event with despair and hostility, turning 'sour' in the last years of life.
>
> *(Schail and Willis, 1991, p. 299)*

What information do we glean from knowing that a person is 70 years old? That they have lived for 70 years is an obvious answer and this knowledge will, in itself, conjure up for us an image of that person. It does not tell us their social or economic situation, their physical or mental health status, their hopes and aspirations or their motivation to change.

> I fancy almost everybody who draws near to the beginning of their seventieth year must be struck by the oddity of the fact that inside their own skull they are aware of so little difference! I have a notion that elderly people have a tendency to forget the fanciful misconceptions about old age that they had when they were young.
>
> *(Powys, 1987)*

A number of assumptions about ageing and the effect it has on people are prevalent in our society and are sometime perpetuated in the media. Generally it is believed that older people suffer a gradual deterioration in both physical and mental health and that age leads to personality changes, often with older people becoming fixed and rigid in their views. Old age is not a disease in itself, yet it is often viewed by society as such. Smith (1990), himself a general practitioner (GP), asks that we reflect on the message: 'Older people are not ill because they are old, they are ill because there is something wrong with them'.

This raises the importance of assessment. As health care professionals we must be clear about how and why we assess, what we are assessing and what we can offer following our assessment. The mental health team at Tameside offers a comprehensive assessment process delivered through the care programme approach model. This is designed to consider every aspect of the person's life, and includes past life events, cultural influences, social, political and economic details as well as the health or ill-health of the person assessed. Without a solid baseline from which to start to work with people, we will be unable to really know the context of our patients' lives.

If we have no starting point, we may be unaware that the 'odd behaviour' observed by carers is nothing more than the person's normal pattern of living – one person who was out of bed wandering around all night and asleep all day had been a night shift worker. The old adage 'You can't change the habits of a lifetime' seems to apply in this instance, but many hours and much energy are often spent by professionals in doing just that.

Referrals are sometimes received for mental health assessment which, when investigated, are no more than the clients exerting their rights and expressing their opinions. It would seem that once you reach 'old age' you are no longer allowed to be bad tempered, express an opinion or disagree, and it is an assumption to believe that older people suddenly become inflexible purely by virtue of age, whereas in reality:

> An imaginative young person becomes an imaginative old person, a sociable young person becomes a sociable old person and so forth. In the few instances of age-related change that seem to occur, the changes are slight and the differences amongst the individuals of the same age are greater than the differences between age groups.
>
> *(Perlmutter and Hall, 1985, p. 273)*

OLD AND GRUMPY?

It may be useful to illustrate this above point by a case study example of an elderly man who was referred for assessment primarily because he expressed an opinion and demanded his rights and a voice within the residential home of which he was a resident. As is shown, this man had in no way changed in personality or in 'mental health' in old age from the man he had been in his youth.

Care profile

> Fred was an 82-year-old man who was referred to the mental health team for assessment by a local residential home. The referral stated that he was displaying 'attention-seeking behaviour', was verbally abusive to staff and other residents and would not have a bath!

At assessment: summary

Fred was in agreement to talk with myself and he quickly took me to his bedroom, which he showed me with pride, so we could talk in privacy. Fred had lived in the same locality all his life, but had moved to live in the residential home recently following the death of his wife some six months ago. The move had happened quickly with little consultation with Fred. His family were concerned around Fred's well-being as they did not believe Fred to be capable of caring for himself.

This was something Fred stated he resented: 'They didn't allow me to try'. He admitted that since his wife had died he had started drinking more alcohol and was neglecting himself somewhat, but he felt it was his life and that he should be able to choose what to do for himself. He also has recurrent bronchitis and the staff, therefore, felt it necessary to restrict his intake of cigarettes. He stated that he had always enjoyed a drink and a cigarette and as his local was just a short distance from the home why shouldn't he go out just when he wanted?

Fred would go to any lengths to get extra cigarettes and he told me of his latest plan. As a keen gardener Fred had been allocated the task of tending the greenhouse tomatoes and his hard work had paid off with a bumper crop of tomatoes. These he had promptly sold to unsuspecting visitors, pocketed the money and funded his cigarettes with this. Whilst this seemed to me a touch of ingenuity, the staff members viewed it in a different way and had informed his son who had taken a strong stance with his father. His son, although very caring, believed his father incapable of deciding for himself how many ciga-rettes he could have in a day. He, therefore, set limits (and funds) on his father's cigarette intake and gave 'permission' for the staff to do likewise. It seemed to some degree that Fred's son had taken over the 'parenting role' and he would often reprimand his father if he did not 'behave'. Some of Fred's anxiety also appeared to be centred around the fact that the residential home may not tolerate his behaviour and may ask him to leave, with the subsequent difficulties this would create for his son.

Fred also believed that as he was paying for being in the home, he should be able to say and do as he wished, and he added, 'I used to be a works manager, I had lots of girls working for me and I was the boss. I'm not going to let these young girls boss me around'.

It must be said that the staff had tried very hard to work with and accommo-date Fred, but sometimes the needs of the 'institution' override the needs of the individual and that left the staff with mixed feelings about how to handle Fred's behaviour.

Some members of staff, therefore, felt that it was the correct thing to do to limit Fred's cigarettes because they saw this as their caring role and saw non-intervention as neglect. Other staff felt that Fred was able to make up his own mind and should be allowed to do so. This was also the case if Fred wished to go out unaccompanied. Whereas some staff had no problems complying with Fred's wishes, others were not prepared to take the risks involved in allowing Fred out alone, partly because of a perceived danger to himself and partly because of the reflection on the home's 'caring'. Fred appeared to believe that this was a 'war' and each day was a 'battle' to be fought and won.

From the information above, we could deduce many possible reasons for Fred's behaviour:

- he had recently lost his wife and perhaps had not fully grieved his loss;
- he had lost his home with the extra losses of security, status and role that this brings;
- he was no longer in control of his own life and destiny;
- he felt constrained by the rules and boundaries imposed on him within the home (rules and boundaries, it must be said, he was not yet fully aware of);
- he had suffered some 'role reversal', especially between himself and his son, but to some degree also between himself and the staff;
- he was no longer 'in charge' as in the past, but was being told what to do by others.

If we add to this Fred's beliefs about women's place in society, i.e. controlled by men, and that he should be entitled 'to get what he pays for', is it any wonder that this situation had arisen? As stated previously, it seems that older people cannot assert themselves without someone assuming that there must be something wrong with them either physically or mentally.

The situation was finally resolved after several meetings between Fred, the staff and his son where issues were raised and negotiated. Staff were able to discuss their fears at these meetings about allowing Fred to go out alone or smoking as many cigarettes as he liked. Fred and his son accepted the staff's point of view, but stated that they were both prepared to take the risks as they perceived them to be reasonable. Fred agreed to smoke up to a maximum of ten cigarettes per day (previously the staff had limited them to five per day).

It was agreed that Fred had much to offer to the residential home, and plans were made to encourage Fred to participate in the life there. He was encouraged to continue with his hobby, gardening, and was enabled to organize some social evenings for the other residents where he would play a leading part as a pianist. Fred felt 'in control' again, the staff began to understand Fred 'as a person' and his son actively and successfully reduced his parental influence over his father. Fred's 'attention-seeking' behaviour reduced, and he now channels most of his energy into the residents committee of which he is chairperson!

FIXED IN THEIR WAYS?

In addition to the idea that we should lose our rights to choice as older people is the myth that somehow our personalities change as we grow older. In order to challenge and question our beliefs a teaching session for students was planned around this issue.

Teaching session

Do we believe that our personalities will alter as we get older and what would we like to remember and be remembered for? These were questions posed to groups of student nurses who were working with older people in mental health placements. During teaching sessions they were asked to examine their attitudes and beliefs about older people and to explore their feelings about growing older themselves. The medium chosen for this work was 'mask work'.

Exercise

Each student was provided with a blank mask on which they were to create an image of themselves as they became older. A variety of different coloured masks were used and a wide range of materials such as paints, jewellery, material, fur and wool was made available. The purpose of providing a variety of colours and mediums was to enable the students to express an honest opinion, either negative or positive, about the experience. This may have been better represented in dark, dismal colours and mediums rather than bright colours and soft fabrics. Whilst the masks were under preparation, the students were asked to consider several questions.

- What is good about being the age you are now (i.e. as an older person)?
- What is difficult for you?
- How should it be for you when you are old?
- How would you like people to act with this older self?
- What do you want people to remember about you?

Although there was much chit-chat and fun during the mask making, when giving feedback to the group about their images it became clear that the students had gained an insight into images of old age.

The suggestion made by the majority of the students was that they could not envisage any changes in their personality when they became older from what they perceive themselves to be now. Comments like 'I'll be the same then as now', 'I'll still want to go to the pub, be with friends, have a laugh, dress up' abounded, and any suggestion of changes in personality because of age were strongly resisted.

It was also interesting to note that during the discussion the question of health status in old age was often passed over quickly with brief comments made such as, 'I hope I'll stay well; be able to look after myself; be active; not be dependent upon anyone', and these appeared paramount requirements to a happy old age.

Financial status was often ignored and did not appear to be the focus or requirement for independence. This may be explained by the group being composed of students who have not as yet encountered financial stability and, therefore, no losses.

The students also voiced the opinion that they would wish to be treated with respect and valued as productive members of society for the skills, wisdom, knowledge and contribution they had made throughout their lives. Often the students stated that their image of old age was influenced by important figures in their own lives, such as grandparents, parents, aunts and uncles who had been positive role models for them.

This exercise illustrated, at the time, that the students had generally adopted positive attitudes to older people, yet this is often not observed to be the case when we enter into the world of 'elder care'. Here it seems people become more like 'products' needing to be 'maintained', that must be fed, watered and clothed to be passed along the 'production line of care' which is never ending and unfulfilling.

Why then do we lose sight of the person as a person? One answer tentatively posed here is that we may lose sight of the person as a human being because (especially with people suffering with dementia) we have no past history of their lives and present knowledge of the person to focus on.

PERSONAL PROFILING

Case studies

Staff caring for one woman with dementia understood her seemingly obsessional behaviour of constantly changing her clothes many times a day because they were aware that in her youth she was a fashion buyer in a large Manchester store. She frequently assisted the models to change their clothing and clothes were her life. One day she went missing, but was ultimately found sitting inside a large wardrobe, indeed she had gone to sleep because she felt safe and comfortable in there. This behaviour would have appeared very odd to those who did not know her past history.

Another man constantly paced the wards and it was difficult to find any way of diverting some of his energy until it was discovered that in his youth he had been a professional footballer. Many pleasurable hours were subsequently spent kicking, throwing or even heading a football around the ward to either the delight or annoyance of the other residents!

Often staff working on wards carry vast amounts of information about the person they are caring for 'in their heads', but this is never committed to paper and, as a consequence, if they leave or move area this valuable information goes with them and is lost. How useful it would be if staff, along with the person and their carers, could build up a 'profile', both in words and pictures, of that person's past life, loves and losses. Perhaps we need to reflect here if we, too, would want our lives now as husbands, wives, partners, friends, employees or lovers to be forgotten or ignored by others if we lose the ability to tell others about ourselves.

Mills and Chapman (1992) advocate the use of a social history form, particularly when working with people with dementia. They believe that it is essential to see the person behind the illness, and that the collection of relevant past life information would be a valuable tool to increase communication with and understanding about the person. As someone who has worked on wards with individuals and groups of severely impaired people, I would have found this invaluable as a starting point for any conversation or activity planned.

WHY GROUPWORK WITH OLDER PEOPLE?

One myth prevalent about older people is that they are unable to learn anything new and are, therefore, unable to initiate any changes in their lives. Another is that severely demented people are, by virtue of their illness, unable to take part in any group activities. A suggestion here would be that it is necessary to find the 'key' to unlock the 'lock', i.e. to discover that person's past interests in order to work with them, and that it is our role as nurses to do just that.

Groupwork

When I worked as a social and recreational nurse on the continuing care wards, most therapeutic work with people suffering from dementia was undertaken in small intimate groups. It soon became evident that the optimal number was four residents to two members of staff and that larger groups were ineffective. It was important that outside distraction and stimulation be reduced to a minimum, so a small room off the ward area was chosen in which to meet. Each group started with a cup of tea and biscuit, as it was found this encouraged people to stay and increased social contact and stimulation. Indeed, this cup of tea was obviously important to one man whose memory recall was very poor, since on one occasion he remarked on entering the ward, 'Here comes the tea lady'.

Each group was planned prior to its commencement, but flexibility was allowed within the group as the conversation often strayed from the planned topic. This was not seen in a negative way by the group leaders who were aware, especially with people with a poor concentration span, that this would, on occasion, happen. As in the planning stage of the dance movement therapy group, cues were taken from the people in the groups and issues which were important to them at that time were explored.

Working from the premise that a group can be planned around the interests and past lives of the group members, it was decided to hold a men's group, focusing on their past working lives. We had discovered that our residents responded better if we brought in 'concrete' objects to the group that they could touch, smell, taste, see or hear. A man in the group had been a joiner in his youth and we thought to use this knowledge to our advantage. Generally this man was very quiet in groups, often going to sleep or getting up to leave early. He had an exceedingly poor concentration span and memory and was very deaf. For this group we had provided a variety of old wood working tools which we passed around for examination and comments. Quite spontaneously this usually quiet man became animated, was able to name the tools and, either by words or actions, to describe their uses. Indeed we had trouble separating him from the sandpaper before he had removed most of the varnish from the chair arms!

In this instance for a short space of time he was able to contribute fully to the group and pass on the valuable knowledge he had learned in his youth. Another benefit was that staff co-working in the group viewed that person differently, which may improve the interaction and subsequently the care that person receives in the future. This refers back to the notion of 'viewing people as people' and not as 'products to be serviced'. Staff become aware that even more severely demented people who, they often believe, cannot do anything for themselves, have something to offer.

Outings are also often good 'teaching sessions' for staff as well as of enormous benefit to the residents. Staff have often remarked how appropriate someone's behaviour is when out in a restaurant or propping up the bar of the local pub. It may, therefore, be useful for us to reflect whether the hospital situation creates some of the behaviour witnessed on the wards if a change in behaviour is observed when people are taken into a 'normal environment'.

Another example to consider was a small group of women who, after a discussion around baking and housework, eagerly set to and were able, with minimal assistance, to make pastry and cakes. These women had been making pastry and cakes for the past 60 to 70 years (most were 80 plus), and had certainly not forgotten how to work in a kitchen or how to be bossy with any nurse who tried to interfere!

Choosing the right intervention often depends on the client's abilities, degree of insight and presentation and it is important that we take into consideration how the therapy may need to be adjusted to take account of these difficulties. Wattis and Church (1986) highlight some of the factors which need to be considered when working with older people in groups:

- less abstract, interpretive approach
- compensate for reduction in memory for meaning
- flexible session length (client comfort)
- flexibility of session location
- time limited contact
- explicit, concrete realistic goals
- awareness of real social and physical limitations
- provision of formal social resources and support
- interpersonal context of problem ('family' or 'institutional')
- active rather than passive therapist
- awareness of age contrast in goal setting and empathy
- absence of ageism in therapist
- awareness of drug effects in older people
- assessment of physical factors which may exacerbate 'psychological' problems.

It requires a great deal of skill and expertise to be an effective therapist working with older people, yet the area of elderly care is often seen as less attractive and rewarding than other 'high-tech' areas.

'PROFILING' LANGUAGE

Whilst forming the social profile of the person, we must also be aware of some of the different language/dialects or sayings which all of us use and how this may be interpreted by us within assessment. The following example may illustrate this point.

Care profile

An 80-year-old woman was being discussed by her GP with a member of the mental health team. The GP was anxious to convey to the community psychiatric nurse (CPN) that the lady was extremely deluded as she believed she had a road running through her body. When assessed, indeed the woman did say she 'couldn't get a road through her', which in the north-west of England means she was constipated and was having great difficulty going to the toilet!

It is, therefore, very important that we are aware of as much information as possible about someone in order to be effective workers with that person. Our aim as professionals should be to build on people's strengths and to utilize these to help them to overcome their own difficulties. We must also be aware of our own preconceived ideas (myths, stereotypes) which we, too, have formulated in our own minds.

A CHANGE OF ATTITUDE

Whilst working with older people, my own attitudes and ideas have changed, developed and been re-evaluated. Myths such as older people being easily embarrassed, less creative, less willing to 'have a go' or express an opinion have all been challenged within my work area. To illustrate each point above it is necessary to describe several groups I have had the privilege to work with.

The women's group

This group evolved naturally from a conversation group which took place in the local day hospital. Although not a 'closed group', it soon became apparent that the same people were attending the group and that these were all women. A decision was taken by all concerned that a women's group would be beneficial and topics of interest were considered. Issues around being women and the changes they had seen during their lives were explored. 'Women's Lib', women's health and health care treatment and what it meant to be an older woman were discussed. The nature of some of the topics was sensitive and personal and a sense of closeness and trust grew within the group. It was very enlightening to discuss how 'strong' these women had been, often in the face of great hardship.

As the group progressed, a suggestion was made by myself that perhaps we could try some simple 'body work' in the form of massage at the next session. My perception (and stereotype) had been that perhaps these women would be embarrassed or threatened by such a suggestion, and I therefore decided that the sessions should be a simple hand massage which would be non-threatening and non-embarrassing to the women. The following week I provided a set of towels, oils, soothing music and various helpers, but I was soon made aware that these women were neither embarrassed nor afraid, as blouses, stockings and other clothing were soon removed, followed by requests for back, shoulder and leg massages. A relaxing, caring time was had by all.

After the group massage we talked about the feelings these women had experienced in the group. The women, many of whom were widows, described how good it had felt to be touched and how this was so sadly missing from their lives. They stressed how the occasional embrace they received from the day hospital staff was so appreciated and was often the only person-contact they had. They described how they missed their husbands, family and friends, not only in an emotional sense but also in a purely physical sense, and this challenges the assumption sometimes made by society that 'after 40 years you are past it!' To them, massage was a totally natural occurrence, as they had been reared in the age when 'rubbing' was the norm and that it was my 'hang-up' or 'professionalization' of massage which was the problem.

The dance movement therapy group

I also had the privilege of being a co-therapist at a dance movement group with older people (see Chapter 7). The image of older people which I carried in my head at that time was that they tended to be less creative and worked more with concrete rather than abstract concepts. This myth was soon dispelled by work I saw undertaken in the group.

One session involved the members choosing imaginary clothing from a rail and parading down the room to the claps and cheers of the other members. The imagination and creativity expressed there was a joy to behold. One woman chose a backless dress in which to get a good suntan, another a glamorous evening dress for a special night out. The movements of the women also reflected the mood of the moment and the cheers they received from the group heightened the mood. On another occasion the members mimed picking fruit from a tree. This 'fruit' signified something they wanted for themselves and something they could share with other members of the group. 'Fruits' such as happiness, peace, love were 'picked' from the trees and were shared with others in total commitment to the exercise.

The two above examples demonstrated to me that older people can be truly creative in the way they work with others and themselves, and that abstract concepts are not only for the young.

Confidence-building group

This group discussed issues around growing older and how they were treated by society. The focus was to consider strategies to enable members to be more assertive and confident in their personal lives, as the group identified that somehow getting older robbed them of these abilities.

It was felt by most people that retirement had had a negative effect on their lives and that perhaps they had not prepared for this event adequately. From this we considered each person's day and each member suggested ways of improving this. By using 'fantasy' each person described how they would like their lives to be 'if they had a magic wand', and it seemed that most people wanted mainly the same things, i.e. someone to share their lives with, to be listened to, taken seriously and respected. We then enlarged on these ideas by asking each person to imagine they were an animal and to then tell the other group members why they had chosen to be this animal. Examples:

> Cat – likes to be cuddled, is loved and needed
> Dog – same as above
> Horse – sleek, proud, fast
> Cow – useful, likeable, reliable.

In order to restore confidence, we aimed to improve the group members' self-esteem by praising them and by examining how they 'treated' themselves when at home. It was interesting how each client identified a lack of self-praise and treating themselves when at home; somehow the process of caring for themselves had stopped. No one thought to buy themselves flowers, books, chocolates, etc. any more. Only everyday articles were ever purchased and this was not dependent on financial considerations.

After several sessions this situation had favourably altered, with some of the women in particular having consciously tried to change their homes into what they described as 'their havens'. This 'inward caring' also had an effect outwardly in that several women started to take more pride in their appearance, with new hairdos, make-up and clothing. It was as though they had to be 'given permission' to be themselves.

CONCLUSION

It is hoped that by sharing some of the thoughts and ideas expressed in this chapter the reader may take some time to reflect on some of the myths which are still around today in the care of older people. It is important we do this, Jeanette Longfield (1984) believes, for three reasons:

- Myths set people against each other.
  If we believe older people 'change' in some way by virtue of growing older, it is easier to have no sympathy for them or their problems. They become the 'scapegoats' and 'not like us' when, in fact, 'they' **are** or **will be** us.
- Myths are an excuse for doing nothing.
  It would be easier to believe that older people cannot or will not change or that there is nothing we can offer to them. In that case we may as well give up now.
- Myths get in the way of solving problems.
  If half truths and prejudices cloud our understanding of problems, then how can we hope to solve them?

Working with older people has come a long way since the author first started in nursing, but the improvements are slow and minute. Let us hope that, like a snowball rolling down a hill, once started it grows and grows, gathers speed and cannot be stopped.

REFERENCES

Longfield, J. (1984) *Ask The Family. Shattering the Myths About Family Life*, Bedford Square Press, London.

Mills, M. and Chapman, I. (1992) Understanding the story. *Nursing the Elderly*, **4** (6), 27–30.

Perlmutter, M. and Hall, E. (1985) *Adult Development and Ageing*, Wiley & Son, New York.

Powys, J.C. (1987) The art of growing old, in *Celebrating Age – An Anthology*, (ed. A. Spokes Symonds), Age Concern, Surrey.

Schail, K.W. and Willis, S.L. (1991) *Adult Development in Ageing*, 3rd edn, Harper Collins, New York.

Smith, R. (1990) Distinguishing medical characteristics of old age (conference paper), in *Understanding Older People*, Age Concern, Scotland.

Spokes Symonds, A. (ed.) (1987) *Celebrating Age – An Anthology*, Age Concern, Surrey.

Wattis, J. and Church, M. (1986) *Practical Psychiatry of Old Age*, Croom Helm, London.

FURTHER READING

Gunter, L.M. (1971) Students' attitudes towards geriatric nursing. *Nursing Outlook*, **19**, 466–9.

Palmore, E. (1982) Attitudes towards the aged. What we know and need to know. *Research on Ageing*, **4** (3), 333–48.

Seers, C. (1986) Talking to the elderly and its relevance to care. *Nursing Times*, Occasional Paper, **82** (1), 51–4.

Advocacy, empowerment and carers

2

Deborah Cavanagh

Advocacy, empowerment and carer involvement have increasingly become a focus for professional staff in the development and delivery of services.

THREE THEMES FOR THE FUTURE

These three themes need to be an integral part of all service provision and planning. To be able to incorporate this effectively, current beliefs and practices need to be challenged. The commitment to the development of advocacy initiatives and empowerment is one that is becoming more obvious throughout social and health services. The challenge is not only to the organization but also to the individual practitioner. Developing strategies and the resulting policy and procedural changes can affect how a service is delivered and in what manner it is received.

Developments in the care of older people and the emphasis on increasing involvement of service users has already started to affect organizational planning. On an ongoing basis it is likely to affect the development and education of staff groups. One way of achieving this is to involve service users and carers in staff education programmes and presentations, an increasingly common occurrence.

With the implementation of the Health and Community Care Act, it is not only staff delivering direct care but also the managers of the service who are concerned about advocacy, empowerment and carer issues. These are no longer theories but real issues to be dealt with in a constructive manner. Many more health and social services departments are working together to achieve coordinated services to meet the identified needs of the user population. Many older people who are involved with the mental health services are also involved with social services.

The encouragement of joint-working through legislation (i.e. National Health and Community Care Act) can produce many positive effects for the person using both services: less duplication of information; coordinated services; knowing who is accountable; and increased communication between disciplines. If done properly, this should reduce the frustrations of service users and carers when dealing with a number of different professionals from different agencies at a time when they are likely to feel vulnerable and powerless. To shift the locus of control to the service users, effective planning, education and development strategies need to be put in place.

The words 'advocacy' and 'empowerment' need to become increasingly common language throughout the whole of the caring community. Mental health service providers are now finding that the empowerment of service users in the delivery of their own care is not just desirable but essential. Wright (1992) spoke of working with people and their carers as partners in care, of sharing the responsibility for caring. It is becoming more common for professionals to regard themselves as having an advocacy role when involved with service users, particularly when caring for those detained under the Mental Health Act. Unfortunately, few staff have had any formal training or education to prepare them adequately for this role.

All too often professionals working in mental health have avoided committing themselves to user involvement (Bell, 1988). Often users of the service who are involved with advocacy groups are labelled as 'non-representative' of the majority of mentally distressed patients. This is just one way in which the opinions and contributions of service users and carers have been ignored and power retained by the professionals.

It is now becoming harder for the issue of user involvement to be ignored. Professional staff involved in service provision should be in the forefront of facilitating these changes.

EMPOWERMENT

Professional charters and codes make it clear that the practitioner's duty is to deliver the highest possible standard of care. Dyer and Block (1987) state that this can only be done through a partnership with the person and not a paternal relationship.

An important part of the partnership is the shifting of power from the professionals towards the users of the service. The current dictatorial atmosphere in which care is prescribed leads to many mentally distressed people feeling oppressed. Where carers or relatives see themselves as acting on behalf of the person, the feeling that they have deliberately been kept in the dark is common. This is not unique to carers and users of psychiatric services, but is also a commonly expressed feeling of users of other general health services. However, for users of social services there has been an increasing emphasis over recent years on consultation and user participation in the planning of services. At a more individual level, these service users are more likely to play an active part in the planning of their own care and participate in decision making.

In the health services there has been a traditional reluctance to allow patients access to information. Within health care, nurses have been dominant in numbers and have, therefore, greatly influenced philosophies of care.

There are many prejudices held by nursing staff which have been allowed to become part of the 'culture' of psychiatric care. For instance, once diagnosed as suffering from a 'mental illness', if a patient refuses to cooperate with the prescribed treatment regime, this could be interpreted as irrational. Empathy may often only be exercised by the nurse when giving consideration to patients' feelings and not their situation. Patients' refusal to accept a treatment regime could be a main consideration for initiating the implementation of the Mental Health Act, rather than patients' perceived level of danger to themselves or others. Despite the assumed role of the nurse to act as the patient's advocate, few actually see this as an active role. Some nurses will encourage a patient to appeal to the Mental Health Review Tribunal, and assist in this. However, few will exercise their role as advocate to the extent of registering their own complaint to the Commission if they feel the patient has justifiable objections to their prescribed care.

These ethical issues are among those considered by approved social workers (ASWs) involved in implementing the Mental Health Act. It is perhaps reflected in this role that social workers receive specialist training and nurses often do not. The approved social worker, by virtue of status and training, acts in an autonomous manner, able to evaluate the circumstances objectively and present conclusions, either to implement the Act or not. However, this is not a role which the nurse could perform and then go on to treat the patient and enforce the Act on a day-to-day basis

The historical picture of psychiatric services oppressing patients and professionals who pursue their own interests (Brandon 1991) needs to be erased. Often the perpetuation of this image is due to the fear and prejudice of those who used the services over two decades ago and the general public who draw much of their knowledge from sensationalist stories in the media. The specific client group which is being considered here, i.e. older people, are, in fact, those most likely to have had contact, either directly or indirectly, with this oppressive system. Many of their memories, not just of how people were treated but also of the buildings of the hospital, will be easily recalled and recounted. Memories of the 'workhouse' and people who were locked away will often be in mind. Mental health services, as this client group knows them, would have existed to hide people away and not to treat them and enable them to return to their own home.

ADVOCACY

Feelings of oppression are felt by patients and carers alike as all are service users. However, what may be apparent is that carers are encouraged to be part of the professional relationship, persuading the service user to comply with a care package, thereby encouraging them to be partners in a relationship which may exclude the patient. This can place vulnerable people at risk of exploitation; only they can say who is the best person to act on their behalf. Common practice should be to ask the service user whom they wish to represent or support them, acting as their advocate.

In all areas of health and social services people should be asked on initial assessment who is their nominated advocate. With this may come the role of educator, explaining the role of advocates and advocacy in organization. The use of independent advocates is becoming increasingly common in psychiatric units, but many hospitals fall short of allowing the advocates a hospital base. Some services (both health and social) employ a professional member of the staff to facilitate the education of staff, patients and relatives with regard to advocacy issues. This can only be a good thing, providing the actual role of patient advocate is not assumed.

Nurses as advocates

The ability of nurses to act as a patient's advocate is debatable (Allcock 1989; Jennings 1991). There are many instances where the nurse is required to carry out professional responsibilities which would present a conflict for the nurse/advocate role: the administration of medication, assistance in the ECT procedure, as well as providing a professional opinion as to the patient's mental state. It is not surprising that patients find it difficult to accept the suitability of nurses to act as their advocates. Psychiatry is still based on the medical model: patients are treated according to their diagnosis, their own feelings and opinions listened to but largely not taken into account. An active multi-disciplinary education programme can help to shift this emphasis.

The obvious conflict between the expectations of the nurse's role and that of advocate is not always as apparent for other professional staff. The unique contribution to the treatment package by nurses, which is offered to the patient and their carers, should enable them to assert their own identity within the multi-disciplinary team. However, it may take some time before the patient views nurses as acting independently from the medical staff. Social workers, psychologists and other paramedical staff do not apper to suffer as much from those prejudices. Much of this is due to the fact that these porfessional staff visit on a sessional basis, are not as closely linked with the medical regime and can clearly identify their unique contribution to a treatment package. Nursing staff, through professional development and training, are working towards this. It must be recognized that the nurse's part in the treatment package delivered potentially presents them with more conflict in their professional role.

Other disciplines are not as directly linked with this perception of the oppressive treatment regime. Social workers, occupational therapists, physiotherapists are more easily identified with their own unique contribution to patient care. Being 'more independent' may assist the service user in seeing them as more impartial than nursing staff. The facilitation of this view and the increasing tendency for nursing staff to be more autonomous within the multi-disciplinary team will assist in breaking down the forceful power base presented to service users.

Professional staff need to draw on their own experience and support networks to develop a consistent approach throughout their own clinical team. To have any credibility with the patients, their carers and other professionals this is essential. A way of achieving this consistent approach is through the use of clinical supervision: the leader of the team can help staff focus on good practices and assist them to reach their own objectives in clinical practice.

Self-advocacy

Due to the conflicts arising between the role of service provider and advocate, the user movement encourages self-advocacy or collective self-advocacy. It is felt that self-advocacy (groups of individuals raising issues and concerns they have collectively identified) is the best form of advocacy (Lawson, 1991)

The facilitation of advocacy groups needs to be carried out by a service which is fully committed to user empowerment. There is no point in supporting people in self-advocacy groups and not empowering them in some way to make changes and contribute to the team. Although staff should play a large part in the facilitation of advocacy groups by offering encouragement and support, it must be the service users themselves who set the agenda for change (Wallcraft, 1992). Staff need to reflect a positive attitude when discussing advocacy and related issues. Service users and their carers will want to feel that their contributions are valued or they will soon become disillusioned and obstructive if they sense that the advocacy group is purely a token.

Staff can support advocacy projects by providing information, informal advice regarding contacts in the hospital and community as well as a venue for meetings. Staff will be naturally curious about the contents of meetings, but it must be stressed that they do not have the right to know what issues are discussed unless this information is volunteered. Medical staff may tend to see the empowerment of patients and carers as a challenge to their power base in the multi-disciplinary team. If other staff are enthusiastic and positive in their outlook, it would be hoped that service users will see these staff as actively promoting and working towards user participation and independent advocacy.

Independent advocates

The overwhelming feeling is that only independent advocates can represent the mentally distressed (Brandon, 1991). Independent advocates are not new to the health service; ombudsmen have been well publicized and utilized for many years. However, the promotion of independent advocacy services and according them status within the social and health care system are much needed.

It is not only the views of users and the public that practitioners have to take into account, but also those of fellow professionals. For instance, medical staff all too often are not keen on their patients holding all the facts regarding interventions and planned treatment. Managers are also not always receptive to the idea of a shift in the balance of power. This is particularly apparent in health care, and may be due to the current climate of insecurity in the NHS or perhaps because managers have little or no contact with service users (Croft and Beresford, 1988).

Social services managers, however, have had to incorporate this initiative. It is important to emphasize to service users and carers who involve themselves in advocacy projects that their contributions will be valued. Lindow (1990) states that many service users find it difficult to realize that their own thoughts and actions are valid and could make a difference. It is possible for professional staff to influence the system from the inside by supporting patients in speaking for themselves, raising the consciousness of colleagues, challenging bad practice and encouraging user involvement (Bell, 1988).

Bell (1988) identifies five main areas which practitioners need to focus on when considering this change in emphasis of their role:

- language and labelling
- information
- choice
- accessibility
- accountability.

All these points are consistent with the National Charter standards, Patient's Charter and codes of professional conduct. These five main areas highlighted are a good focus for a clinical team when they are considering increasing both user and professional awareness.

It is not just the group labelled 'mental patients' who have traditionally found barriers to participating fully in the prescription and delivery of their own care. Croft and Beresford (1992) point out that participation has never been a particularly strong theme when challenging exclusions faced by women, black people and other minority groups. Specific initiatives need to be taken to ensure that such groups are involved and encouraging the empowerment of service users through the facilitation and support of advocacy projects is one such way.

One group of consumers who are becoming an increasingly higher proportion of the population are those people over 65 years of age. People in this group who are suffering with a degenerative organic illness will rely almost solely on others to represent their needs and views adequately. Currently, carers and voluntary organizations perform this function. However, with the Government's initiative to transfer the care of long stay patients to the private sector this informal arrangement may need to be formalized. This particularly vulnerable group of people will require representation both in their own residences and in a more public forum, where their views and those of their carers can be taken note of and acted upon.

Many health and social services have acted together to begin addressing this issue. With the increasing number of older people being cared for in residential and nursing homes, some areas have joint registration and inspection units. Advocacy initiatives for those people in homes who do not have visitors or advocates are being addressed. Formal procedures for contacting an advocacy group need to be put into place to ensure that the people using the service have 'a voice'. It is important that policies are put into place as many of this client group will be unable to refer themselves. This is an issue that joint mental and social services groups could address by involving independent home owners, service users and carers, as well as organizations such as Age Concern. In this way feedback can be gained from those experiencing the service that could affect future provision. Instead of being provider-led, services can be increasingly consumer-led.

It is obvious from research that people (both patients and carers) want to be more involved and want to have more say (Croft and Beresford, 1992). Patients and clients want to influence service provision, decisions and outcomes, alter the balance of power in their favour and ensure equal opportunities.

Although many staff may appear keen on the emergence of advocacy groups, their motivation should be examined. Some will use it as part of their role in promoting the quality of service provided; others, however, may see advocacy groups as fighting the battles professionals shy away from within the workings of the multi-disciplinary team (Lowson, 1988) The aims of advocacy groups must clearly be those set by the participants of the group and not the facilitators. It could easily occur that advocacy groups fall into the same category as 'ward meetings'. These are frequently cited as evidence of an involving approach, but are dominated and controlled by staff members (Campbell, 1990). These meetings are often used to raise issues that are focused by staff and then rationalized and justified rather than discussed constructively and critically examined: this is more likely to be a reflection of a lack of planning and consultation with members of the group than an attempt to manipulate the forum.

POWER

One of the central themes to consider when examining the emergence of advocacy projects is that of power and powerlessness. In the current mental health system, the power lies with the professionally qualified staff. The patients' most basic human rights to privacy and freedom can be challenged. Even though this may be done with the best of intentions,it is still an infringement of civil liberties.

Many professionals find participation uncomfortable for themselves as powerholders. This needs to be recognized and the true worth of their role identified. Providers of health and social services need to focus on being enablers, assisting service users to reach the maximum level of independence identified as desirable by everyone, including themselves. Practitioners should be focusing on their unique and valuable skills. There may be differing ideologies between professionals as well as between carers and service users, and these differences need to be confronted. Professionals must be prepared to share the power they hold with carers, service users and voluntary organizations.

Barriers and prejudices

This theory of the barrier between professionals and service users is one reflected in many areas. Departments are largely white dominated with black workers in low status jobs. Recruitment is often biased towards younger staff, with ageist views regarding mature applicants common.

With the implementation of the Community Care Act there is a greater emphasis on user involvement. Many social services departments have developed initiatives to increase participation and consultation in service development and delivery. The Health Service has much to learn from these models.

In hospitals there is a tendency for middle managers to be clinically based. This should enable the views and concerns of patients, carers and staff to be considered and acted upon promptly and appropriately. Procedures to facilitate this good practice need to be negotiated by all parties involved. The rights of the user must be clearly established and it is important to make the connections between the experience of the provider and the user. This will obviously present practitioners with some uncomfortable situations which will have to be addressed. It could be argued that no matter how difficult the situations arising may be, the relationship between the professional and the service user can only benefit.

Building on these experiences and sharing with service users and carers should enable the breaking down of barriers and prejudices. It will give the practitioner a chance to empathize with individual situations and to break down the labelling of people as diagnoses, dependencies or disabilities. This will facilitate the promotion of service users to the status they should be accorded. There are many who object to the labels given to people, even those meant to be sensitive to their situation. For instance, the label 'mentally ill' is no longer considered to adequately represent users of the psychiatric services. Many organizations focusing on patient advocacy now promote the use of the phrase 'mentally distressed' to represent their members.

A commonly held belief is that rather than service use or disability being used to describe people, they should be regarded as citizens. The use of an alternative label may make people feel more highly regarded, but this does not really challenge any overriding beliefs or reflect how people are cared for. Bell (1988) states that we all have the ability to recover from stressful situations, given sufficient support and a valued and respected role in society. Much distress is socially perpetuated. All minority groups are overrepresented in the mental health system, particularly women, people from ethnic backgrounds other than European and the elderly. This does raise the question as to who or which group can adequately represent these groups who have complex needs. The obvious answer, of course, is that the people should represent themselves wherever possible. For this to be effective, they need to feel confident when expressing their views, both as users of the service and as their representatives.

AUTONOMY

The medicalization of mental distress is actively perpetuated by psychiatrists who dominate service provision. It is all too easy for medical staff to trivialize challenges made to their practices by patients, particularly when they are often surrounded by supportive fellow professionals. They are traditionally reluctant to provide the patients with detailed information regarding their treatment. Older people commonly come into contact with physicians as well as psychiatrists. Therefore the frustrations and anger felt at a lack of information are highlighted with increased contact with several professions.

Medical staff often feel uncomfortable when challenged or requested to provide more detailed information. This is particularly so when the challenge comes from outside the multi-disciplinary team. With the current emphasis on patients' rights, highlighted in the Patient's Charter, and legislation such as access to health care records, such demands for information can no longer be easily ignored. People should not have to portray themselves as making an aggressive challenge to the system to obtain information which is rightly theirs. Clear, accurate information and its availability, either written or verbal, should be a qualifying standard set by and for the service.

It is easy to identify that the movement of personal autonomy is a greater threat to the medical profession than to practitioners. The practice of psychiatry especially has remained largely static over the last 30 years, and it no longer reflects the liberation that modern society is encouraging consumers to explore.

Empowering users of the service, however, is not always a welcome ideal. There is a theory of medical sociology which suggests that persons who are most disadvantaged by oppressive social systems often come to believe in the legitimacy of the system which is oppressing them (Hall, 1978; Simon, 1991). Rogers and Pilgram (1991) pointed out that people who suffer from mental distress tend to be socially withdrawn. Consequently, many patients/clients do not wish to join or feel uncomfortable when taking up membership of user groups. As with any representative group within society, it is the more confident, demonstrative participants who will speak out on behalf of others. Although the carers of elderly people have many supportive voluntary organizations there are few independent advocacy groups.

In the early 1980s decentralization was claimed to herald greater accessibility. This, together with subsequent legislation, has helped to encourage open policies and practices. Decentralization should allow the service provider at local level to respond to consumer needs. This has obvious advantages: organizations providing and managing the services are more accessible to the consumer of the service; assessment of need should be much more accurate and the response quicker. This shift in power to the purchaser should ultimately empower the user. As many social services departments devolve their budgets down to individual practitioners, it can be envisaged that the service user will be able to discuss with the care manager just how the budget allocated for their care is spent. This will extend a great deal more power to the user and, hopefully, allow the package of care to reflect truly the individual's needs.

Presently the National Health Service and Community Care Act, 1990, goes some way to bringing the decision making for service provision to a more local level. Through the Act, social services departments are assuming lead responsibilities for community care arrangements. It stresses the need for health and social service departments, as well as other agencies, to work together to ensure appropriate provision of care. Good practices such as the involvement of service users and carers in decision making, the availability of choice and the giving of clear information are all focused upon. This is the first major legislative step towards empowering carers and service users. The Community Care Act is particularly important for the carers of elderly people. It gives them a more formal framework through which to express their views and influence care provision.

PLURALISM AND PARTICIPATION

This new legislative framework also encourages the mixed economy of care. This draws on socio-political theories regarding the mixed economy of welfare. Included in this are the themes of pluralism and participation. Different organizations can offer a wide range of services, allowing local groups to participate in the provision of welfare. Although this obviously has implications for providing a service which is responsive to local need, it also has an effect on the budget.

The burden to provide a consistently high standard of care within the public sector has increased greatly over recent years as consumer power has been encouraged. It is, therefore, economically sound to encourage the voluntary and private sector to assist in the provision of care. With the increase in the voluntary sector, it could be argued that services are indirectly being provided by the community and service users. Douglas Hurd promoted the idea of the 'active citizen' who would be more involved in the provision of welfare. The difficulty is that due to labelling of mentally distressed people and older people, they are often considered incapable of making a valuable contribution. Although in periods of crisis people may undoubtedly lose their capacity, either physically or mentally, to decide what is in their best interests (Campbell, 1990) this state of body or mind is a temporary one and not permanent.

It should, therefore, be seen as both politically and morally correct to actively encourage user participation. This is not a new idea in psychiatry. 'Therapeutic communities' have functioned for many years, where clients are supposed to be equal if not sole decision makers. Where in-patient services are concerned, a starting point is the acceptance of the principle that everyone who uses health services has a right to be heard, however unpopular or unusual their views might be (Lawson, 1991).

The anger and frustration experienced by many service users is an understandable response to their experience of disempowerment and not the product of a presumed psychopathology (Lowson, 1988). Where professionals have set limits on the nature and extent of user involvement, this has prevented users from having any effective influence on service provision. The greatest allies for professionals when trying to improve the service offered are those who experience it first hand. Problems highlighted within the services need to be considered with an open mind and strategies formulated to implement any changes.

CARERS

Pressure groups and voluntary organizations have a valuable role to play in focusing on issues. However, this is not a substitute for carers voicing their opinions to encourage planners and providers of services to hand over some of their control of resources to the people who know best how they may be utilized (Cobb and Wallcraft, 1989).

Increasingly, carers are being consulted regarding changes in provision, but providers of services do not need to wait for larger scale changes before going through the consultation process. Carers should be asked for their contribution and their views listened to at every stage. This emphasis on the partnership in care should not be exceptional but integral to good working practices.

Carers often find assistance through voluntary organizations. These groups may provide individuals with the support they need to represent themselves to professionals. The Association of Carers is a national organization which attempts to make connections with local groups to strengthen its case, whether or not they have time to campaign themselves. This type of organization provides some structure and coordination which carers can draw on if they wish. Local action is important, however, if carers want to shape services directly affecting them (Cobb and Wallcraft, 1989). Representation on local forums may have to be fought for but it is essential to ensure the views of service users are heard. With the increasing emphasis on carers, health and social services are encouraging carer support, not only in conjunction with service user support but also in its own right.

In the absence of truly independent advocates working for patients in the psychiatric and medical services, carers can provide a valuable contribution on behalf of the patient. There is currently an increasing emphasis on the facilitation of 'patient advocacy'. These groups are generally stimulated and organized by professionals, and they involve people who collectively share the same user 'label' and access the same health and social service provision (Sang, 1989). This philosophy is contradictory and can only detract from the active facilitation of self and independent advocacy.

An essential ingredient in the facilitation of such advocacy projects is the active support of staff. People who may use many different services need to have access to a forum in which they can effectively reflect their views. However, it needs to be asked whether in all cases a different forum is needed for different services. Consultation with service users when discussing the development of these forums is essential. Staff need to be prepared to be open to challenge. Professional staff, too, will need education and support that could involve carers, service users and voluntary organizations.

Staff need to feel confident with this part of their role. Part of the confidence-building process will involve skills development. Staff will need assistance in building the skills they need to participate and develop their own alternative approaches to involvement. Advocacy groups themselves also require practical support: they may need information (collating and disseminating), child care, transport and meeting places. Not all these resources will be on offer, but it is important that they are not dismissed and that the groups, carers and professionals identify these as common objectives. Support groups can also facilitate the sharing of information by service users. This has obvious benefits for mutual education as well as for identifying subjects for which they wish to seek further details.

USER-INVOLVEMENT PROJECTS

Writers such as Croft and Beresford (1988, 1992) have for many years warned against token user-involvement projects which encourage users to participate in trivial decision-making issues that do not address questions of disempowerment. They argue instead for the development of models of consultation and involvement wherein 'service user' is not a permanent status, and where there is recognition that the same people may at different times work in a service or use it, care and support someone and need support themselves.

For such a system to work effectively, mental health workers must always remain aware of the power and status accorded to them by the socio-political system, and recognize that when they work alongside service users in campaigning for the rights of these users the relationship is a delicate one. The role is a particularly stressful one for nurses due to their position in the organization. They will be called upon to support the position of many of the key participants due to their accessibility and powerful influence. It is essential that nurses keep their integrity and draw on the multi-disciplinary team for support. This will give all staff the opportunity to discuss issues and reflect on professional practice and protocols.

When offering support to people involved in advocacy projects, the staff may consider the following suggestions presented by Bell (1988): the promotion of a philosophy of user participation throughout the service; allow the group full participation in the setting of the agenda for change; listen to people's anger at existing systems without being defensive; be sensitive to and respect the need for user-only meetings.

An agreement of mutual respect and cooperation is the most important 'contractual agreement' between staff and group members. One concern of staff members may be that group participants will use the forum of user groups to complain about personal issues and attempt to get these resolved with the power of the group. Although this may be a legitimate course of action for complaints, advocacy projects would be better served by aiming to improve the standard of service to all consumers.

Participation in groups can bring its own unique set of problems for both carers and clients. People who are already dealing with their own stressful situations may feel burdened by the expectations that they will not only represent other service users' views but also their problems. It is important to consider the cost there may be for people 'getting involved', particularly if participatory groups become an obstacle course due to barriers and conflicts presented by professionals. Such a struggle may be damaging and intolerable for service users already overburdened with illness anxieties, social insecurity and deprivation. Advocacy groups should be an exercise in collaboration, a chance to build a partnership on the basis of good practice and identified need.

Advocacy and empowerment, although very different from each other, cannot be viewed in isolation when considering their application in clinical practice. Wright (1992) promotes the philosophy that professionals should share their knowledge and skills with those who have need of it, be a force for empowerment of others and not over others.

Many governments now are pursuing the ideals of empowerment and self-help (Shulamit, 1991). This appears to be due to concerns regarding the crisis in the welfare state which has been common throughout Europe since the 1970s. Although the phrase 'user empowerment' is a popular one with Government representatives there are no systems or assistance provided by them to support changes at local level. The changes have been given legislative support through policy statements such as the Patient's Charter, but tangible support through education and resources has not been forthcoming.

CHANGES IN PRACTICE AND PROVISION

The current emphasis is on the quality of the service offered and the monitoring of that service. Quality must be for staff and consumers. At the heart of real quality initiatives is the direct experience of service users, therefore the basis of good practice is to involve them in policy making and standard setting, and in some authorities they are invited onto interview panels when appointing staff. This kind of involvement would give service users and carers some ownership of the way in which services are provided, lending credibility to it and removing the feeling of an imposed oppressive system.

Through this involvement people will have higher expectations of services and will feel more able to express their disappointments fully (Brandon, 1991). This should enable constructive evaluation of services and changes which are negotiated, not imposed.

Croft and Beresford (1988) describe a service culture that is receptive, where agencies and their workers support, listen and respond to the accounts and definitions of people who use them. The gap between services and the user needs to be bridged from both sides; this will take commitment and a recognition that all parties have common aims.

Professional staff will need to be able to balance the delivery of their professional skills with the ever changing emphasis on empowerment of service users and carers. This will take experience and flexibility together with an open-minded, non-judgemental approach. Rather than waiting to see if their client group takes up the idea of an advocacy project, staff should commence the education/information initiative immediately. It would be advantageous if these initiatives were not seen as being the result solely of pressure exerted by users and carers but as part of good practice. Brandon (1991) points out that the training of professional staff places the emphasis in both training and education on socialization and on desirable qualities such as reliability, respectability and responsibility. In the past this may well have been so. In the health service, schools of nursing trained nurses to work within the system and not to question it, the emphasis being on hierarchy, discipline and conformity.

Another great change in practice is the giving of information to carers and clients. Traditionally, health care professionals especially have been encouraged not to share information; secrecy is power (Brandon, 1991). In mental health services, secrecy is due in part to the belief that it is detrimental to a person's psychological well-being to have access to medical and nursing notes describing mental state and diagnosis. This is not research based and has often meant that labelling and judgemental comments regarding users and their carers have gone unchecked. Practitioners need to seize this opportunity to work together with users and carers to develop and evaluate care plans, to give and receive positive feedback and in so doing build an honest partnership to benefit the service user. Within social services there has been a more proactive move towards consultation and involvement in assessment and care planning.

Brandon (1991) comments that professional staff find it easier to treat people described as the 'worried well'. Older people, with Alzheimer's disease for instance have, in the past, not been a popular speciality for newly qualified staff. There is a tendency for practitioners to retreat from experiences that make them feel impotent, so consequently there is a tendency for staff to move away from close contact with the very disabled person. The positive aspect of the role on seeing clients recover is greatly reduced. It must be remembered that carers will also feel this sense of powerlessness and will often be unable to distance themselves from their situation. Older people would undoubtedly prefer to have their own relatives and friends as their carers. However, the majority of informal carers feel that care should be provided by health and social services (Cornwell, 1989). Professionals and carers alike need to be informed of the full range of services, so that accurate information can be given to service users promptly. Carers need to be empowered to identify their own needs and encouraged to work with professionals to develop care plans. In collaboration with the service user this should enable a positive plan for the future to be devised that will benefit all parties involved in some way.

The overall aim of advocacy projects and the empowerment of carers and service users is to effect positive change in provision to do this. It will be necessary for all staff to draw on support from fellow professionals as well as service users. The implementation of advocacy projects, the promotion of empowerment and sharing of information can only strengthen the position of all practitioners within the clinical team, but the implementation of these initiatives needs to be done in a strategic manner. If projects are started and people are ignorant or prejudiced regarding the aims, support will not be forthcoming and people may deliberately set out to sabotage the projects. A sense of ownership for the principles and their application needs to be fostered, then the wish to see the projects succeed will dominate. Providing information and education will enable people to be knowledgeable participants, and will ensure the service is accessible to the majority and not just a vocal minority. Managers of the service at every level need to involve all relevant parties at every stage of planning services. This responsibility should come right down to the level of service provision.

To facilitate the partnership in care between professionals and service users, staff can promote a positive relationship through involvement in philosophies, formulating policies and procedures and care planning. Each team of service providers could ensure that aims and objectives common to both professionals and users are identified. In this way all parties are moving forward sharing responsibility and power. As a result, advocacy and empowerment will become an integral part of professional practice and service provision.

These issues should eventually no longer be regarded as initiatives but a routine part of the professional role. Service users and their carers should be able to expect these principles to be incorporated in their package of care and not have to request their inclusion.

REFERENCES

Allcock, D. (1989) The psychiatric nurse as advocate. *Nursing Standard*, **37** (37).

Bell, L. (1988) *User Participation: The Challenge to Mental Health Workers*, paper circulated by Survivors Speak Out.

Brandon, D. (1991) Listen to real experts. *Nursing Times*, **87** (4).

Campbell, P. (1990) Psychiatry and personal autonomy. *Critical Public Health*, No. 4.

Cobb, A. and Wallcraft, J. (1989) Women's needs, in *Mental Health Care in Crisis*, (eds A. Brackx and C. Grimshaw), Pluto, London.

Cornwell, J. (1989) *The Consumers' View: Elderly People and Community Health Services*, The King's Fund Centre, London.

Croft, S. and Beresford, P. (1988) Time to build trust between them and us. *Social Work Today*, 8 September.

Croft, S. and Beresford, P. (1992) The politics of participation. *Critical Social Policy*, **12** (2).

Dyer, A.R. and Block, S. (1987) Informal consent and the psychiatric patient. *Journal of Medical Ethics*, no. 13.

Hall, S. (1978) *Policing the Crisis*, Macmillan, London.

Jennings, K. (1991) Speaking up for patients. *COHSE Journal*, **3** (5).

Lawson, M. (1991) A recipient's view, in *Beyond Community Care*, (ed. S. Ramon), Macmillan, London.

Lindow, V. (1990) Participation and power. *Openmind*, no. 44, April/May.

Lowson, D. (1988) *User Empowerment*. Unpublished paper circulated by Survivors Speak Out.

Rogers, A. and Pilgram, D. (1991) Pulling down churches: accounting for the British Medical Health Users' Movement. *Sociology of Health and Illness,* **13** (2).

Sang, R. (1989) The independent voice of advocacy, in *Mental Health Care in Crisis*, (eds A. Brackx and C. Grimshaw), Pluto, London.

Shulamit, R. (1991) Policy issues, in *Beyond Community Care*, (ed. R.Shulamit), MIND, London.

Simon, R. (1991) *Gramsci's Political Thought*, Laurence and Wishart, London.

Wallcraft, J. (1992) User empowerment, *Mindwaves*, no. 15

Wright, S. (1992) Nursing in its own image. *Nursing Standard*, **7** (9).

FURTHER READING

Campbell, P. (1991) In times of crisis. *Openmind*, **52**.

Ingelfinger, F.J. (1972) Informed (but educated) consent. *New England Journal of Medicine*, no. 28.

Rogers, C.R. (1951) *Client Centred Therapy*, Constable, London.

Spandler, H. (1992) To make an army out of illness. *Asylum*, **6** (4).

3 Assessment of an older person with mental health problems

Elaine Stott

For purposes of clarity all references to the therapist will be to 'she' and the client will be addressed as 'he' throughout the chapter.

ASSESSMENT

When dealing with mental health problems in older persons, assessment is based on a multi-disciplinary approach. This is because the problems of individual clients tend to be wide-ranging and may include physical and social problems as well as mental health. In addition, the degenerative effects of ageing need to be taken into account: time can lose meaning when an older individual has been an in-patient for a few days, away from their normal daily routine.

Due to effects of ageing, older persons are less agile than their younger counterparts and, therefore, it is likely that they will perform tasks more slowly. Some are also less likely to be able to deal with the execution of tasks where they have to divide their attention, for example when they are undertaking several tasks in a kitchen environment. All these factors must be taken into account during assessment of this client group.

A key element in work with elderly people is the individual assessment (Coleman, 1982). Older people are said to be more affected than young persons by such factors as time of day, fatigue, digestive upset, drug reactions and the test environment (Burton, 1989). They are also said to be more influenced than younger adults by the quality of the client/therapist relationship and may perform differently for a strange therapist. For this reason, formal testing should always be carried out by the same therapist, as should continuing informal assessments.

All assessments have a significant bearing upon the future placement of older clients. If evidence of cognitive deficit is identified it is necessary to reinforce the results of informal assessments with data obtained from standardized cognitive assessment procedures which have been tested for reliability and validity.

If clients wear spectacles, then it is essential that the therapist ensures that these are worn during any assessment which involves visual tasks. Before conclusions are reached regarding the older client's ability to receive, assimilate and process verbal information, any hearing deficit present must be taken into account.

REASONS FOR ASSESSMENT

In broad terms, assessment is necessary in order that the therapist and the client may together recognize the client's functional deficits and also his areas of ability.

Assessment provides the therapist with the means to identify a baseline for treatment as well as indicating realistic and achievable aims that are seen as being of value to the client. By contrasting positive and negative aspects to arrive at an estimate of the client's possible potential for improvement, assessment also helps the therapist to determine the degree of assistance a client may require in the future. Unless a baseline can be established, the therapist has no way of determining the point from which treatment can be planned and against which progress and improvement can be compared.

When assessing the client's current level of functioning, pre-morbid ability is an important baseline. A client's normal ability may be overridden by the symptoms or consequences of the presenting illness or level of dysfunction.

A good assessment is usually structured around the pattern of an initial assessment, ongoing assessments and a final assessment. These provide the therapist with important data concerning an older person's social situation, individual needs and cognitive, psychological, emotional and physical status.

Initial assessment

During the initial assessment a database may be produced and the required baseline prior to treatment can be established. Background information, such as the client's personal history, interests and abilities along with an indication of their pre-morbid personality or ability, can be gained during this stage.

These initial stages of assessment provide the therapist with the means to observe and record data and make use of a wide range of appropriate information resources. This is invaluable as assessment must view the client holistically, i.e. mind, body and environment. In this way the assessment, which has to be fair and valid, is able to be based on a multidimensional picture of the client's status.

The initial contact between therapist and client is of great importance in determining the quality and nature of the relationship that is to be developed between them.

The initial assessment of clients suffering functional illness is carried out in an informal interview, aimed at establishing the client/therapist relationship and the acquisition of baseline data. Where clients suffer organic dysfunction resulting in short-term memory loss, confusion and/or confabulation the interview is conducted for rapport-establishing purposes only. After the client has been given a few days to adapt to the hospital environment and a rapport has been established, further one-to-one assessments can be implemented.

The whole assessment process can be classed as a communication process between a therapist and a client. Assessment provides a valuable opportunity for the therapist to let the client feel that she has both heard and understood what he is communicating. The therapist can also show that she is not only empathic towards the client but also possesses the knowledge and skill necessary to help him with his problems. Therefore, the amount of rapport gained during initial contact and the degree of confidence the therapist displays in both her abilities and her profession may be crucial in setting the tone of all future interactions.

Ongoing assessment

Assessment forms an integral part of treatment. Ongoing assessments are therefore carried out throughout the treatment process. Each treatment session is evaluated in order to monitor a client's progress continually. The results of different forms of assessments can also be examined in order to provide a comparison of results, which in turn provides the therapist with a continuous flow of information that keeps her work current.

Treatment does not always continue uniformly. The client's level of ability may decrease, remain static or improve. Continuous assessment, therefore, incorporates a building process during which the therapist can determine whether treatment methods require modification. Information gained from the assessments also provides the therapist with an indication of the most appropriate adjustment to her intervention, assists her in the planning of future strategies and stages of treatment and helps her to make recommendations for the client's future. It may be found that referral to other agencies is indicated.

Final assessment

Later assessments can be carried out pre-discharge. The final assessment gives the client an opportunity to see what progress he has made and to experience positive feelings about himself. Of course it is possible that there has been no improvement and this may be distressing for the client. Reassurance and further discussion is indicated in such circumstances. Recommendations for the future can now be made, based on any differences between the client's existing level of skills and those he needs to carry out his expected roles. Further treatment or advice regarding input from other agencies can also be given.

This system of evaluation provides a multidimensional picture of the client and ultimately determines the feasibility and effectiveness of treatment.

Comprehensive assessment

The objective of a comprehensive assessment is to select a combination of approaches which will provide the most complete and distinct picture of an individual's ability and thereby assist in the profiling of any identified problems. However, the amount of time, energy and cost expended must be contained within reasonable boundaries. Therefore the therapist must carefully consider the utility and validity of any assessment approaches before they are implemented.

Assessment and reassessment of a client by the therapist in her treatment programme, and the necessary informed interpretation of the consequences plays a significant part in the effectiveness of the total treatment programme of the multi-disciplinary team. It also provides valuable input in monitoring the effectiveness of medical, physical, psychological and/or social therapy interventions. Add to this the peer review available through the medium of case conferences and staff feedback on the contribution to the whole treatment process, and you have an evaluation on the outcome of the whole service provided. This assists standard setting and measuring of achievement whilst also defining the skills of each discipline and the experience necessary to achieve these skills.

It can, therefore, be appreciated that when multi-disciplinary assessment data is pooled this global view provides a general indication of how a client is progressing and the team can, if necessary, explore possible alternatives and solutions in relation to a client's presenting problem.

The assessment process, with its extensive scope, multifaceted capacity and its integral and indispensable part of treatment, provides a cornerstone for quality care.

ETHICS

Ethics as a subject can be extremely complex because as a subject it does not have the certainty of natural sciences and ethical issues may be concerned with moral circumstances and situations which do not fit into universal laws and principles. In a general sense, ethics refers to a deliberation on how best to conduct one's life and, in the case of professional matters in relation to assessment within health care, intervention to the highest moral degree. Aristotle believed that deliberation was the essence of ethics.

It is important that the therapist remembers the need to see every client as an individual with individual needs. Assessment is a vital factor in determining these unique needs. However, in order to practise according to ethical and moral standards, the therapist must acknowledge that a client's background and lifestyle may be different from her own and thus she cannot impose upon him her views regarding what she personally considers to be 'normal' or desired behaviour. This should be taken into account when forming treatment plans from assessment results.

Ethical guidelines may be laid down, but there is always the exception to the rule where no clear-cut solutions can be found. If all selected options or solutions can be justified as satisfying the highest degree of morality, then there is a good chance that the client's standing as a human being and person with essential rights will be neither undervalued nor diminished. Seedhouse (1988) believes that ethics is the key to a new era of health care and that the work for health is a moral endeavour.

The ethics of health care is generally concerned with caring for and respecting people and recognizing their potential, preparing them to help themselves and empowering them to take greater control over their lives. An essential human need is to be treated with dignity and respect. Careful consideration of both cultural and ethnic issues when dealing with clients is an important component of this latter point.

Ethical abuse

As a client group, older persons are particularly vulnerable to ethical abuse. Very often they are isolated or have limited support networks and may be unaware of their rights within society. An excerpt from literature written about privacy and dignity for the elderly provides food for thought.

> If clients are to be docile parts of a well-oiled machine they cannot be seen as people – as individuals clinging to the vestiges of personality, choice and dignity and independence – and the message transmitted all too easily becomes: 'We are caring for your body, but you as a person do not really exist'.
>
> *(Norman, 1987)*

Halperin states that privacy is the control that individuals have over the distribution of information about themselves and is to be maintained because 'irrespective of its utilitarian benefit to society it serves and enhances our sense of self' (Halperin, 1989). Thompson's (1990) view is thàt invasion of privacy strikes at the very heart of a person's dignity and he goes on to say that the right to privacy includes respect for a person's physical privacy, intimate secrets and for confidential information.

The first of the nine standards of service stipulated by the Patient's Charter, which the Health Service states it is aiming to provide for patients, is 'Respect for dignity, privacy and religious and cultural beliefs'. Awareness, attitudes and respect determine how we deal with and talk to individuals.

Labelling

The way in which the therapist actually addresses the older client is most important. Terms of endearment such as 'darling', 'sweetie' and 'lovie' are belittling, patronizing and, in some cases, degrading for the client. Older adults may have rigid role values and this degree of familiarity might be something that they are just not used to. They may not have been addressed in this manner since childhood and, whilst they do not object for fear of being labelled 'difficult', they may build up feelings of resentment and anger and fail to comply with assessments or treatments.

Labelling an elderly person as a 'sweetie', 'lovie' or 'dearie' conjures up images of passivity and lack of motivation or volition on the part of that person. This form of labelling may lead to a self-fulfilling prophecy of learned helplessness and for this reason also should be avoided. During assessment and treatment of a client it is the therapist's aim to encourage motivation and volition, not to unwittingly discourage a client's active participation.

Throughout all assessments, clients should be encouraged to be as independent as possible and be provided with opportunities to problem solve and make decisions whilst receiving guidance, prompting, reassurance and assistance where necessary.

Competence of therapist

Assessment is a crucial factor in providing an accurate knowledge of the needs and abilities of an individual, and the therapist's intervention must be effective and efficient in order to provide treatment that will benefit and not harm them. As Creek (1990) points out, vague and inaccurate assessments lead to vague and imprecise treatment which is unacceptable for both ethical and practical reasons. It is essential that a therapist learns to function within the parameters of individual competence – do what she does do well, and know when to delegate to others of higher competence/experience or do nothing at all. It would be unethical for the therapist to implement any assessment or treatment process which she felt either too inexperienced or lacking in knowledge to carry out competently. Assessment must always be carried out by a qualified therapist.

Testing

Standardized testing is a form of assessment which greatly assists in the forming of inferences and, ultimately, decision making regarding a client's ability or aptitude. When using this type of testing it is again important to remember that the client is an individual.

A standardized test provides a quantitive assessment of a client's particular attributes or deficits. This type of testing may be used to assess factors such as personality and higher cortical functions – language, naming, memory, constructional ability, calculation, and so on.

During administration of standardized testing, it is highly unlikely that any two people will score exactly the same. With this fact in mind the therapist can use standardized testing to continue to see a client as an individual in the knowledge that this form of testing will provide a unique picture of an individual's level of functioning.

The purpose of any assessment should be explained to the client, even if it is the therapist's view that a client with a dementing illness may be unable to grasp this concept or have little insight. It is good practice to accept that clients have a right to refuse to participate in any assessment. Another important ethical point is that ownership of test results must lie jointly with both therapist and client. At the very least, the client must be given some indication of how he fared during testing and what implications the test results have for him. When using test results as an aid to decision making about a client, this feedback is an important component of the client's right to information about himself.

Testing should also provide some measure of prediction regarding a client's future level of function. Test results can be used in conjunction with data acquired for diagnostic purposes and applied within the acknowledged frame of reference for treatment of a particular clinical condition.

The British Psychological Society (BPS) stipulates that adequate training is essential for the correct administration, evaluation and interpretation of any psychological test, as without this the individual upon whom such a test is used may be gravely prejudiced especially if decisions concerning his future placement or treatment are to be based, even if only in part, upon the results of the tests or assessments.

One of the foremost ethical concerns regarding the use of formal assessments is that it is vital all standardized tests used for assessment purposes are only used on the population for which they are intended. Testing protocol procedures must be strictly adhered to when using formal standardized testing, as any deviation from stipulated guidelines would render any reported scores invalid and unreliable.

Occupational therapists are now being encouraged to undertake specific training in order to achieve registration with the British Psychological Society to enable them to be registered as competent to administer such testing.

Ethical codes and principles

One of the characteristics of a profession is that professionals are governed by a code of ethics and professional practice. These state the duties of professionals and lay down guidelines regarding professional conduct and responsibilities.

The oldest known code of professional ethics, which was written for physicians, is the Hippocratic Oath (147BC). The Code of the World Federation of Occupational Therapists (WFOT, 1985) and that of the British Association of Occupational Therapists (BAOT, 1985) are both modelled on this ancient oath.

There are three essential principles involved and these are respect for persons equally, justice and beneficence; a duty to promote good and prevent harm is the principle of beneficence (Thompson, 1990). Each individual is entitled to be treated accordingly. Therefore, because of the ethical considerations involved, assessment must be based on these principles. If they are adhered to, they should control the conduct which guides the actions of an assessor.

When working with clients with mental health problems, there may be many difficulties in translating ethical principles into practice: trying to uphold a person's rights and, at the same time, attempting to comply with societal expectations. Problems may also occur in relation to a client's desire to live an independent lifestyle of his choosing, if that individual is considered to be suffering from such a 'mental disorder' as defined under the Mental Health Act, 1983, which would contraindicate such independence.

It is not beyond the realms of possibility that a therapist may have to act on behalf of a client against his will under the terms of Section VIII of the Mental Health Act, 1983. This part of the Act deals with proceedings for power of guardianship which may be implemented if results of assessments indicated that a client was incapable of living independently in the community and where residential care was indicated. Fortunately, it is said to be rare for therapists to be caught in a true dilemma in which there is a direct clash between two equally valid moral principles of duties (Thompson et al., 1987). This may be due to the fact that if enough time and trouble is taken to consider and discuss all the pros and cons when faced with moral dilemmas then they can be satisfactorily resolved. Thompson et al. have suggested that the therapist must adopt the same problem-solving approach that is used within the assessment process, i.e. assessing the data, planning strategies based on informed decision making and monitoring the process, thus providing a basis for evaluation and modification of outcomes.

An occupational therapist working within her profession's code of ethics is expected to demonstrate a concern which will provide beneficial results for her client. She is expected to show respect for, and safeguard the rights of her client. She must also preserve the client's confidence that she is concerned with his welfare. She is bound by certain ethical considerations regarding the effectiveness and efficiency of her therapeutic input.

RELEVANCE OF ASSESSMENT TO CLIENTS

Occupational therapists are concerned with standardized cognitive assessments, because they are constantly confronted with the issue of the cognitive status of a client regarding the degree to which it affects the level of functioning related to activities of daily living. Occupational therapists are involved in helping the client and his family to adjust to the level of cognitive function/dysfunction. The client is also taught compensatory techniques where necessary.

The assessment process which necessitates the client being placed in different social or environmental settings in order to gain comprehensive data must be a positive experience for that client. It must not only highlight areas of deficit but must identify strengths as well as weakness. If only areas of weakness are identified then this can be a demoralizing experience for the client.

Dressing assessment

Problems involving self-care are often assessed by means of dressing assessments. Cognitive deficit can very often be identified from this type of assessment as the dressing process involves extensive use of thought processes, orientation and interaction with the environment. During the assessment a client's level of volition/motivation can be determined. If this area of functioning and/or level of confidence is low then a prioritized graded programme designed to overcome areas of deficit and build upon areas of strengths can be implemented. The therapist might also take this opportunity to spend time thinking about how it must feel to have reached later life and to struggle with activities of daily living.

All assessments are geared to normalization as far as is practicable and allowances made for any unfamiliar aspects of the environment when interpreting results of assessments. Normalization has been defined as 'the utilisation of means which are as culturally normative as possible in order to establish and/or maintain personal behaviours and characteristics which are as culturally normative as possible' (Wolfensberger, 1972).

The environment in which practical assessment of older people is carried out is one in which activity would usually occur or as close a simulation as possible. In this way a more accurate prediction about their ability to function in that environment can be gained.

Dressing assessments are carried out at an appropriate time of day, such as in the morning, rather than expecting the client to demonstrate self-care abilities at an unreasonable hour.

Throughout the dressing assessment the client's dignity and privacy is preserved and respected as, of necessity, the assessment involves very intimate aspects of the older person's functioning.

The role of the therapist is a key factor. The presenting condition of the client may affect his ability to communicate and understand. The client must be treated with tact and sensitivity. Both what the therapist says and the way it is said are equally important.

Helper skills

A major role of the therapist is concerned with the helping process which, according to Carkhuff (1969), consists of the core dimension of the helping relationship, helper skills and client learning. Research has shown that helpers who can offer high levels of interpersonal skills are more likely to help clients (Carkhuff and Berenson, 1977; Truax and Carkhuff, 1967).

Helper qualities – empathy, genuineness, respect and concreteness – are important components of these core dimensions. Carkhuff states that these qualities, together with the helper skills of attending, responding, personalizing and initiating, guide the client through the process of exploration, understanding and action.

All the attributes necessary to facilitate working practice can be acquired through experience. The therapist who is prepared to develop both professionally and personally is better equipped to be a more effective therapist.

Assessment procedures

Because the assessment process is such a vital factor in intervention, certain factors have to be borne in mind when choosing assessment procedures. These include resources available and the time which can be taken over the assessment – client fatigue, distractibility, sensory loss and physical handicap are going to be limiting factors.

Group activities are frequently employed as a means of assessment. Once a client's level of functioning has been determined via one-to-one assessment, he can then be included in appropriate group activities designed to facilitate demonstration, practice and maintenance of any areas of strength/ability. The group setting can thus be used equally well as a treatment and assessment medium.

An important aspect of the therapist's role involves the assessment of the suitability of particular activities for her clients. The therapist has to consider what she intends to do and why; who she hopes will benefit and how; what she needs to do to ensure this; what skills both she and her clients require to carry out the activity. She also needs to consider the appropriate size of the group and its composition, as well as the number of staff required, time, place and location.

Further considerations include the physical, emotional, intellectual and mental demands that particular activities will make on each individual participating within a group activity.

At the end of group sessions the therapist evaluates the outcome of the group sessions: what were the aims/objectives of the group? Were they fulfilled? And if not, why not – what went wrong and why? Can this be either prevented or rectified in future?

PHILOSOPHICAL CONSIDERATIONS

Before deciding to use a particular assessment, it is necessary to consider if it will yield the particular type of information required. It is also then necessary to further consider if that information will facilitate treatment planning and intervention.

Standardized tests should reflect the process of scientific enquiry which determined its acceptance as a standardized and valid form of assessment. The manual should make it clear what client groups were used during standardization and what process was followed in order to validate the test and substantiate its results. The philosophical perspective of the author of the test should also be determined. This is important because administration of a test which is badly designed would be an injustice to the client on whose behalf the test is being used.

The model or frame of reference used in developing assessment forms should be considered before these are incorporated into the assessment process; for example forms based on Beck's cognitive therapy are suitable assessment instruments when assessing depressive illness, but a neurodevelopmental frame of reference would be contraindicated as the latter is used with those suffering from neurological conditions such as cerebro-vascular accident or cerebral palsy rather than psychiatric conditions.

If any degree of uncertainty exists regarding the appropriate usage of a particular assessment tool, a list of its strengths and weaknesses or positive and negative features could be compiled in order to put matters into perspective. Questions that may be asked could include:

- Is it easy to use? (Take into consideration the suitability for the client/client group in terms of literacy level required or complexity of instructions, cultural bias or physical ability required.)
- What is its cost in terms of both time and money? (Include training therapists in its use and administration.)
- Is there ample scientific/statistical evidence of its validity/reliability? Is there a sample against which it is fair to compare the client?
- What does the test measure?
- Is the assessment procedure explained in clear and precise terms?
- Are there guidelines relating to its correct usage/ interpretation, and are these easy to understand and administer?
- What sort of environment is necessary for the successful application of the assessment?

When making a decision regarding whether to test it is useful to ask, 'Will the test tell us anything new?' and 'Will the results have practical implications for the client?'.

Certainty and judgement

When considering the ethics of the degree of certainty with which decisions are made (i.e. principles of informed decision making), the question 'Do we have the right to make judgements about clients, particularly on the basis of one or two formal assessments?' is, in Finlay's view (Finlay, 1990), worthy of consideration. This is very often the case in practice, as a therapist's caseload is usually such that only a certain amount of time can be spent in assessing each individual client. Therefore, each individual assessment should be as thorough as possible in order to provide the optimum amount of data. All results of assessments should be carefully considered to provide the most accurate and effective interpretations, and so facilitate unbiased and informed decisions and recommendations. Past experience of similar cases and learning acquired from experiences is a valuable asset when attempting to reach an informed decision regarding the outcome of assessments.

Finlay believes that we do have to make judgements and these cannot be avoided. However, she goes on to say that judgements should be contained within the limits of professional requirements and not personal, moral standards, religious beliefs or political views. The interrelated nature of assessment and treatment provides therapists with the opportunity to monitor judgements and/or assessments constantly in order to confirm, deny or adjust to changing circumstances.

Care should be taken that any conclusions arrived at from interpretation of results of scores obtained via standardized assessments are within the limits of the data obtained, i.e. conclusions should not contain inferences, personal views or be based on information obtained from any other source which is not directly relevant to the client's performance. However, in evaluating a test score the therapist must take account of any information from other sources which might have some bearing upon the subject's performance on the test in question.

The term validity centres upon the fact that an instrument or strategy truly measures what it claims to measure. Reliability is concerned with how accurately the scores of assessment data reflect the true performance of the client.

CONFIDENTIALITY

All results of assessments should be treated with the strictest confidentiality. The issue of security of test results is also important – these should be stored in such a manner that their confidential nature is maintained.

Any correspondence about clients should always be sent from one professional to another in a sealed envelope, even when being transported internally. Any discussion regarding a client should never take place in a public place where it may be overheard.

There are certain ethical considerations concerning who should have access to diagnoses and other information. Wherever possible this should be limited to relevant personnel only.

Privacy includes the principle of the individual's right to have control over personal information and to confidentiality of information about themselves. Clients should always be informed if any information is to be disclosed to others. Whilst there is no statutory right to confidentiality, the professional should not disclose information to others unless the client wishes it. Therefore, unless the client has been declared legally incompetent their privacy and confidentiality should be respected.

Individuals now have the right of access to their case notes. Since 1987 clients have had the right of access to any health records held in a computerized form and the Access to Health Records Act gave them the right of access to manual health records. Therefore, care should be taken in the way that recording is carried out.

When recording, all data must consist of objective fact which is specifically related to assessment results. This may be augmented but not replaced by subjective feelings, i.e. value judgements or personal views.

Reports

Reports compiled using data obtained from assessments should be factual, accurate, unbiased and objective. Where a value judgement or opinion is made, it should be supported by a description or explanation of the facts which have led the professional to form such an opinion. Reports should be succinct. They should be comprehensive enough to provide sufficient information to enable the professional to justify her actions and be professionally presented. Any unnecessary use of jargon should be avoided. Reports must be worth accessing and, whilst they must be succinct, they must also be as comprehensive as possible in order that professionals from other disciplines can interpret them, use them to obtain a clear picture of a client's presenting problem and assist them in their own informed decision making.

Clients are entitled to be given the opportunity to be able to read through reports related to their level of function, such as at case conferences and discharge planning meetings. The client has a direct interest in his records and the accuracy and confidentiality surrounding them. It is crucial that any report can be understood by them and contains factual content which is neither subjective nor biased in any way, and which cannot be construed as defamatory.

ASSESSMENT TECHNIQUES

Principles of informed decision making

The diagnosis provided in medical notes may help a therapist to formulate speculative ideas regarding a client's expected level of functioning and may provide an element of guidance for the therapist when choosing specific assessment tools. However, the medical diagnosis deals with areas of deficit rather than strength regarding a client's abilities. In addition to assessing the extent of presenting problems, the occupational therapist assesses the patient's potential to overcome any identified deficits/dysfunctions, so the problem setting, framing of problems and outcome-orientated information incorporated into the assessment process are invaluable.

Conceptualization

This process requires a knowledge of the presenting clinical condition, along with an understanding of various concepts including selection of a framework for organizing and interpreting information.

Certain simple concepts relative to an individual may be identified through observation and/or the therapist's past experience of similar circumstances. Data gained from these observations or experiences may enable the therapist to make tentative inferences. As the assessment progresses and a wider picture is gained of presenting problems, more complex concepts may be formulated, during which time the active process of hypothesizing takes place. During this process earlier inferences may be either discarded or improved upon as the client's progress is monitored.

Rigorous conceptualization of a problem provides the therapist with a sense of confidence in her clinical decision making, as well as maintaining professional credibility. Clinical decision making must entail systematic conceptualization and examination. According to social scientist Donald Schon (1983): 'Problems must be constructed from the materials of problematic situations which are puzzling, troubling and uncertain'. In order to convert a problematic situation into a problem a practitioner must make sense of a situation which may be far from clear. In this way the therapist can say what is wrong and what needs to be done to remedy the situation.

The preliminary stage of assessment was termed 'problem setting' by Schon. This involves the gathering of data about events/occurrences surrounding the onset of presenting problems of dysfunction and how these affected the client's performance or behaviour. The client's presenting condition is then considered. Much of this information can be obtained from both the client and his family.

Assessment strategy

An assessment strategy is the implementation of a process which will yield information about the nature of a given problem via assessment techniques, instruments or tests designed to facilitate the acquisition of sufficient data to provide a wide-ranging assessment and assist in the formulation of a comprehensive understanding of the nature of a problem. Significant data is thus collected, organized in order to make sense of it, and interpreted to ascertain what information the assessment gives. Questions which can be asked are: What is the problem? How does it affect the client? How can it be dealt with? and Which problem needs to be dealt with first? The problems which affect a client's level of functioning can thus be named, prioritized and dealt with within the context of an individual client's needs.

Significant factors to be considered are the client's feelings and values concerning the reality of his situation or goals for himself with regard to his future. Discreet questioning and the provision of opportunities for the client to vent or discuss his feelings can facilitate the acquisition of such information.

In most cases, an occupational therapist will employ several different strategies in order to frame a problem which has been identified from assessment. To do this, she must have a sound knowledge of presenting clinical conditions, along with a basic understanding of appropriate models of reference and what instruments or strategies will provide more information regarding a particular presenting problem. Assessment must always be carried out by a qualified therapist.

The therapist may make inferences and informed guesses based on previous experiences with similar clients before an assessment has been completed. This intervention, before a full picture has been gained, was termed 'reflection-in-action' by Schon (1983).

The assessment procedure

The assessment procedure can be grouped into three sections which cover a wide area and provide numerous options.

Section 1

Assessments which test the functioning of an individual, utilizing questionnaires, observations, interviews and performance checks
(i) Questionnaires

These may be:
>   self-rated – incorporating the client's view of the situation, progress, treatment or home environment.

Within psychiatry it is necessary to consider the client's level of insight. Although a client's perceptions of a presenting problem should always be taken into account, the client's view alone can be subjective, and it is vital that the therapist maintains an objective view of a situation.

An elderly person's expectation of success or failure can differ somewhat from that of a younger person. Turner (1987) states that the elderly are prone to both overestimate and underestimate their abilities. This tendency is borne in mind by the occupational therapist during her assessment. Actual performance, which can be assessed during direct observation, rather than self-reporting should, therefore, always be used.

It must be appreciated that very often older clients present with somatic symptomatology and feel too ill to cope with such assessment tools. In the case of clients suffering from organic dysfunction, where confusion and confabulation are often presenting symptoms, the questionnaire would prove an unreliable source of information.

therapist-rated – in which the therapist's view of the situation, and the client's progress, etc. are recorded.

The therapist asks the questions and puts her own interpretation upon the client's answer. However, this form of assessment may lead to inappropriate answers from or misinterpretation/misunderstanding of the questions by the client. This form of assessment is open to subjective interpretation by the therapist, and it is again imperative that the therapist is objective in her views in order to give any real meaning to any presenting conditions.

When dealing with unresponsive, uncooperative clients, or those who suffer hearing or visual deficits, it may be impossible to assess validly via questionnaires.

(ii) Observation

The therapist can observe the client's level of functional and cognitive ability. All clients, whatever their presenting problems, are observed to some extent by the multi-disciplinary team. Observations include social and interpersonal factors such as communication and socialization, expression of need and coping skills. These factors may be observed during a client's everyday interactions with staff and other clients or during group treatment settings.

A client's demonstration of confidence and expressions of satisfaction with self can provide information regarding interpersonal factors such as self-esteem and self-worth. In the case of clients suffering from extreme organic impairment, it is often impossible to assess by any means other than observation. Unless these clients are actually continually observed, it is impossible to know what they can or cannot do, or how well they undertake a particular activity.

Some functional disorders prevent a client from communicating well verbally and, therefore, observational assessments are often carried out during the acute stages of functional illness. A great deal of information can be gained about a client by careful observation of body language, such as eye contact or lack of it, gestures, posture and interpersonal interactions. This may provide significant clues regarding a client's underlying mood. An interview between therapist and client can always be carried out at a later date.

Observations can be either general – for purposes of gaining an overall impression, or local – for purposes of concentration on specific areas.

Observation is frequently a form of assessment employed within a behavioural approach, which concerns itself with observables, and may take place over a number of weeks.

In order that observation can be made easier and more reliable, decisions must be made regarding what aspect of behaviour the therapist is interested in: which specific behaviours are to be observed and which are significant. These can then be pinpointed and a clear definition of behaviour decided upon. It is necessary to define a behaviour for information about its frequency and characteristics to be gathered.

One of the shortcomings of observation is that when behaviour is observed by several members of the multi-disciplinary team, two people can see different things while watching the same sequence of behaviours – either because they have different expectations or because of a decrease in concentration. In addition to deciding what specific, defined behaviours are to be observed it is, therefore, also necessary to decide who will observe, and when and where the behaviours are to be observed.

When assessing by observation, progress can often be slow and changes difficult to discern. It involves time and effort to ensure that definitions or descriptions of behaviour are communicated clearly to other staff members who need to know exactly what is happening.

However, if the therapist wishes to know how well a client copes with various situations then observation is vital before any attempt to change aspects of behaviour. Why is behaviour to be changed? Who will benefit from behaviour change? These are questions that may also be addressed when using observations to assess.

Over a longer period of time, a client communicates a great deal of information via behaviour observed in a wide variety of settings and in a variety of circumstances. This assists in building up a picture of what clients can or cannot do, and helps in the treatment plan to meet specific client need.

It would be impossible for a therapist to observe all behaviours thoroughly; therefore, in addition to observation, it is often useful to listen to and ask questions of a client. One of the best ways of discovering a person's unique perspective of his problems or views is to invite him to tell you about it, and establish whether his perspective is different from that of the therapist.

Reliable observation is a skill which must be acquired through practice.

(iii) Interviews

Interviews between the therapist and client usually have three major aims: to obtain information about the client; form or develop a relationship with him; and briefly explain the purpose of the therapy in relation to his individual problems.

It is essential to have an outline plan for discussion and to be clear about objectives prior to conducting the interview, because this helps to clarify what information needs to be gained and why.

Beginning the interview

The interview should be planned carefully to provide a relaxed atmosphere and reasonable comfort in a setting which is private and quiet and likely to remain free from interruption. It is helpful if the venue is familiar to the client.

It is good practice for a therapist to introduce herself, state which department she is from, address the older client as, for example, 'Mr Smith' or 'Mrs Jones' and request permission to use the first name.

It is important to put the client at ease: there may be feelings of embarrassment or stigma related to the seeking of psychiatric help. A therapist should, therefore, aim for an atmosphere of openness, sensitivity and trust.

In order to build an effective working relationship, warmth, genuineness and respect are necessary attributes. It is important that the therapist meets clients in a genuinely friendly, even-tempered way. It is difficult to fake attitudes. If we do then clients may come away with a vague feeling of uneasiness, some suspicion and perhaps mistrust. The forced smile serves no purpose because clients need genuine friendliness: the false attitude is usually spotted very quickly.

During the initial minutes of an interview observational skills can be implemented to gain a general impression about a client's general appearance or personal hygiene. These first few moments of active vigilance can also provide important data regarding a client's thought processes, evidence of hallucinatory experience or subtle behavioural clues. Evidence of low mood, language problems, paranoia and level of concentration and attention can be gained at this time.

Communication

Talking with clients is an important aspect of building relationships because it is the most reliable form of communication (Calman, 1983). In this respect, the outline plan for discussion should not be too restricting.

Interviews with certain clients – those suffering from moderate to severe dementia, those with high anxiety levels or significantly decreased affect – will, of necessity, have to be very informal and of short duration.

The pattern and content of the interview will more than likely be influenced by the mood of the client, and this in itself will provide a considerable amount of information for the therapist.

Both parties should have equal opportunity to speak. It is essential that the client feels free to ask questions and not just answer them. It is also important not to take decisions out of the client's hands.

Clients should be encouraged to talk and vent their feelings and be allowed to control the points that they consider to be important.

It is particularly important that language should be understood by both parties for, as Drucker (1975) says, 'We can't perceive unless we conceive'.

Questions

Questions comprise 25% of most conversations and 9/10 will usually get an answer. In order to gain the optimum level of information required to make an informed decision as a result of assessment, it is necessary to have an awareness of the differing characteristics of interviews. There are two types: structured questions are determined and call for simple and direct responses, e.g. 'How old are you?'; **unstructured** questions allow the client to voice opinions, beliefs and attitudes.

There are certain prefixes to sentences which a therapist can use to best advantage. These can be summed up in the following quote: 'I keep six honest serving men (they taught me all I knew), their names are what and why and when and how and where and who' (Rudyard Kipling, 1902). Why, what and how questions are open-ended. They establish rapport, a first superficial or 'getting to know you' relationship and put the client at ease. Who, when and where are closed questions where the answer can be expected to be short. Questions can be initially open-ended to gain information and then closed and unstructured in order to gain wider information.

Phrases such as 'tell me about', which is neutral and gives no indication of what sort of answer will win approval, usually invite more than a yes/no answer. Link words such as 'then what' may encourage the client to enlarge upon or carry on with a conversation.

Listening skills

Listening skills are also vital when assessing. Listening is an integral part of caring, and the therapist must listen as one human being to another and then respond professionally. Listening to a client is both valuable and therapeutic; it may be just as important for the client to unburden himself of fears and worries as to provide important information about himself. Clients are more likely to do this during relaxed conversation, and so a therapist has to appear relaxed also.

If the therapist discloses herself genuinely and constructively in response to clients, communicates an empathic understanding and a respect for their feelings and guides discussions along specific and relevant lines, she communicates confidence in what she is doing.

Active listening by the therapist facilitates the opportunity to reflect, summarize and recap a client's feelings and views during interview. In this way the therapist can show the client that she has heard, understood and has a genuine interest in what is being said.

Feelings and responses

Both therapist and client may experience feelings of ambivalence. The client's feelings may or may not be related to embarrassment or a fear of the outcome of assessment. It is not unknown for a therapist to experience difficulties striking up a rapport with a patient due to personality clash, no matter how hard she tries. It is, therefore, easy for the therapist to fall into the trap of making erroneous assumptions regarding any remarks the client might make. It is important to clarify any responses that the therapist is not sure about and explore the origins of any remarks or client behaviour.

During the interview, it can be valuable to observe a client's non-verbal communication. Gestures can convey emotion more quickly and appropriately than words; as Goffman (1959) observes, 'Impressions are given off as well as managed'.

Towards the end of an interview any problems identified may be jointly prioritized by therapist and client.

Ending the interview
It is also useful practice to be especially alert during the last few minutes of an interview – the tension should be relaxed by now, and in an off-guard comment from the client a therapist may discover significant clues to his personality.

Inference and interpretation
According to Heider (1958), interviewees are only too well aware that the interviewer is likely to be making inferences concerning their motives, intentions, etc. on the basis of what they say and do during an interview. Therapist and client do not always share a common view, and it is unwise to deny that clients sometimes deliberately set out to deceive. A further difficulty is that a client may think that he is telling the therapist what they want to hear rather than what he, in fact, wishes to say.

The therapist, therefore, having elicited the required information, has to decide whether the client's statement can be accepted at face value or whether information gained needs to be interpreted, and whether oral accounts in interviews can be used as a basis for predicting behaviour in contexts outside the interview.

According to Harre and Secord (1972) this can be 'negotiated'. The perspective of the interviewer is often different from that of the interviewee, and this divergence in perspective is an adequate basis on which to 'negotiate'. The client's perspective can be checked out with that of their relatives or other professionals who may have had lengthy prior involvement with the client. The therapist can also take into account any experience she may have gained from involvement with clients presenting with similar problems.

(iv) Performance checks
Checks are widely used to discover what a client can or cannot do. Well-designed check lists can assess such skills as activities of daily living when carrying out dressing assessments, domestic assessments or home visits. They can be designed to ensure that no skill area is omitted from a particular assessment, and to incorporate yes/no answers under a series of headings, such as personal care, cognitive functioning, safety in aspects of kitchen work, sequencing and organization. Provision may be made for more generalized comment, where this is felt to be appropriate.

Section 2

Assessments aimed at others in contact with the client, i.e. which focus on relatives or friends and on staff involved in direct care

This facet of the assessment process can provide an invaluable source of information. Carers are often the best source of information about the problems that a client is experiencing and how the problems affect the life of that client. The carers can also relate how the problems affect them, personally, in their role as carers.

An assessment of carers themselves is a vital component of the whole assessment process. It is important to recognize 'carer strain'. The carer may be striving to put on a brave face and not admitting that they find things difficult. How carers feel is important; if they are supported they will feel and cope better.

Carers are themselves individuals, and the ability of a carer to cope will vary from one person to another. They are, therefore, likely to respond differently to the stress of caring. Many carers may themselves be elderly and under considerable strain, due to the ageing process and the demands of caring.

It is possible that the relationship between client and carer has broken down or been poor. Carers may have other difficulties such as financial worries or marital problems, or the elderly client's behaviour may be difficult to cope with.

Section 3

Assessments which look at the environment in which the person functions,
particularly at the ways in which this helps or hinders daily activities
A therapist is concerned with helping a client to realize his potential, and must achieve this through careful assessment and often deliberate manipulation of the person–environment fit. The therapist thus becomes part of the social environment of the client and may assume a variety of roles as indicated by client need: assessor, teacher, supervisor, confidante and supporter.

A client's performance during assessment may be affected by the fact that he is being observed by the therapist. This introduction to an environmental condition which influences client functioning may be lessened if the therapist aims to be as unobtrusive as possible.

Different perspectives on values, interests and functional levels may be gained via assessment in different environments. As all clients take on different roles and demands within their daily lives they are provided with opportunities to demonstrate their abilities in a variety of settings.

Community environment
Assessments out in the community can provide information regarding ability to purchase goods and whether this differs according to whether shopping is undertaken at small local shops or large stores. Aspects of road safety can also be assessed in the community setting. During social activities a client's social skills can be assessed and, during group discussions, an insight into individual client's views and opinions can be gained.

A client's appraisal of different situations and the ultimate coping strategies employed can provide a wealth of information which can be incorporated into the assessment process.

Hospital environment

A person's behaviour is influenced by the surrounding environment as well as by attributes which the person brings to that environment, such as personality, ability and attitudes (Orford, 1982).

In certain cases, hospitalization disrupts the familiarity of a particular environment by placing the elderly person in unfamiliar, less meaningful environments – he does not recognize an allotted locker as being his and cannot understand that clothes will be stored here. The elderly client may also be disorientated within the ward environment.

It is an extremely traumatic experience for some confused elderly clients when they are admitted onto an assessment unit. They have been subject to a move from familiar to unfamiliar surroundings and have sacrificed a previously independent life. They must, therefore, be given the opportunity to reorientate before any assessment is implemented. In this way a truer picture of clients' level of functioning can be ascertained.

It is extremely helpful to advise the client what adverse effects are due to the normal ageing process and what is illness related. Recognizing what is illness related may help the elderly client to cope better with day-to-day feelings of dependence and loss of control.

Hazards

Sensory, physical and cognitive changes in the client may mean that the environment can become hazardous to elderly people, and these factors form a part of assessment.

Responses to environmental cues are important safety factors when considering levels of functioning. Environmental cues are elements which provide information about the environment and require interpretation and responses in an appropriate, purposeful manner, i.e. is the client aware of the risks involved when heated elements of a cooker are left switched on and this leads to pans boiling dry and burning, etc.?

Social networks

When assessing the client's environment and predicting their envisaged future level of functioning, it is important that the therapist takes into account the client's social network. If it is found that this is limited or not conducive to the client's future functional, emotional and psychological performance then it must be either changed or adapted. The client's opinion and views regarding the adaptation of the social network are vitally important. The therapist's role is to strengthen existing social networks, whilst not forgetting the client's wants and needs. The assessment will have provided information about what the client will be able to do and what forms of support are required.

The therapist can inform the elderly person of what help is available, and also help them to use whatever resources are available to enhance their performance.

Society's expectations can affect our sense of well-being and self-esteem: are elderly people considered to be valuable members of society or useless, expendable and non-contributing or non-productive? An older person with a serious infirmity/impairment may often be an unwelcome reminder of what may lie ahead for many of us.

Life changes

Figure 3.1 below shows the types of adjustments to life changes that an elderly person has to contend with.

Requirements for psychological health include adequate standards of living, financial and emotional security, health, regular and frequent social interaction and pursuit of personal interests.

Resources

All living systems must interact adaptively with the environment and have their needs met. Resources which the therapist can use to help meet these needs include volunteers, self-help groups, Age Concern, local facilities and home care schemes.

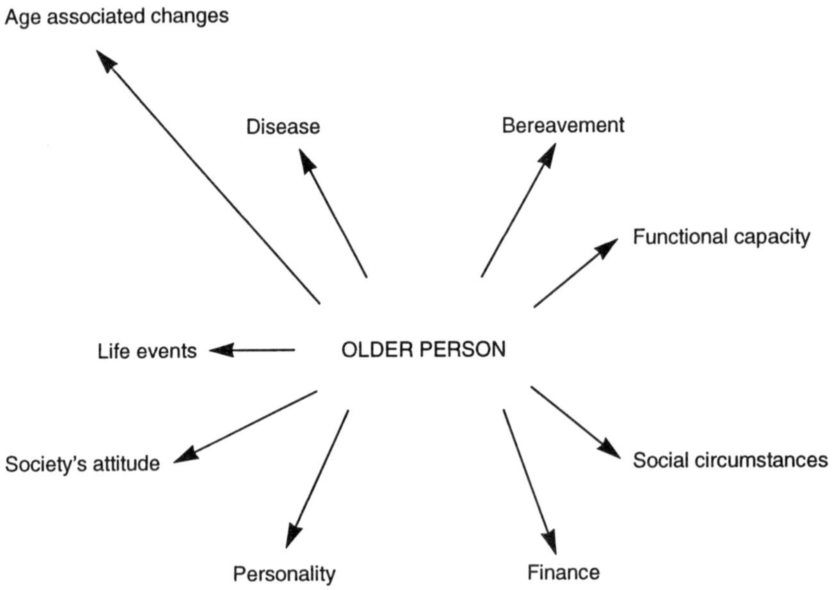

Figure 3.1 Adjustments to life changes

The therapist should assess the family to ascertain what support they c/ provide and what other commitments they may have.

All the services of the multi-disciplinary team can be coordinated to give the best results when considering social networks. Close liaison between services will avoid overlap or omissions of service and provide a better quality of care for the client.

It would be wrong to say that any one assessment technique is inferior or superior to another. In practice they all have an important part to play. However, the interview has been found to be an extremely valuable initial assessment, where rapport can be established between a therapist and her client and where essential background history can be obtained.

Assessment through observation provides crucial first-hand information regarding a client's actual level of functioning. A major factor in its favour is that it can be used in all cases, as it must form the basis of assessment of all forms of human behaviour.

Questionnaires can be used as additional methods of gaining information – notably clients' own views of a situation. Performance checks and formal standardized testing provide a source of information which can assist the therapist to justify or clarify results of informal assessments.

Where one particular facet of a client occurs consistently in interview, observation, questionnaire and carer's comments it is most likely to be a true reflection of the client's characteristics.

Assessment of carers and different environments all have their place. When used in conjunction with each other, all these forms of assessment together provide a global view of client ability and a comprehensive range of information from which the therapist can make decisions about and provisions for treatment.

LEGISLATION

In the White Paper *Caring for People* (DHSS 1989), which formed a basis for the NHS and Community Care Act, 1990, it was stated that the objective of assessment is to determine the best way available to help the individual, and should focus positively on what he or she cannot do. It suggested that assessment should not focus on the user's suitability for a particular existing service, i.e. it should be needs led not service led. Additionally, assessment should take account of the wishes of the individual and his/her carer and of the carer's ability to continue to provide care. These stipulations are mirrored in the Disabled Persons (Services, Consultations and Representation) Act, 1986, which resulted in part from the concern over the deficiencies of the Chronic Sick and Disabled Persons Act, 1970.

The advent of the NHS and Community Care Act has seen the implementation of the Level I and Level II assessments – the latter requiring a package of care from the multi-disciplinary team. An important aspect of a hospital assessment now involves the changes in community care legislation. Since April 1993, anyone entering residential or nursing home care will receive a full assessment and the changes have affected hospital discharge policy. Clients with complex care needs are now referred to a discharge coordination team which consists of a health worker, social services worker and support staff. Occupational therapists have an important part to play in the identification of Level II triggers during their assessments.

Assessment is the keystone to the provision of means of identifying and establishing a range of needs which require further assessment or intervention, or identifying more complex needs which are presently not being met. A need for a care coordinator can also be identified.

Triggers which indicate the necessity for a Level II assessment are:

- people whose care situation in the community is breaking down;
- service user and/or carer requesting admission to residential care;
- people who are homeless or who need alternative accommodation and who have physical and/or mental and/or psychological difficulties which limit their ability to care for themselves;
- people subject to frequent hospital or residential care admissions because of instability in their care arrangements;
- people at risk of harm or severe self-neglect, particularly where this requires support from more than one organization;
- people who are being abused as defined by the Adults at Risk procedure;
- people suffering from progressive, long-term, chronic or terminal illness with multiple resource requirements, or in hospital with acute illness, requiring multiple resources on discharge;
- people suffering from long-term mental health problems;
- carers who are being abused;
- carers under severe stress which may be demonstrated by their emotional state, risk of self-harm or neglect, or where the person being cared for is at risk of harm or neglect;
- carers who are no longer able/willing to continue with their caring role, for whatever reason;
- multiple/complex factors in a household, e.g. carers who are older or suffering from ill health.

There are also specific criteria for admission to either residential or nursing homes and assessment is, therefore, necessary to ascertain what level of caring input is required, taking into full account the client/carer's wishes, choices and preferences.

Various changes in legislation may occur in the future. However, assessment carried out along the lines outlined previously, which deal with specific needs and unique situations, should provide the necessary information and format required for an effective and efficient appraisal of client and/or carer need, whilst adhering to appropriate ethical criteria.

REFERENCES

British Association of Occupational Therapists (1985) Code of Professional Conduct, BAOT, London.

Burton, J.E. (1989) The model of human occupation and occupational therapy practice with elderly patients, Part 2. *British Journal of Occupational Therapy*, **52**(6), June.

Calman, J. (1983) *Talking with Patients – A Guide to Good Practice*, Heinneman, London.

Carkhuff, R. (1969) *Helping with Human Relations*, Vol. 11, Holt, Reinhart and Winston, New York.

Carkhuff, R. and Berenson, B. (1977) *Beyond Counselling and Therapy*, 2nd edn, Holt, Reinhart and Winston, New York.

Chronic Sick and Disabled Persons Act (1970), HMSO, London.

Coleman, P.G. (1982) Ageing and social problems, in *Psychology for Occupational Therapists*, (ed. F. Fransella), British Psychological Society, Macmillan Press, London.

Creek, J. (ed.) (1990) *Occupational Therapy and Mental Health. Principles Skills and Practice*, Churchill Livingstone, Edinburgh.

Department of Health (1989) *Caring for People*, HMSO, London.

Disabled Persons (Services, Consultation and Representation) Act (1986), HMSO, London.

Drucker, P. (1975) *The Practice of Management*, Heinneman, London.

Finlay, L. (1990) *Occupational Therapy in Practice in Psychiatry*, Chapman & Hall, London.

Goffman, E. (1959) *The Presentation of Self in Everyday Life*, Penguin, Harmondsworth.

Halperin, E.C. (1989) The right to privacy and the duty to protect. *Southern Medical Journal*, October, **80**(10), 1286–90.

Harre, E. and Secord, P.F. (1972) *The Explanation of Social Behaviour*, Blackwell, Oxford.

Heider, F. (1958) *The Psychology of Interpersonal Relations*, Wiley, New York.

National Health Service and Community Care Act (1990), HMSO, London.

Norman, A. (1987) *Aspects of Ageism. A Discussion Paper*, Centre for Policy on Ageing, London.

Orford, J. (1982) Institutional climates, in *Psychology for Occupational Therapists*, (ed. F. Fransella), British Psychological Society, Macmillan Press, London.

Schon, D. (1983) *The Reflective Practitioner: How Professionals Think in Action*, Basic Books, New York, pp. 40, 46–69.

Seedhouse, D. (1988) *Ethics. The Heart of Health Care*, Wiley & Sons, Chichester.

Thompson, I.E. (1987) Fundamental ethical principles in health care. *British Medical Journal*.

Thompson, I.E. (1990) Ethics, in *Occupational Therapy and Mental Health. Principles Skills and Practice*, (ed. J.Creek), Churchill Livingstone, Edinburgh, pp. 132.

Thompson, I.E. et al (1987) *Nursing Ethics*, 2nd edn, Churchill Livingstone, Edinburgh.

Truax, C. and Carkhuff, R. (1967) *Towards Effective Counselling and Psychotherapy*, 2nd edn, Holt, Reinhart and Winston, New York.

Turner, A. (1987) *The Practice of Occupational Therapy: An Introduction to the Treatment of Physical Dysfunction*, 2nd edn, Churchill Livingstone, Edinburgh.

Wolfensberger, W. (1972) *Normalisation: The Principle of Normalisation in Human Services*, National Institute on Mental Retardation, Toronto.

World Federation of Occupational Therapists (1985) Code of Ethics for Occupational Therapists, WFOT, South Africa.

FURTHER READING

Barrowclough, C. and Fleming, I. (1986) *Goal Planning with Elderly People. Making Plans to Meet Individual Needs. A Manual of Instructions*, Manchester University Press, Manchester.

Bean, P. (1988) *Mental Disorder and Legal Control*, Cambridge University Press, Cambridge.

Bruce, M.A. and Borg, B. (1987) *Frames of Reference in Psychosocial Occupational Therapy*, Slack Incorporated.

Christiansen, C. (1977) Measuring empathy in occupational therapy students. *American Journal of Occupational Therapy*, **31**(1), 19–22.

Christiansen, C. and Baum, C. (1991) *Occupational Therapy Overcoming Human Performance Deficits*, Slack Incorporated.

Cooper, J. (1990) *The Legal Rights Manual*, Gower Publishing, Aldershot.

Cummings, E. and Henry, W. (1961) *Growing Old: The Process of Disengagement*, Basic Books, New York.

Denham, M.J. (1991) *Care of the Long-stay Elderly Patient*, 2nd edn, Chapman & Hall, London.

Dimond, B. (1988) Mental health law and the occupational therapist. *British Journal of Occupational Therapists*, **51**(9).

Ellis, M. (1987) Quality: who cares? *British Journal of Occupational Therapists,* **50**(6), 195–200.

Finlay, L. (1988) *Occupational Therapy in Practice in Psychiatry*, Chapman & Hall, London.

Fransella, F. (ed.) (1982) *Psychology for Occupational Therapists*, British Psychological Society, Macmillan Press, London.

Gillett, N. (1968) *Principles of Evaluation*, AOTA Regional Institute.

Hanley, I. and Gilhooly, M. (1986) *Psychological Therapies for the Elderly*, Croom Helm, London.

Jones, R.M. (1983) *The Mental Health Act 1983. With Current Law Statutes and Annotated Reprints with Annotations*, Sweet and Maxwell, London.

Keilhofner, G. (ed.) (1985) *A Model of Human Occupation*, Williams and Wilkins, Baltimore.

Lemon, B. et al (1972) An exploration of the activity theory of ageing: activity types and life satisfaction among in-movers to a retirement community. *Journal of Gerontology*, **27**.

Lloyd, C. and Mass, F. (1992) Interpersonal skills and occupational therapy. *British Journal of Occupational Therapists,* **55**(10).

Maddox, G.L. (1963) Activity and morale: a longtitudinal study of selected elderly subjects. *Social Forces,* **43**.

Maslow, A.H. (1970) *Motivation and Personality,* Harper and Row, New York.

Moorhead, L. (1969) The occupational history. *American Journal of Occupational Therapy,* **23**(4), 329–34.

Munby, H. and Russell, T. (1989) Educating the reflective teacher: an essay review of two books by Donald Schon, *The Reflective Practitioner: How Professionals Think In Action* (1983); *Educating the Reflective Practitioner* (1987). *Journal of Curriculum Studies,* **21**(1), 71–80.

Norman, A. (1987) The confused elderly. Risk or restraint. *Nursing Times,* **83**(30)

Reed, K.L. and Sanderson, S.R. (1983) *Concepts of Occupational Therapy,* 2nd edn, Williams and Wilkins, Baltimore.

Rees, L. (1988) *A New Short Textbook of Psychiatry,* Hodder & Stoughton, Sevenoaks.

Steering Committee on Test Standards (1990) *Psychological Testing ... A Guide,* British Psychological Society, London.

White, R. (1960) *Competence and the Psychosexual Stages of Development,* Nebraska Symposium on Motivation, pp. 1–2

Willard, H.S. and Spackman, C.S. (1988) *Occupational Therapy,* 7th edn, Lippincott, Philadelphia.

Willson, M. (1987) *Occupational Therapy in Long-term Psychiatry,* Churchill Livingstone, Edinburgh.

ACKNOWLEDGEMENTS

My thanks to all who have assisted me in obtaining relevant literature related to the various topics discussed in this chapter.

My special thanks to Dr Jeanette Kenyon for her expertise and practical help, advice and support regarding the compilation of this chapter at its various stages, and to both Jeanette and Andrew Reid (my colleagues at Forest House) for reading and commenting on the completed chapter.

<table>
<tr><td>4</td><td># Risk and decision making</td></tr>
</table>

| 4 | # Risk and decision making |

Steve Pugh

This chapter has been produced in order to examine the concept of risk and the associated issues of risk assessment, risk minimization and risk taking. In addition, the chapter will look at decision making in relation to risk. The purpose of this chapter is to achieve a common or shared understanding of the nature of risk, to establish objective measures for assessing risk exposure and to explore the rationale employed in determining whether such exposure warrants specific reaction, which may include statutory measures.

Risk and decision making is a complex area involving the application of theoretical concepts to situations which are, in themselves, difficult. Carson (1990) brings together those two areas and relates them to people with mental health problems who have undertaken some form of criminal activity. Few practitioners become involved with deciding whether a patient or service user, who is the subject of a hospital order, should return to the community.

It is more likely that practitioners who are working with people who have mental health problems will be involved in decisions about their discharge. In order to assist the reader through this complex area the chapter has been illustrated by two different processes. The first involves a consistent illustration throughout the chapter, applying risk and decision making to the issue of abuse directed towards older people. The second mechanism of illustration employs short examples which places the more abstract points in practice reality.

RISK AS AN EVERYDAY EXPERIENCE

Everyday life exposes us to varying levels of risk by the simple fact of interacting with the environment. Risk is integral to our lives and the way we conduct ourselves on a day-to-day basis; it must inevitably be reflected in the perception of the quality of life. Few people willingly expose themselves to unnecessary levels of risk, and daily we ensure that the risks to which we are exposed are reduced as much as possible or we have extra awareness of that risk. The inclusion of various expressions of disability in the equation of everyday life interacting with the environment may change the nature of the risk to which we are exposed. This change may be reflected by the addition of other types of risk, may directly increase the potential of harm from existing risks or, conversely, minimize other risks.

Example A

A person who has taken to bed because they are not feeling well minimizes the risk from household accidents in the kitchen by simply not being there, but may be exposed to risks associated with the deterioration of an existing lung disorder and become exposed to the new risk of pressure sores.

For many people who experience disability and who are in contact with health and social service staff, an additional element is added to the equation of everyday life interacting with the environment, that being the workers' perception and tolerance of risk activities. Whilst the principle of self-determination is an integral part of working with adults, we have a responsibility to ensure that the risks to which people are exposed are identified and relevant minimization undertaken. However, when such risks become unacceptable by 'everyday' standards, appropriate action, which could include statutory action, may need to be initiated.

DEFINITION OF RISK

In establishing a common basis upon which good practice can be based, it is important that a shared understanding is achieved. The British Medical Association, in their guide *Living with Risk*, maintain that risk is ' the probability – likelihood that something unpleasant will happen ... the hazard is a set of circumstances which may cause harmful consequences, and the likelihood of its doing so is the risk associated with it' (BMA, 1987, p. 13).

The Royal Society, in its deliberations on risk in 1980, identified a hazard as 'a situation or activity involving events whose consequences are undesirable to some unknown degree and whose future occurrence is uncertain' (RS, 1981, p. 5).

David Carson (1992) maintains that risk is 'an occasion when two or more outcomes whether perceived to be beneficial or harmful are possible'. It is not a risk if it is certain; he goes on to say that 'risk has two variables; outcome which may be good or bad and likelihood which may be high or low. Risk also has a dimension – time. Outcomes have value, degrees of importance or desirability, positive or negative' (Carson, 1992, p. 7).

Risk can be defined as the likelihood that an unpleasant outcome will occur because of the presence of a hazard. The outcome may be unknown in character, in extent or even when or if it will occur. A hazard is a situation or activity which may give rise to something happening.

Example B

A wet floor is a hazard. Risk is experienced whilst walking over it, because there is a likelihood that you may slip – an unpleasant outcome. You may slip backwards, forwards, or on to your side. You may slip and bruise yourself or break a bone; you may knock others over. You do not know if you will slip or when – it may be the first step on to the wet floor, the last or at any time in between.

RISK ASSESSMENT

In practice, Brearley (1982) maintains that most decisions with regard to risk in the realms of health and social services are those which have high degrees of probability – they are likely to occur – and have high consequences – the outcome will be unpleasant, possibly leading to death, injury or future illness. In making decision about these risks, those who are involved – service users or patients – undergo a process of risk assessment.

Brearley (1982) argues that there are two broad elements to assessing and responding to risk, risk estimation and risk evaluation. Risk estimation involves posing two questions.

- What are the possible effects, given what we know of a situation?
- What is the likelihood that each of these effects will occur? Risk evaluation involves placing a value to the known effects and balancing these values relative to each other so that the effects which are most unwanted can be clearly identified.

Brearley's framework aids clearer decision making and specifically addresses risk estimation.

This type of framework is further developed by Brearley to include four possible approaches which may assist in identifying potential but specific risks:

- problem balance sheet – listing problems as well as strengths, building upon existing strengths;
- measure of functional capacity – what tasks can be performed, including activities related to self-care, role requirements and relationship activities;
- adaptation – how does the person behave and feel about the events;
- identifying the match between needs and the environment/resources to meet these needs.

Example C

Mr C.

Predisposing hazards	Situational hazards	Strengths	Danger
Age	Burst pipes	Social worker	Further deterioration of
Poor health	Faulty wiring	GP	health
Isolation	Deteriorating	Willingness	Depression/suicide
Lack of social	physical condition	to discuss	Cold/hypothermia
contact, etc.	Poor heating, etc.	problems	Loss of right to self-
			determination
			Self-neglect

(Brearley, 1982, p. 5.)

Risk assessment involves decision making in terms of recognizing potential risks, but also in evaluating the relative significance of one risk against another. Brearley advocates placing a value against specific risks, thus establishing their relative importance. Whilst numeric values may be employed, problems will be encountered because of the lack of shared consensus with regard to what these values actually mean.

Two potential resolutions to these difficulties may be:

- the application of generalized categories of values, grouped from most important to not too important; or
- a hierarchy of response identifying those risks which need to be responded to as an indicator or urgency.

Table 4.1 outlines a framework for prioritizing risk by identifying those activities or elements of a present situation which may be regarded as most important to the life and health of service users.

Table 4.2 represents a schema for identifying and tabulating the risks to which an individual may be exposed and the mechanism for minimizing or responding to such risks.

Accountability of health and social services staff, particularly when working with complex and difficult situations such as abuse, requires that they recognize and respond to identified risks.

Employing schemas such as outlined in Tables 4.1 and 4.2 provides a facility for the thorough examination of the situation in which a service user or patient is located, thus providing links between risk areas and identifying who takes specific action. This ensures that the process of accountability is based on a set of objective measures, rather than relying on memory or recording, the primary purpose of which is not one of risk assessment.

Table 4.1 Framework for priorities in risk assessment

	Priority 1	Priority 2	Priority 3	Priority 4
Service user needs	The life or health of the service user *will* be threatened from the identified aspects of their present situation or the activities they are undertaking	A threat to the life or health of the service user will occur from further deterioration of identified aspects, or the activities they are undertaking place them at considerable risk	The identified aspects may have long term implications for either the life or health of the service user, and/or may result in an improvement in the quality of life, or the risk activities undertaken do place them at some risk	An improvement or addition to the quality of life may be achieved or the activities undertaken place them at minimal risk
Carer needs	A threat exists to the life or health of a carer as a consequence of their caring activities/responsibilities, or the stress being experienced by the carer is having a detrimental effect on the service user	Considerable stress is being experienced by a carer from either this or another situation which may have implications for the carer or the service user, and which may give rise to the caring role being withdrawn	An improvement in the quality of life may be achieved for the carer, or in their relationship with the service user, which may enable them to carry on caring	An improvement in the quality of life may be achieved for the carer or in their relationship with the service user
Service implications	1. Requires an extremely urgent response from all those who are working with the service user and carer	1. Requires response that is urgent from all those who work with service user and carer	Response should be considered as important by all those who are working with the service user and carer	Response should be made as soon as possible by all those who are working with service user and carer
	2. May necessitate an admission to hospital or residential care in order to stabilize the situation by an assessment and/or treatment for a health-related problem	2. Temporary admission to residential care or hospital for assessment in order to establish the nature of a health-related problem or to stabilize the situation may be required		

	3. Statutory measures may need to be pursued 4. Referral to emergency services may be necessary 5. Failure to respond will place service user or carer at extreme risk, and may possibly result in admission to nursing home or residential care, which is not the preferred option	3. Failure to respond may result in admission to nursing or residential care		
Decision making	1. Opinion of service user and carer must always be sought 2. Referrals to GP and/or ASW undertaken without consent should be discussed with line manager 3. Multi-disciplinary forum or case conference may be used to share assessment and decision making. Outside of these forums, consultation with line managers should take place 4. The need to consult should never delay seeking assistance from the emergency services if the life and health of the service user or carer is immediately threatened	1. Opinion of service user and carer must always be sought 2. Multi-disciplinary forum/case conference may be used to share assessment and decision making 3. Consultation with line manager should take place	1. Opinion of service user and carer must always be sought 2. Consultation with other workers should be undertaken 3. Consultation with line manager may appropriately be made during supervision	1. Opinion of service user and carer must always be sought 2. Consultation with other workers may be undertaken 3. Consultation with line manager may appropriately be made during supervision

(Source: Based upon "Priorities for domiciliary services", Tameside Metropolitan Borough Council Social Services Department.)

Table 4.2

Name: D.O.B.   Compiler:

Address:

Predisposing hazard	Situational hazard	Strength	Opinion of service user	Risk activity	Priority of risk	Risk minimization	By whom?	Service user consent	Consultation
Chronic confusional state	(a) Gas fire being left on	Some potential to relearn with repetition	Unaware of risk but likes specific source of heat	Risk of explosion from inappropriate use of gas fire	1	(a) Disconnect gas	Social worker	Yes	Manager Service user Family Home care worker
						(b) Fire with coal effect but not radiant bars	Family	Yes	Manager Service user Family
	(b) Wandering	(a) Routinized behaviour involving putting appropriate clothing on	(a) Unaware of risk but likes to go out walking (b) Relatives very worried	(a) Risk of hypothermia	1	(a) Ensure availability of suitable clothing	Family Home care worker	Yes	Service user Family DCO Home care workers
				(b) Risk of getting lost	1	(b) Advise home care staff in patch	DCO	Yes	Service user DCO Family Manager Family
				(c) Risk of mugging	4				
				(d) Risk of getting locked out	3	(c) Key to neighbour	Family	No Carer making decision	Family Service user Manager DCO Home care workers

Whilst the tables look daunting, they are straightforward to complete and become a mechanism which presents risk assessment in an accessible format. The following represent a guide to completing the assessment.

- Identify predisposing hazard(s) – the condition or element that may potentially give rise to a risk situation, e.g. confused state.
- Identify specific situational hazard(s) – the consequence of the interaction of the predisposed hazard with specific situations such as confused state and gas fire.
- Outline positive elements which may influence the situational hazard, e.g. some potential to relearn activities.
- Identify how the service user feels about the risk to which they are exposed – do they recognize the risk? Does it concern them? Are they prepared to live with the risk? Or wish nothing to be done about it?
- Identify the **specific** risk activities and not generalized statements about risk – risk of explosion, risk of hypothermia, risk of getting locked out, etc.
- Using the framework for priorities in risk assessment, identify the priority of the specific risk activity.
- Having prioritized specific risk activities, identify the direct risk minimization needed to be able to address the specific risk activities.
- It is important to nominate a specific person whose responsibility it is to organize the individual risk minimization response.
- Finally, identify whether the service user has given consent for the minimization activities to take place and who was consulted in the process, which should at least equate to the decision-making format in the framework for priorities in risk assessment.

Table 4.2 has been completed for a fictitious situation which may be familiar to many practitioners, of a person experiencing a dementing illness interacting with the misuse of a gas fire and 'wandering'. Each problem area is broken down into specific steps which assist practitioners in working through such problems and also provide the mechanism by which the decisions made can be recorded and become accessible to line managers, relatives and the legal system should any form of legal action be taken.

Carson (1992) compiled a risk assessment format which involves:

- identifying the proposed risk;
- identifying how long the risk will last in the review period;
- analysing the decision as a risk;
- recording possible outcomes, either positive or negative;
- identifying the value of the outcome;
- identifying the likelihood of each outcome;
- exercising a judgement as to whether the benefits sufficiently outweigh the harms.

Carson's (1992) guide is more detailed and should be referred to if this format is employed in practice situations.

Monitoring and evaluation

Risk assessment highlights specific risk activities which may be prioritized and responded to by identified measures which minimize the harm that may be a consequence of such activities. However, it is important to maintain a monitoring and evaluating role to establish whether the minimization measures have addressed the specific risk activities. In such instances it may be necessary to refine or review the measures to be undertaken in order to minimize risk exposure.

Whilst previously identified risk activities have been addressed, this will generate a different situation which will contain its own risk activities requiring further assessment as part of a monitoring and evaluation procedure. This does not take into account the specific consequences of the measures which have been applied in order to reduce risks. Thus risk minimization may actively create new risks or exacerbate existing ones. Monitoring continuing risk minimization measures is demonstrated in terms of:

- ensuring the effectiveness of the measures;
- responding to new situations which are a consequence of the minimization measures;
- ensuring that the minimization measures do not in themselves directly increase exposure to risk.

RECOGNIZING EMERGENCIES

Changing situations will continue to affect the risk assessment and the steps required to minimize the risk, even though identified risks have been recognized and responded to. One such change in circumstances is an emergency or crisis. 'An emergency is a situation in which serious danger is imminent and action must be taken to avoid loss, damage or further damage following recent loss' (Brearley, 1982, p. 50).

The most common response, particularly among people who are viewing such a situation, is to seek admission into hospital or residential care. It would appear this response is based upon the perception of the risk takers as unable to cope or care for themselves.

Example D

The carer of an older person who has a dementing type illness has been admitted to hospital as an emergency. Domiciliary care and day care services have been supporting the relationship. In response to this emergency, should the older person be encouraged to have a short stay in a residential home? What happens if the hospital admission becomes extended? How long before the skills of the older person are lost? Alternatively, a thorough risk assessment, with appropriate risk minimization strategies and frequent monitoring with evaluation, may assist the older person to remain at home at a time that may be anxiety provoking.

Undoubtedly, medical emergencies will occur and should be responded to appropriately but, in balancing risk, further measures of risk minimization and additional community resources may address this new situation. Sharing decision making within the agency and with the person who is affected, family and friends is extremely important as a response to emergency situations, not least in advising people of what is happening and what is being considered.

RISK AND MENTAL ILL-HEALTH/LEARNING DISABILITIES

The responsibility of the health and social services will be influenced by the provision of the Mental Health Act, 1983, which gives a duty to act if the person is a danger to self or to others. This assessment is confined to an approved social worker (ASW), but other workers have a responsibility to recognize such situations and to advise the managers in order that appropriate action may be taken.

Not all situations where mental ill-health/learning disabilities are a factor require the intervention of an ASW or the acute mental health services. People who experience chronic confusional states because of memory and orientation problems do require the input of comprehensive risk assessment in order to reduce the risks to which they are exposed.

DECISIONS AND RISKS

Whilst a scheme may be employed to identify the source of specific risks to which an individual may be exposed, it cannot adequately reflect the subjective elements involved in more significant decision making in response to the identified risk situation, i.e. whether to move home, give up specific activities, etc.

Example E

An older person is living alone in his/her own home. The house is cluttered with dirty dishes and pans, dust is thick on surfaces, the walls are yellow with nicotine stains, the carpets are threadbare and the house is cold. Is the older person at risk? The older person has always lived like this and does not perceive any changes; has no mental health problems and is physically very well; has a very busy social life, goes out with friends most days and for the biggest part of the day; and maintains that such household tasks are insignificant, what matters is friendship and going out. Should there be intervention? The social worker feels that the person is at risk. Who is the risk taker and who the risk avoider?

Service provision to adults has traditionally involved front-line workers – social workers, home care workers, district nurses and domiciliary care organizers exercising a high degree of autonomy in decision making derived from considerable levels of skill and knowledge. These workers have usually had the freedom to decide their own objectives and methods, often working independently in a close relationship with service users.

WHAT IS A DECISION?

It may seem facile to ask such a question, particularly given the context of the many decisions being made on the basis of the professional competence identified above. However, it alludes to a much more complex theoretical analysis of decision making, the processes undertaken and, of equal importance, the issues which are eliminated from the decision-making agenda, i.e. non-decision. Etzioni (1968) defines a decision as ' making a conscious choice between two or more alternatives in selecting the most appropriate means to achieve the end' (Etzioni, 1968, p. 30). Whilst attempting to define a decision, Etzioni identifies that, in fact, a decision is the end state of a much more dynamic process.

The process would suggest there may be a set of logical steps which involves inputting the conditions that establish a problem exists and receiving the output in the form of a decision. In such a process the decision maker would become a technician. Real decision making involves uncertainty and resource constraints, it involves identifying those who participate in the process and the mechanism which provides legitimacy for the decisions made.

Decisions and the process by which they are reached are not undertaken in political and social voids. It is important to recognize that there are biases reflecting dominant interests in society; the location in which the decisions are made and the decision makers' own personal agendas. Given such biases, Grenson (1971) and Lukes (1974) identify the importance of non-decisions, which will be addressed with particular regard to the recognition of abuse.

MODELS OF DECISION MAKING

Rational decision making

This classical model of decision making identifies a set of logical steps which move through the process of making a decision.

1. Faced with a problem,
2. A rational person first clarifies his *(sic)* goals, values or objectives and then ranks or otherwise recognises them in his *(sic)* mind.
3. He *(sic)* then lists all important possible ways or policies for achieving his *(sic)* goals.
4. And investigates all the important consequences that would follow from each of the alternative policies.
5. At which point he *(sic)* is in a position to compare consequences of each policy with goals.
6. And so choose the policy with consequences most closely matching his *(sic)* goals.

(Sinclair, 1984)

Simon (1957) maintains that the model in essence involves establishing desired goals or objectives; identifying methods of achieving them; evaluating the options and then making the decision ' which maximises goal attainment or minimises costs' (Hitchens 1990). This model is recognized as an 'ideal type' because it is unrepresentative of what actually occurs in practice, reflecting primarily the limitations and the tasks which can be performed simultaneously.

In order to overcome these problems, the concept of limited search and 'satisfying' was proposed by Simon (1957); thus decision makers do not seek optimal solutions but those that solve the problem satisfactorily. Hardiker and Barker (1981) have applied this model to rational decision making in evaluating social worker assessment in cases of suspected child abuse. Their model, similar to that of Drezner (1973), involves five distinct stages:

- understanding the problem
- identification of objectives
- identification of alternative solutions
- evaluation of alternatives
- choice.

Incremental decision making

An incremental or successive limited comparison model of decision making is one in which a limited number of alternatives are considered, differing from existing choices by only small amounts. Analysis of each alternative is limited to a number of important consequences which are subjected to re-evaluation on successive occasions. Change is achieved in small steps – incrementally and on the basis of consensus.

Other models

Rational and incremental decision-making models represent the two most significant models. Others have been developed from these, namely the optimal rational model (Dror, 1964); mixed scanning (Etzioni, 1967) and iterative mixed scanning (Genstrung, 1978).

DECISIONS AND JUDGEMENTS

Dowie (1990) asserts that decisions are easy to make, but that judgements are the most difficult component of decision making. The judgements are as to:

1. what **choices** or courses of action are **available**;
2. what final **outcomes** are **possible**, via different sequences or scenarios of chances and choices;
3. the **chance** of each of these scenarios and its associated final outcome occurring;
4. the **un/desirability** of each of the possible outcomes.

In constructing the tree, he identifies judgements which are qualitative and quantitive. Thus judgements 1. and 2. above are brought together to form the qualitative aspect of the decision and 3. and 4. form the quantitive aspects or, as he puts it, the fruit on the tree.

TYPES OF DECISIONS

The assumption has been that each decision has equal importance in terms of outcome; however, the concept of decision differentiation enables the identification of a number of different levels of decision making. Case conferences or reviews will involve several different types of decisions, some of which may be new or fundamental whilst others are more routine.

Etzioni's 'mixed scanning' model of decision making combines rational and incremental approaches, enabling more fundamental decisions to be separated from less important decisions, and each decision is subjected to a different process. Fundamental decisions are examined in a broad search manner which concentrates on the analysis of alternatives – evaluating and rejecting them until only one remains, whilst minor decisions involve less examination of alternatives but greater attention is paid to the detail, with the intention of constantly improving rather than radically changing the way in which things are done.

A fundamental decision in an abusive scenario may involve an input from the domiciliary support services. More minor decisions may involve an examination of what tasks are to be undertaken when, where and by whom. Further reviews may consider the input of domiciliary support, possibly changing times, tasks and personnel.

Weekes (1980) identifies a distinction between (i) routine and programmed and (ii) non-routine and non-programmed decisions and responses. Programmed responses are invariably determined by people other than front-line workers and involve low levels of discretion. They represent regular answers which are available to familiar or regular problems. A procedural guide may stipulate a case conference should be convened within a specific period following an abusive incident. As such this decision – a fundamental decision within Etzioni's model – may be programmed and determined by people other than front-line workers.

A non-programmed response remains the workers' responsibility, where discretion is required in order to cope most effectively with complex, irregular and unfamiliar problems. Thus a referral to the police of an abusive incident is a fundamental decision which could not be programmed but would rely on the discretion of the worker involved, reflecting the high levels of competency and professional skill which these workers exercise.

The distinction between programmed and non-programmed decisions appears to establish a dichotomy: if both types of responses are regarded as ideal types and placed at either end of a continuum, it becomes impossible to place most decisions within the framework of the continuum. The decision to refer to the police is placed towards the non-programmed end of the continuum, because it relies on the expertise and knowledge of individual workers. Such a decision moves towards the programmed end if procedural guides maintain that such a referral be made only after broad consultation is undertaken.

Achieving consistency of response at a high standard of practice relies on a greater understanding of the processes and issues involved in a complex area. Consistency through time and amongst workers could be achieved with the greater use of programmed decision making within procedural guides. The assumption that prescription equates to consistency in decision making does not take into account the flexibility of response required by abusive situations and by the workers who are located within these wide varieties of situations. Such over-prescription will also undermine the professional autonomy and competency of many of these workers, and would be in direct contradiction to achieving consistency at a high standard of response and decision making.

The manager's skill and knowledge is crucial in responding to abusive situations. Working with front-line workers will broaden the basis of decision making and provide some degree of legitimacy for the decisions made. If this relationship is fundamentally prescriptive based on a lack of confidence in the workers, the likely outcome would be dissatisfaction amongst workers and managers at a time when a unified and consensual response is required in order to develop intervention strategies aimed at protecting abused individuals. In order to achieve a high standard of practice consistently, an interaction of programmed and non-programmed decision making is required. Procedural guides need to maintain a sensitive balance between programmed decisions and respecting, facilitating and encouraging professional autonomy and competence.

DECISION MAKING AND THE ORGANIZATION

Decisions and decision making are not made or undertaken in political voids, and many agendas and biases affect these processes. Front-line workers are invariably located within organizations which maintain objectives and exercise duties and responsibilities.

The establishment of control and the maintenance of professional autonomy results in an inherent conflict between the needs of the bureaucracy and the professional worker. This is particularly so with regard to the qualitative aspects of service delivery and has been recognized by the Barclay Report (1980) and many other commentators, notably Wilding (1982). Various techniques have been employed to achieve accountability to the profession and to the organization, as well as to ensure that policies and objectives are implemented and achieved. Hierarchical supervision has been one method used within the social and health services, whereby a worker informs a relevant manager of the progress of service delivery or intervention strategy.

The case conference procedure provides a wider basis for consensual decision making and has taken on an increasingly multi-agency or multi-disciplinary format, providing some legitimacy for decision, but demarcation becomes a problem when trying to establish who should and should not be invited to a conference.

Whilst hierarchical supervision and case conferences provide frameworks within which decision making may be extended to include others and some degree of legitimacy, case recording represents an aspect of professional accountability, the accuracy of which assumes greater significance, given Home Office Circular 60/1990, *Domestic Violence*, or where legal or quasi-judicial review may be taking place.

Abusive situations require case recording to be accurate, up to date and extensive, and should include:

- analysis of the information;
- decisions made or being made;
- discussion of the options/alternatives considered;
- nature of the proposed intervention strategies;
- referrals undertaken and not undertaken;
- measures which may be used to assess the effectiveness of any intervention strategies employed.

If case recordings are to be used as a tool of accurate accountability at certain moments in the development of the response to abusive situations, and to assist in achieving a broader consistency in decision making, procedures need to be developed which respect professional autonomy and facilitate flexibility rather than over-prescription in decision making. The development and use of a proforma which **guides** and **prompts** decision making may assist in achieving this balance, and should be included within or represent part of case recording notes.

Practicalities of decision making

Recognizing abuse

The publicity and comments surrounding the case of the Nye Bevan Lodge and Beverley Lewis represent the public expression of an increasing recognition within the health and social services of abuse directed at adults. The emergence of social problems and the acceptance of the need to respond is a complex process; it is not unreasonable to assume that abuse is a problem countless adults have had to cope with and has been expressed privately for many years.

Why then is it only recently that abuse of adults is receiving professional interest, and what was happening to those situations, some of which involved service input, prior to this interest being shown? Failing to recognize abuse or to act following recognition refers to the importance of the non-decisions identified by Grenson and Lukes. Not recognizing that someone is being subjected to abuse is extremely important and has a reflection in the development of intervention strategies (possibly non-intervention), thereby leaving someone at further risk of abuse.

Most abusive situations, however, were responded to on an individual basis, reflecting a belief in an individual pathology. Much abuse was not recognized, being regarded possibly as the expression of psychological processes and consequently dismissed – 'they bruise easily don't they' – or, if recognized, a belief that little could in fact be achieved to reduce the risk of further abuse would inform decision making and the response to the situation.

Recognizing that abuse is taking or has taken place involves a fundamental decision and should be made taking into account the events, explanations, circumstances and acts in question. Such a decision could not be 'programmed' but would be towards the non-programmed end of the continuum, reflecting the complexity and variety of the situations and circumstances within which abuse may take place. It relies on the skill and knowledge of the worker in establishing, from various indices, that abuse may form an aspect of a particular relationship.

Case conferencing

The use of case conferences as a method of working with adults has increasingly become accepted within the health and social services. As an aspect of the response to abuse it has many clear advantages, both in providing a forum for sharing information and developing a coordinated interventive strategy.

The decision to convene a case conference is a fundamental decision, although it would probably be programmed within a procedural guide which would maintain that following recognition or reporting of abuse a case conference should be held within a specified period, possibly three working days.

Where establishing that abuse has or is taking place is unambiguous, the decision to conference, as set out in a procedural guide, is quite clear. However, where uncertainty may exist with regard to particular actions or sets of conditions, then the decision to convene a conference may also be unclear.

Information gathering during a case conference may assist with deciding whether or not abuse has taken place; the forum also provides an opportunity for a broad-based consensus to be achieved, as well as ensuring some legitimacy for the decisions made.

A case conference would also represent a mechanism for formally recognizing sets of conditions or events, whether or not they are abusive, which may prove useful when legal or quasi-judicial review may be taking place.

Information gathering, broad-based consensus, legitimacy and recognition of events provide a number of very convincing reasons for convening a case conference, and it may be useful to suggest that where doubts exist a conference should be convened.

Recognizing abuse and calling a case conference both represent fundamental decisions. Case conferencing will, however, also involve a number of minor decisions: who should take part; levels of participation; where it should be held; and the information which is relevant for the objectives of a case conference. Decisions are made at different levels – decision differentiation. Some of these will be programmed, others will be at the discretion of the worker(s).

Referral to the police

Referrals to the police provide a great deal of anxiety for many workers, and consequently may be differentiated from most other referrals. Much of the anxiety may be attributed to the decisions which will or will not be made by the police, and are, in turn, informed by the professional model maintained by the police which facilitates an understanding and rationalization of the situations that they encounter. The police force and its officers on the whole maintain an adherence to a justice model, social services a social welfare model, and the Health Service operates a medical model. A social welfare model, with its emphasis on the processes which brutalize and alienate people, does not rest comfortably with a justice model.

Relationships between the police and social services have, on the whole, reflected the antagonisms which arise from substantially different methods of working with and understanding of the various situations within which we become involved. However, social workers and other front-line workers cannot place themselves above the law, and consequently must work within the framework of the established legal system.

Situations which involve physical abuse, financial abuse and sexual abuse may involve the police defining these events by using different terms such as assault, fraud, rape, indecent assault or incest. These terms involve harsh images and may give rise to a substantially different picture than an overstressed, ill carer hitting the person they are caring for in a moment of exasperation. However, the act is the same as someone hitting a stranger in the street. The differences may exist in the reasons for the assault and its location, i.e. not in the privacy of the home. The anxieties provoked by referrals to the police may, therefore, be based on a perceived powerlessness experienced by front-line workers, as investigations and legal proceedings occur based on the perception of the act(s) rather than the situation. The very opposite may occur when the police and the legal system undertake not to respond or proceed with any action, against the expectation of the front-line workers.

What is clear is that front-line workers and the police have to work together if abused individuals are to receive the response and the degree of protection they require. A greater understanding of roles, achieved by training and working together, may facilitate increased cooperation. Social services employees refer to and work with Health Service staff who operate a different model and maintain different responsibilities. In many ways this is not too dissimilar from working with the police, who are another agency exercising a responsibility in a similar area.

The decision to refer, given the above, is another fundamental decision (so, too, is a referral for domiciliary support – it establishes a principle), and under some circumstances the basis upon which the decision is made will be clear and unambiguous, i.e. an assault giving rise to serious injury. However, most abusive situations will not be so clear-cut. It is important, therefore, that the decision is made on the basis of as broad a consensus as possible, and it may be an appropriate decision for a case conference.

A procedural guide could not reflect the numerous situations which may involve a referral to the police. However, it may offer advice regarding referrals, and the decision would move further away from the non-programmed end of the continuum.

Nursing perspective

Miers (1990, p. 4) highlights the role that the nursing process plays in assisting nurses to make assessments and decisions. She maintains that 'the nursing process is a systematic approach to patient care whereby care is planned, implemented and evaluated by following a series of steps. These are observation, assessment, planning, implementing and evaluation'.

The nursing process is responsive to changing situations and is, therefore, capable of evaluating and reacting to the changing nature of the risks which are presented in a patient's situation. Recognizing such changes, Miers maintains, is a consequence of the 'daily knowledge of the nurse'. This 'daily knowledge' has parallels in other professions, such as social work, where it is referred to as 'practice wisdom'. As Miers points out, there is a need for such knowledge or wisdom to be made explicit.

In making such knowledge explicit by identifying the basis upon which it is based and how it is expressed in terms of outcome, Miers believes that the contribution which nurses make in decision making can become more valued. Given that the medical profession is highly structured, with lower status individuals having daily contact with purportedly higher status groups such as doctors, the status of the former group gives rise to their observations, comments and assessments being regarded by many doctors as having little impact on clinical decisions.

Miers argues that in a ward situation nurses are in an excellent position to get to know patients, to observe their changing situation and responses. These elements are crucial components of the decisions which are made. Presenting such information in more objective terms may assist in recognizing the role which nurses have to play in decision making within interdisciplinary teams.

PROFESSIONAL RESPONSIBILITY AND RISK DECISION MAKING

Professional responsibility in the area of decision making rests with the quality of that decision making. Many professionals, particularly in the area of human service, the health and social services, rely on intuitive or instinctual feelings in the decision-making process. This chapter has been dedicated to objectifying the process through which decisions are made by professionals about other people's lives.

To service users or patients and their carers, professional responsibility may be expressed in terms of getting decisions right, or as close to right as possible. People who are ill or tired and exhausted from their caring responsibilities are invariably worn down and maintain levels of dependence on professionals who they believe know what they are doing. At a time of vulnerability they require the exercise of professional judgement to be based on expertise. Such expertise may be demonstrated by the individual performing optimally and applying the full body of knowledge available to the professional, such is the faith placed with the professionals, particularly doctors and nurses.

Second best is not good enough. Increasingly, service users or patients and carers are seeking more information alongside professional decisions, which includes information and the process by which information is analysed, all of which inform the decisions made about them. Instinctive decisions based on gut feelings are difficult to accept. How would you feel if your doctor made a decision based on how he or she was feeling? Wouldn't you want decisions to be more objective?

Making a decision to release a person who is detained under the provision of a hospital order and who has a record of violence can be very difficult. Pickersgill (1990) identifies that some 1700 people are subject to a hospital order with restrictions and are in hospital, with a further 500 people in the community.

The Baxstrom case, heard in New York in 1966, led to the conviction of Johnnie Baxstrom for assault. He was imprisoned but, having been diagnosed mentally ill, was transferred to a New York State Hospital. When his sentence expired he was not released but kept in hospital. The Supreme Court in America upheld his petition of denial of equal protection under the Fourteenth Amendment of the American Constitution and he was released. It was subsequently found that 967 people were also detained in a similar manner and were released.

Steadman and Cocozza (1974) carried out a follow-up study and found 50% were in hospital, 27% discharged to the community, 14% were dead and only 3% were in a prison or secure hospital. Only 16 convictions had been noted and these involved nine people, 968 people were regarded as needing to continue to be in hospital – decisions were made to detain them, but only nine went on to offend further.

Undoubtedly, the newspaper headlines are not going to report 959 people successfully released from secure hospital, but nine people who put society in danger. The tolerance is nil if the decision gives rise to harmful consequences.

The other area of professional responsibility rests with the courts. It would appear that we are or may be entering a litigation culture, with professional decisions either being directly challenged in the courts or subjected to judicial review.

Freeman (1990) comments that at present 'a judge, indeed any other kind of decision maker in the legal context, is forced to make a snapshot decision. It is a decision about what is right there within' (Freeman, 1990, p. 46). He goes on to comment that there is no mitigation to take into account; you are either guilty or not guilty (the law in Scotland is different).

Carson (1992) identifies that the law of negligence is very important in the area of risk assessment and decision making, and associated with this are five core concepts:

- existence of a duty of care;
- breaking of standards of care in relation to the duty of care;
- identifiable causation of the loss;
- compensation assessment as a result of the loss;
- nature of the losses *vis-à-vis* whether they were foreseeable.

As professionals within health and social services we do have a duty of care and what matters is whether our actions fall short of the standard of care which would be supported by professional bodies. Whilst other areas of law can apply to our decision making, it is clear that we have a professional and legal duty to act in a manner which is not negligent, and our mere involvement with service users or patients ensures that we have a duty of care. Exercising this duty necessitates employing all the professional knowledge available to us.

CONCLUSION

As professionals, we not only have a legal duty to service users or patients and their carers, we also have a professional duty. This requires us to be responsive, informative and to employ the relevant professional body of knowledge.

Acting intuitively or instinctively, justifying such action in terms of daily knowledge or practice wisdom, clearly is not good enough. Our service users or patients should have confidence in our decisions and have access to the information upon which we have based our decisions.

Employing schemes does not restrict our decision making in terms of options, but may liberate us from the confines of well-trodden paths of problem solution to be more inventive, to seek more imaginative and satisfactory methods of resolving problems. They will enable us to break down problem areas into their component elements and allow more purposeful risk taking, primarily because the risks are outlined in front of us without appearing to be overwhelming.

REFERENCES

Barclay Report (1980) *Social Workers: Their Role and Task*, National Institution of Social Work Training.

Brearley, C.P. (1982) *Risks and Ageing*, Routledge and Kegan Paul, London.

British Medical Association Guide (1957) *Living with Risk*, BMA, London.

Carson, D. (ed.) (1990) *Risk Taking in Mental Disorder; Analyses Policies and Practical Strategies.* Proceedings of an Inter-disciplinary Conference, University of Southampton.

Carson, D. (1992) *Risk Taking in Community Care – One Day Workshop*, University of Southampton.

Dowie, J. (1990) Clinical decision making; risk is a dangerous word and ... is a sin, in *Risk Taking in Mental Disorder; Analyses Policies and Practical Strategies*, (ed. D. Carson), Proceedings of an Inter-disciplinary Conference, University of Southampton.

Drezner, S.M. (1973) The emergency art of decision making. *Social Casework*, **54**(1).

Dror, T. (1964) Muddling through – source or inertia. *Public Administration Review*, **24**, 153–7.

Etzioni, A. (1967) Mixed scanning: A 'third' approach to decision making. *Public Administration Review*, **27**.

Etzioni, A. (1968) *The Active Society*, Collier-Macmillan, New York.

Freeman, M. (1990) How might the courts respond to alternative analysis of risk?, in *Risk Taking in Mental Disorder; Analyses, Policies and Practical Strategies*, (ed. D. Carson), Proceedings of an Inter-disciplinary Conference, University of Southampton.

Genstrung, J.T. (1978) Policy making P...: a reformation. *Policy Sciences*, **9**, 295–316.

Grenson, M. (1971) *The Unpolitus of Air Pollution*, Johns Hopkins Press, New Haven.

Hardiker, P. and Barker, M. (1981) *Theories of Practice in Social Work*, Academic Press, London.

Hitchens, B. (1990) Case management decision making in a local authority. Unpublished dissertation.

Home Office Circular 60/1990 *Domestic Violence*, HMSO, London.

Lindblom, C.E. (1975) *The Policy Making Process*, Prentice-Hall, Englewood Cliffs, NJ.

Lukes, S. (1974) *Power: A Radical Review*, Macmillan, London.

Miers, M. (1990) Daily risks and daily decisions: a nursing perspective, in *Risk Taking in Mental Disorder; Analyses Policies and Practical Strategies*, (ed. D. Carson), Proceedings of an Inter-disciplinary Conference, University of Southampton.

Pickersgill, A. (1990) Balancing the public and private interests, in *Risk Taking in Mental Disorder; Analyses Policies and Practical Strategies*, (ed. D. Carson), *Proceedings of an Inter-disciplinary Conference*, University of Southampton.

Royal Society (1981) *The Assessment and Perception of Risk*, London.

Simon, A.A. (1957) *Administrative Behaviour*, Macmillan, New York.

Sinclair, R. (1984) *Decision Making in Statutory Reviews on Children in Care,* Gower, Aldershot.

Steadman, H. J. and Cocozza, J.J. (1974) *Carers of the Community Insane*, Lesington, Lesington Bodes.

Weekes, D.R. (1980) Organisation and decision making, in *Control and Ideology in Organisation*, (eds F.W. Salamen and K. Thompson), OU Press, Milton Keynes.

Wilding, P. (1982) *Professional Power in Social Welfare*, Routledge and Kegan Paul, London.

FURTHER READING

Guttman, D. (1978) Life events and decision making by adults. *The Gerontologist*, **18**(5), 462–7.

Howe, D. (1986) *Social Workers and Their Practice in Welfare Bureaucracies,* Gower, Aldershot.

McGrew, A.G. and Wilson, M.J. (1982) *Decision Making Approaches and Analysis*, Open University Press, Manchester.

Norman, A. (1980) *Rights and Risk: A Discussion Document on Civil Liberty in Old Age*, National Corporation for the Care of Old People, London.

to see how easily nurses can feel out of control if they were not to make it their own personal responsibility to find out about a forthcoming change.

Nurses are in an ideal position to direct the implementation of change as they are the ones with the working knowledge and are, therefore, often best suited to make informed decisions about it.

Using the basic principles of implementing change the nurse needs to ensure:

- change is planned and implemented gradually;
- it is based on knowledge and discussion with the other team members;
- that all alternatives have been explored;
- that all staff feel they have some control in the change and responsibility for it;
- that a trial period is allowed;
- that the change makes sense – that it is for the better and the benefits are highlighted.

It was refreshing to discover that these simple ideas on implementing change were shared by some nurse theorists.

PRACTICE AND THE THEORY OF CHANGE

There are many books which discuss nurse theory in general and, specifically, the theory of change is discussed at length in Lancaster and Lancaster (1982). It is not the intention here to discuss theories of change, but to give a clinical example of how a change has been implemented in practice and, by explaining the process of implementation, it is hoped that ward-based nurses can see its roots in the theory of change and how both practice and theory complement each other. Therefore, practice can be based on theory and theory can emerge from practice.

A brief overview of Lewin's theory of change (1958) will be given, as it is well known and often used in conjunction with Lippitt's (1973) seven steps of implementing change. Lewin saw the process of change occurring in three main stages: unfreezing, moving to a new level and refreezing.

Unfreezing During this stage there is a need to recognize the necessity for change and to have a general idea about the specific change needed. This is a time when promotion of the need to change and becoming motivated to change is important, alternatives should be explored, group cohesion should be formed and there should be mutual trust and respect.

Moving to a new level We move on from the identification of the need to change to thinking about the goals to be achieved and the formulation of an action plan to which all agree. The goals and action plan can come from two sources. First, they can come from someone who is trusted and respected or in a position of power; this method is referred to as identification. Secondly, they can come from looking at all the options open to a given group and making a choice from these options, a method referred to as scanning.

Refreezing This is the time when the new behaviour becomes accepted to such a degree that it becomes the new norm.

During the process of unfreezing, moving to a new level and refreezing there are two opposing forces at play, one driving nature to succeed and one restraining.

In Lippitt's theory of change, there are seven steps to enable the implementation of change.

1. Diagnosis of the problem: An open mind and exploration of all possible causes are essential in diagnosis. It is a stage of data collection, during which all those that are concerned with the change should be involved and the problem identified.
2. Assessment of motivation and capacity: This includes all the resources needed for the change and any constraints that may hinder change. From the information gathered so far, it is possible for solutions to be identified and prioritized.
3. Assessment of the change agent's motivation: It is essential that this is honestly assessed, and that in circumstances where there are a number of individuals seeking change they all have the same goals, etc.
4. Selecting progressive change objectives: This is the formulation of a step-by-step guide for the implementation of the change. A trial period is recommended because evaluation can then take place.
5. Change agent's role: awareness of role, which will be dictated by individual circumstances, is needed to enable effective change.
6. Maintenance of the change: During this stage it is easy to fall back into old habits, so it is essential to keep channels of communication open, that regular feedback is given and success promoted to other areas which may want to adopt the change.
7. Termination of the helping process: This should be done gradually and in a planned way.

One example of change on my current ward is the implementation of 'flexishifts'. The process of flexishift implementation will be described and, in doing so, it is hoped that the similarities between the process of change implementation and the theories of change are highlighted. It is important to show that theories are not prescriptions that have to be followed to the letter, but that they are merely guidelines available to help in the process.

The first six steps of Lippitt's theory of change can be seen in the example of flexishifts.

Flexishifts

The ward I currently work on is a 22-bedded continuing care ward for older people who have some form of dementia. Due to the degree and prognosis of the dementia the residents live on the ward and are dependent upon nursing intervention to carry out most or all the activities of living. All the staff on the ward have chosen to work with this client group and, therefore, are highly motivated and open to new ideas. It is the ward's philosophy to strive continually to improve the care given. One example of this is the flexishift system.

Background to the introduction of flexishifts

The ward is adequately staffed throughout the day and all staff on the ward do internal rotation.

Step one

During one of the weekly ward meetings, attended by all staff on the ward, several problems with this system were highlighted.

Due to the ward's philosophy, the residents get up and have their breakfast on an individual basis. This results in the whole morning shift concentrating on the specific needs of individual residents, therefore recreational activities are performed in the afternoon.

Problem identification

- With the present shift system there is only an overlap period of one and a half hours during the day when the majority of the staff are on duty, in which time a handover needs to take place and in giving an adequate handover the amount of time left for recreational and other activities is reduced.
- The time available for recreational activities was limited. It was felt that the recreational activities were very important to both the residents and the staff. On a continuing care ward it is essential for staff motivation and morale to ensure that the staff have a balance of activities, with recreational activities being used to counterbalance the nursing activities which are both mentally and physically tiring.
- From a ward management perspective, this is not an efficient use of nursing time. It is not necessary to have five members of staff on duty at 7.00 a.m. when the residents only require nursing intervention from approximately 8.00 a.m. when they start to wake up. Similarly, there are certain times during the day when more staff are needed on duty, for example at lunchtime.

Once problems had been highlighted at the meeting, all staff members were given an open forum to enable them to contribute to the collection of relevant data and to propose possible solutions to the identified problems. Brainstorming sessions were used to identify possible solutions, each being explored for its viability with regard to resources, constraints, possible advantages and disadvantages, etc.

Step two

There was an overall agreement that we needed to increase the amount of overlap time, the amount of recreational activity occurring on the ward, the numbers of staff on duty at the busiest times of the day, reduce the amount of wasted staff time and, most importantly, have a shift system that was geared to the needs of the residents.

Step three

There were a number of viable solutions highlighted, and ward consensus suggested that the most popular solution should be implemented for a trial period of three months. The situation would then be reviewed by assessing its effectiveness using a questionnaire. Having a trial period allowed all staff members to participate in the change willingly, in the knowledge that it would be reviewed prior to its permanent implementation. The change was positively promoted and perceived as a challenge by everyone, and because all the ward staff were involved and had been consulted, genuine commitment to its success was visible.

The whole process of the identification of a problem and possible solutions occurred over a number of meetings. It was an ongoing process where good communication channels encouraged the change to be seen as a challenge rather than a threat. The process allowed all the ward staff to have ownership of the problem, possible solutions and the desire to do something about it, and by having this ownership they felt they had some control over the situation.

Towards a solution

The solution was seen in the form of a two-pronged approach. The shift system would become 'flexible'. On an early shift, two of the five staff members who would normally start work at 7.00 a.m. would start at 8.00 a.m. and, therefore, would finish working at 3.30 p.m. On a late shift, one staff member would come in to work at 12.00 noon to be available to help with the residents' lunches and would, therefore, finish at 8.00 p.m. instead of 9.00 p.m. The second prong of the solution entailed a rigid activities programme, in which named nurses would have responsibility for ensuring that a specific activity would happen each day.

To assist in the success of the implementation of this change, the effect of the change on individual staff members was intentionally minimized. All staff were consulted as to their preference in working the new shift patterns and no member of staff was made to participate in them. A duty request book was issued so that the staff doing the alternative shifts could volunteer to do specific shifts, and, before an off-duty was completed, all staff were asked if it was convenient for them to do the rota. This assisted in the implementation of flexi-shifts, as coercion was not an issue and, therefore, could not adversely affect the implementation of the change. Similarly, in the activities programme, all staff members were consulted about what they had to offer with regard to recreational skills and, therefore, participated in activities they personally enjoyed. The ward staff also formulated the weekly activities programme.

Step four
Goals were set.

- The overlap period during the day would increase from one and a half hours to three hours.
- The number of staff available in the afternoon to participate in activities would increase and, therefore, the activity programme would be adhered to.
- There would be sufficient staff on duty at the busiest time of the day and less nursing time wasted.
- The residents' needs would be firmly related to the shift system in operation.

A three-month trial set a deadline for when assessment of the effectiveness of the flexishift system would occur using a questionnaire; therefore a system of evaluation was built in.

Step five
Due to the motivation of the ward team, I, personally, had only to act as group leader and facilitator, and ensure that the trial period was implemented.

At the end of this period a questionnaire was circulated to all staff members, who were given two weeks to respond and return the completed questionnaire anonymously.

The response to the questionnaire was generally favourable. The main advantage was seen to be that flexishifts created time for staff to implement a planned activity programme, to spend time discussing and formulating care plans and allowed more time for handovers. More staff were on duty at the busiest time of the day, nursing time was used more constructively and the actual time at work seemed to pass more quickly.

The disadvantage of the trial period was that the activities were dependent upon individual staff involvement and non-nursing duties took a large chunk out of the potentially available nursing time. Some nurses felt that the trial period was a way of making staff work harder and felt the loss of quiet times that were an essential part of the day. There was a core group of staff that were resistant to change, justifying their resistance by expressing concerns about flexishifts intruding on personal commitments, that they had to work harder for longer and about the loss of special duty payments between the hours of 8.00 p.m. and 9.00 p.m. when doing a 12–8 shift.

Review

Step six
A report on the questionnaire's findings was given to all staff members prior to an arranged meeting to enable them to comment upon them. The meeting was

then used to discuss the trial period and to explore the staff's motivation to proceed with the new change. All staff agreed that the actual benefits to the residents outweighed the inconvenience to staff members, especially if their individual circumstances were considered when formulating the off duty. The trial period highlighted a problem with regard to the use of nursing staff to do non-nursing duties (putting laundry away and washing up, etc.). The solution of a housekeeper post was suggested. The meeting was attended by nursing management who were able to legitimize the introduction of flexishifts and the possibility of a housekeeper post being advertised.

Due to the nature of the clients' illness, it was impossible to ask them formally whether they had benefited from the change in nursing practice. However, observation from nurses and relatives suggested that they had done so, and they were likely to have a nap in the afternoon. During the actual sessions the clients would say they were having a good time, participated well in the activities and were able to function on a more personal level (in that they could be themselves).

Throughout the trial period the positive aspects of flexishifts were promoted both on the ward and to other health care professionals.

Implementing a change into the clinical setting is not as easy as it would appear. In practice there are many variables that can affect its success that are beyond the control of those wishing to implement the change.

Flexishifts is an example of a change which was implemented for the benefit of the residents. It was also supported by the staff making the change and was practice led. It is also an example of a change that was not maintained past the trial period due to uncontrollable variables. In flexishifts, the uncontrollable variables were changes in overall structure of the hospital which resulted in all vacant posts being temporarily frozen, therefore a housekeeper was no longer an option. In addition, the staffing levels on the ward were not stable enough to be able to plan flexishifts without potential problems with low staff numbers throughout the day.

It is also important to bear in mind that it takes a lot more than a vocalized desire to change to enable change to occur. If the change interferes with the individual's present lifestyle without actual perceived benefit to them, they will not allow change to occur.

To maintain change, it is necessary to keep the channels of communication open, manage the situation so that old patterns of work are not lapsed into and feedback about the positive aspects of the change is relayed to all staff members. The new work patterns will eventually become the norm, at which time the change agent withdraws.

When trying to implement a change in a clinical setting, it is essential to realize that there are never any failures, that lessons can be learned and success celebrated. It is far more challenging and interesting for staff to become actively involved in a change project that does not succeed in its eventual implementation than it is to sit back and do nothing.

CHANGE IN CARE OF OLDER PEOPLE

In a very personal account of the changes that I have seen in the care given to older people with dementia, I intend to concentrate on the clinical setting of a continuing care ward.

My first placement as a student nurse 10 years ago was on the 'psychogeriatric' ward. Because of the similar client group to this that I currently work with today, I feel it is appropriate to compare and contrast the two wards. Both wards had training status, therefore both were considered 'good' examples of good practice.

It is interesting to examine the language used when describing this client group. Presently it is acceptable to refer to them as having some form of dementia with the diagnosis of Alzheimer's disease being perceived as a genuine illness by the general public. Ten years ago the same client group were referred to as being either 'senile' or as 'psychogeris', and popular terms of reference during the interim period were ESMI or organic brain disorder. Different terms of reference will always come in and out of vogue and, no doubt, the term dementia may be seen as a degrading term in years to come. It is very important that this client group is referred to in a 'positive' and non-offensive way, but a move forward would be to see the individuals that make up the client group and to move away from negative terms of reference.

To enable a clear comparison of the 'then and now', I will refer to nursing undertaken 10 years ago as 'factory' nursing and the nursing undertaken today as 'free-range' nursing. Factory nursing seems an appropriate description because the general philosophy was to provide quick, cheap, basic nursing care in a situation where the importance of 'jobs to be done' resulted in task allocation. In free-range nursing the emphasis has been shifted on to the patient's individual needs and to providing quality care which allows for more flexibility.

Attitudes to the client group

One major difference between factory and free-range nursing is the nurses' approach to the client group. Ten years ago, as today, there were a number of staff who cared very much for those in their care but were misguided in their expression of this care. Many of the staff felt that the patients needed to be protected, and that due to their illness they had returned to being a child or infant which affected how they cared for them. They cared for them as they would care for a child or baby, and this resulted in the patients being 'wrapped up in cotton wool' and 'de-skilled' for 'their own good'. Today, on a free-range ward, the staff have a genuine desire to work with this client group and generally aim to protect the residents' independence, dignity and privacy. They treat the residents how they themselves would like to be treated, or how they would expect their own parents to be treated in a similar situation.

The job

In factory nursing, the 'job' was seen very much in terms of coming to work, performing tasks and then going home; indeed very much like working in a factory. To be placed on a continuing care ward was often used as a punishment for previous 'crimes', with the sentence being 'hard labour' on a psychogeriatric ward. Because of this unwritten policy, the staff on continuing care wards were often a collection of troublemakers or hard-to-place nurses which, in turn, did not assist in the positive promotion of the speciality as worthwhile. Motivation on the factory wards was poor, attitudes and actions were not challenged and, therefore, change did not occur. Staff status was obtained by being a 'good worker' rather than how the nurse interacted with the patient.

On a free-range ward, the job is seen as a speciality, with nursing staff actually applying for jobs on the continuing care ward. The client group is seen as having potential and very much as a challenge. Staff motivation and attitudes are high (which, in turn, allows for staff to value their work), and are maintained by giving all grades of staff regular updates, teaching sessions and clinical supervision, combined with a clear say in how the ward is run. The actual work is still very hard, especially when emphasizing the need to maintain a resident's independence, but it is also rewarding with status being given to the nurses who are able to communicate well and appropriately with residents.

The philosophy

The general philosophy of the two types of wards is very different. In factory nursing, important issues were to get the job done as quickly and efficiently as possible, because only then could the staff sit down and have a drink together, usually round a big table with the exclusion of patients. Task allocation was the norm; daily tasks were broken down clearly, bath and bowel books and toilet lists were used.

Patients were viewed collectively; their privacy, dignity and independence were not seen as being important because 'the patient did not know what was going on anyway'.

The environment was sparse, with chairs covering the outer walls of the huge day areas and plants and ornaments non-existent because the patients would eat or break them. Restraint was used indiscriminately, in the form of buxton chairs and cot sides, their use being justified as in the patients' best interest and for their safety.

Individuality was not evident, the patients wore shared 'pool' clothing, used the same toiletries and hair brushes and did not possess any distinguishable personal space or belongings. The patients' money was used collectively to buy the ward biscuits and sandwich fillings and, although these items were given to the patients, no individual preference was sought. Toileting was undertaken en masse: all the patients were seen as being incontinent, therefore they were rarely given the opportunity to actually use the toilet and their 'nappies' were changed instead.

In contrast, in free-range nursing the most important concept is individuality. Residents are seen as individuals with specific needs; this meant that many of the unwanted nursing practices undertaken in factory nursing were automatically diminished. Residents have individual care plans, are given choice in all activities, wear their own clothes, have their own toiletries, and can individualize their bedroom with personal effects. Bathing and toileting are undertaken on an individual basis and privacy is maintained at all times.

The environment is homely; residents are encouraged to bring their own personal artifacts on to the ward so that they can see familiar things. Small clusters of chairs are used to encourage resident communication, with the staff taking their brew time with the residents rather than isolating themselves. No restraint is necessary on a free-range ward.

The residents have their own money which is used to purchase clothing, toiletries and special items that they like. Relatives are consulted when purchasing items for them so that the personality pre-dementia is maintained. The terminology used when talking or referring to a resident is age appropriate. Terms such as 'nappies', 'babies' and 'feeders' are not condoned; instead 'incontinence aids', 'highly dependent' and 'residents who require assistance when feeding' are used.

Daily routines

In factory nursing, the main focus was to get the job done as quickly and efficiently as possible with the minimum of fuss. The patients were treated as a whole, with all daily activities being performed on all patients at the same time. The clothing belonged to the ward and was, therefore, shared by everyone. In the morning patients were helped to get up and dressed, were washed using the communal back trolley, and then brought to the breakfast table in a wheelchair because it was quicker than assisting someone to walk if they were slow or unsteady on their feet. Breakfast was only served when all the patients were at the table. This was a set meal with no individual choice available. Each subsequent meal followed the same pattern as breakfast. When everyone had finished eating, they were moved to the day room. In the day room a trolley would visit each person in turn to enable them to have their hair brushed (using the ward brush) and their faces washed, using a disposable cloth.

The day was punctuated with toilet rounds, meals and brew time. There were no structured activities available. All the patients would be taken to the toilet at the same time, usually prior to a meal, so that they could be taken straight to the meal table afterwards, thereby killing two birds with one stone. All the ward toilets were occupied simultaneously, the patients sitting on a toilet with the door wide open and having their 'nappies' changed. Time was never allowed for the patients to use the toilet, as it was considered a waste because they were 'incontinent'.

'Brew time' consisted of a cup of tea, made in a large kettle and to which milk and sugar were added, no consideration being given to whether a patient liked tea, milk or sugar.

In factory nursing there are a number of rituals that occur: the use of the bowel and bath books, the preparation of 'bundles' (clothes, stockings and an incontinence pad rolled up into a ball) ready for the following day; and the belief that to manage a wandersome patient buxton chairs have to be used to restrain them from walking about. These rituals are deeply imbedded into the ward's philosophy, with no explanation to back up their use.

In free-range nursing the emphasis is on the individual resident; all of the negative activities of factory nursing are eroded. Basically, residents are given choice in every area of life. They have their own clothing, get up when they would wake up naturally and when they get up they are served their breakfast immediately and a choice is offered. Residents have individual toileting programmes based on extensive assessment of their individual needs. Bath and bowel books are not necessary because residents bathe when they wish and will be given time on the toilet to be able to use it.

Structured activities are provided, both on the ward and in the community setting, and the residents are able to participate in them if they want to. The residents are viewed as worthwhile people and, therefore, restraints are no longer seen as desirable or ethical.

CONCLUSION

During my nursing career I have been very lucky to have worked on wards that have provided excellent nursing care for older people with dementia. Change has been an integral part of each of the wards that I have worked on, and this change has been supported by an investment in quality nursing care and a commitment from the management.

For change to occur on a continuing care ward, the client group has to be valued by those giving the care, therefore all staff have to want to care for people with dementia and possess a positive attitude towards the residents in their care. On my current ward this has been achieved by conducting interviews specifically to recruit staff to work with people who have dementia, and by selecting only those staff who have a positive attitude to work with older people. Once the staff were selected, a multi-disciplinary 'team-building week' was arranged to enable staff relations to be built, to open channels of communication and to begin work on a shared philosophy. The unqualified nurses were also provided with a week set aside to concentrate on cultivating a positive attitude to their work and client group, and to stress the importance of individuality, privacy and dignity. A follow-up bi-weekly programme enables these issues to remain on the agenda. On a day-to-day basis, staff motivation is maintained by attending regular ward meetings, being involved in change initiatives and having a real say in what happens on the ward.

Unfortunately, factory nursing still exists today and, therefore, change is necessary to improve the basic standard of care on these wards. Many nurses are afraid of change, especially when it is seen as a theoretical exercise. It is for this reason that I have concentrated on practical examples of change with flexi-shifts and on giving real examples of positive changes in the care of the elderly over the past 10 years. Change needs to be demystified. It needs to be seen as achievable by the ward-based nurse and that theories are not essential requirements. It is far better to use common sense and have a well-thought-out plan that everyone agrees upon. It is also hoped that it is not viewed as a waste of time as lessons can be learned, for example in the trial period of flexishifts where communication channels were encouraged and used well and alternative solutions to the problem were discussed.

There have been many changes in the care of older people over the past 10 years. It is hoped that by highlighting some of the changes that ward-based nurses have achieved, it will encourage others to participate in change. There are many nurses who have taken on board the need for change and have actively sought to improve the quality of nursing care given to patients. There appears to be a lot of motivation to change, and this motivation could act as a catalyst and encourage other nurses to undertake similar approaches.

REFERENCES

Lancaster, J. and Lancaster, W. (1982) *Concept of Advanced Nursing Practice – The Nurse as a Change Agent*, C.V. Mosby & Co., Missouri.

Lewin, K. (1958) Group decisions and social change, in *Readings in Social Psychology*, (ed. E. Macoby), Holt, Reinhart and Winston, New York.

Lippitt, G.L. (1973) *Visualising Change: Model Building and the Change Process*, University Associates Incorp., LaJolla, Calif.

Purposeful activity as a treatment medium

6

Carol Ainsworth

The purpose of this chapter is to consider the factors which influence the therapist's choice and use of activities to promote the highest degree of competence in an individual's functional performance of life roles.

INTRODUCTION

Mrs Waite is a smart elderly lady. She had been diagnosed as having Alzheimer's type dementia. Initial assessments suggested that she was unable to learn new information, had short-term memory impairment and marked receptive and expressive dysphasia. She experienced difficulties in sequencing and organizing once routine tasks and required prompts to commence any functional activity. Her life roles had been taken over by her husband, the principal carer.

During assessment, Mrs Waite was invited to participate in a craft session. She noticed a sewing machine and stated, 'I use one of them'. She was able to demonstrate considerable skill in using the sewing machine. This was nothing remarkable in itself, but during the activity marked changes occurred in her behaviour. She was able to sequence and organize the task, determine her own standards for competence, her posture became more erect, her speech clear, direct and formed into complete sentences. Two hours later Mrs Waite was able to recall the experience sufficiently to relate it to her husband, who confirmed that it was five years since she last attempted to use a sewing machine. Mrs Waite was able to repeat this skill performance on other occasions.

The clinical anecdotes throughout the chapter are based on actual occurrences, although the names of the clients have been changed.

Purposeful activity can be defined as the tasks or experiences in which the individual actively participates. It has been said that 'occupation is the very life of life'. Individuals engage in purposeful activity as part of daily life. Engagement in activity requires and elicits coordination between the individual's physical, emotional and cognitive systems. The individual who is involved in purposeful activity directs attention to the task itself rather than to the internal process required for the achievement of the task.

The 'purpose' in purposeful activity is to produce a calculated response from a client to the activity that addressed his or her treatment goals. The performance of an activity can provide the means to encourage social interaction, decrease anxiety, stimulate cognitive function and improve performance in self-care depending upon the stated treatment goals.

The use of purposeful activity represents a positive approach to intervention. It emphasizes the functional abilities and potential of the individual. Engagement in activity or activities facilitates normal functioning.

The philosophy which guides the use of activity can be encapsulated by three basic principles:

- humans have an occupational nature, i.e. need to participate in a balance of work, rest, play and sleep in everyday life;
- humans can experience occupational dysfunction;
- occupation is a natural means of restoring function.

As 'doers', people are so dependent on meaningful occupation they often overlook just how important activities are to a satisfying and productive life. The 'doing' process, which necessarily involves activity, is the process by which individuals promote their own well-being by active participation in meaningful activity.

The process commences with a choice of model. A model can be used to organize knowledge, direct assessment and information gathering, guide management and treatment strategies and ultimately activity choice. Based upon the philosophical assumptions already listed, Keilhofner's 'model of human occupation' (Keilhofner and Nicol, 1989) is one model currently generating interest. A detailed knowledge of Keilhofner's concepts and terminology is not required and in briefly introducing this model some of the subtlety has been simplified.

The model as presented highlights many of the features which the therapist must understand in relation to a client to enable activities to be used in a therapeutic manner.

MODEL OF HUMAN OCCUPATION

Humankind has an occupational nature, a need to explore and master the environment that leads to engagement in occupations or activity.

A person is perceived as an open system, composed of interrelated functions organized into a coherent whole, in constant interaction with the environment and capable of maintaining and changing itself through engagement in activity. Activity or occupational behaviour is that which an individual carries out on a daily basis. The individual's beliefs, past experiences, preferences, environment and specific patterns of acquired behaviour will shape the manner in which activities are carried out.

The person is represented by three interdependent subsystems – volition, habituation, performance – which are organized into a hierarchy, the higher governing the lower, and in constant interaction with the environment.

Volition is the choosing or initiating of occupational behaviour. It consists of belief in self and one's skill values and interests.

Habituation is the organizing of occupational behaviour, i.e. daily life skills, into patterns or routines. It consists of roles which define who one is and habits which guide and pattern the way a person performs.

Performance is the producing of occupational behaviour. It consists of skills – sensory motor, cognitive and psychosocial – which are the abilities the individual has for the performance of purposeful behaviour.

Each of these three skills requires constant monitoring in order to guide the performance. This monitoring is composed of an image of the action to be performed and judgement to assess how closely actual performance approximates to the inner images.

Environment is the final component in this model, and where human beings (the three subsystems) are in constant interaction. The environment is the site for the practice of performance skills, the maintenance of roles and routines, and is the source of positive reinforcement of the volitional subsystem.

FACTORS INFLUENCING ACTIVITIES AS THERAPY

Participation in activity is essential if individuals are to maintain and change themselves. They can experience physical, cognitive and emotional deficits arising from changes in their health status, and these may affect their ability to participate in a balance of normal occupational behaviours. When individuals experience difficulty in changing or readdressing their normal balance of occupation, intervention may be required to help them, either directly or indirectly, to take part in activity.

Activities as a therapeutic medium must be realistic and appropriate. Their effective use depends upon the therapist's knowledge and understanding of:

- the client
- characteristics of normal ageing and disability
- activity analysis and synthesis.

The client

Before activities can be used therapeutically, we require knowledge of the individual elderly person. Assessment is necessary to determine what the client would like to accomplish, and to evaluate the limitations arising from the condition, i.e. dementia, which interferes with the client being able to carry out chosen occupational behaviours, that is to engage in activities to maintain life roles. Assessment should also provide information upon a person's background, interests, strengths and weakness. This information is important because activities are most effective when they are relevant to the client's experience, consistent with their skills and interests, supportive of their strengths and appropriately compensated or adapted to their functional level.

Assessment, therefore, should establish a baseline from which the client's individual programme of activities can be planned, and allow measurement of the changes occurring in the client during and after engaging in activity.

The assessment consists of:

- **an occupational history** which examines the client's history (through employment and as a homemaker) and family history – this allows an understanding of how roles in self-care, work and leisure have been developed and maintained, will highlight which roles have been important and give the client a feeling of independence and achievement, and features from these roles can be incorporated into activities;
- **an assessment of routines or patterns** of a person's daily life activities which will enable the therapist to explore what adjustments or alterations the individual has had to make as a result of his/her illness, and learn what the person would most like to be able to do now;
- **a performance assessment** which determines how the client is able to perform such activities as bathing, dressing, toileting, mobility, object manipulating, home management and leisure interests, and helps the therapist to evaluate the individual's functional capabilities.

Having collected the above information treatment, goals are set through discussion with the client that is dependent upon their comprehension of the situation. The ability to contribute and make decisions is a necessary part of gaining and maintaining one's individual identity. The key focus of using activities therapeutically is on improving and maintaining the quality of life by assisting the client to obtain meaning, in the here and now, through recognizing his/her functional potential.

Case examples

Two case examples have been used to highlight how information gained from the client during the assessment process is used to influence the choice of activities to meet treatment goals.

Table 6.1 Individually planned activities based upon the results of assessment

Client	Lifestyle and interests	Routines and patterns	Performance skills (cognitive)	Goals	Suggested activities
Mrs Kirkpatrick (age 81) Lives alone	Machinist, recently retired Routines now imbalanced since recent retirement Enjoys social outing to family and church-based activities (no avoiding same) Was actively involved in many community groups, taking on many organizing responsibilities Enjoys caring for others Homemaker Likes to be busy, especially with others High standards for competence in activity	Daily routine now very rigid, centred around self-care activities Has difficulties if routine interrupted Marked social behaviour patterns, formal but friendly	Disorientated for time Short-term memory impairment New learning limited Difficulty comprehending verbal information	Maintain existing memory skills by practice of skills required of short-term memory (attention, concentration, comprehension, rehearsal, recall) Maintain existing ability to comprehend verbal information Consider alternative methods of structuring time	(a) Indirect Craft activities using existing skills (activities to be graded as to amount or component skill of short-term memory required) (b) Direct Practice of daily life skills requiring memory skills – cooking, shopping, budgeting Cognitive activities – puzzles, quizzes, memory games – either individually or as group member Social activities in hospital and community – dancing, flower arranging, whist drives Client's own suggestions
Mr Benson Resident in elderly persons home	Worked outdoors and enjoyed activities, sports, gardening, fishing and walking Enjoyed drinking with friends in local pub	Social routines and patterns intact, but limited by cognitive impairment Unable to structure own time or activities	Long-term memory impaired Unable to remember family names Concentration for short periods only Has difficulties integrating cognitive skills	Maintain existing long-term memory skills by involving client in familiar activities which rely on long-term memory for competence Maintain existing skills and devise methods of compensating for loss of performance skills	Practical skills group based on past interests (gardening, walking with others) Social activities (dominoes/cards), preferably in appropriate environment (pub) Working with others allows for compensation of deficits

Characteristics of normal ageing and disability

Normal ageing

An understanding of normal characteristics of the older person will assist in ensuring choices of activities which reflect the features of the client group.

Normal development spans a lifetime, and the older person's occupational behaviours are shaped by their past experiences. The characteristics of normal ageing will be described in relation to the model already discussed.

Volition

The older person has many negative and loss issues to deal with – death of friends and relatives, effects of ageist attitudes, decrease in energy and strength and so on. Despite these factors, there is little evidence that self-esteem is negatively affected except following a traumatic loss. Belief in skill and the usefulness of that skill are maintained except when disability occurs. Regardless of the number of events over which the older person has no control, there is little indication that the individual's locus of control shifts to an external orientation.

The older person's expectation of success or failure differs from that of younger people. They are more prone to overestimating or underestimating their abilities. As with other age groups, the older person is affected by the loss of work following retirement. Since the value placed upon working is high, depression is not uncommon following retirement if no plans to replace work are made.

The healthy older person has the same time orientation as any other age group, focusing first on the present, second on the future and third on past experiences. This process can be disrupted if the individual lives in an unstimulating environment. Some hold values about old age such that they believe they should cease to engage in certain activities purely because they are old, but independence, social acceptance, adequate resources, the ability to cope and having significant goals are meaningful values commonly held by the older person.

Life is given meaning through a sense of one's place in the community and the purpose of work, and this is enhanced if one's values are rooted in a philosophy or religion.

The older person:

- spends less time planning than the young and they are more efficient;
- has goals which tend to be short term but maintain a commitment to the future;
- adjusts better to the effects of age if able to maintain personal standards; and
- is subject to a number of restrictions which prevent the pursuit of interests.

Older people also demonstrate an interest in a broad range of activities, especially those which have a social component. Maintenance of social contacts has a strong correlation with life satisfaction. Restrictions may stem from limited resources or fear of going out at night.

Habituation

Roles provide love, identity and self-esteem; old age is characterized by role loss. Leisure and social roles become important sources of companionship and meaningful occupation.

Established roles developed over a lifetime assist in structuring time and can compensate for loss of some skills and give meaning and purpose to the day. Older people resist changing routines even when circumstances alter, because they provide comfort and security. Changes to routine can occur in response to biological changes and social expectations.

Performance

The performance skills require constant monitoring in order to guide performance; the constituent which performs this function remains intact during the normal ageing process. The monitoring of performance may be impaired by deficits in the sensory organs, notably vision and hearing.

Physically, loss of muscle strength, tone and diminished range of joint movement will affect mobility. Communication skills remain intact except when disrupted by neurological deficits, e.g. reduced ability to hear. Speech may be impaired due to shrinkage of the jaw and to surrounding tissue. Sensory motor skills show some slowed reaction, as more time is required to process information, but this is not of functional significance except in an emergency.

Verbal ability, general knowledge and mathematical ability, e.g. cognitive skills, do not change with age. Learning is prominent, adjustment to changes in life roles and changed customs involve new learning. Learning is not impaired but takes longer.

Memory skills do not inevitably deteriorate with age, although some factors may contribute to poor recall, a source of some considerable anxiety. These factors include distortion of incoming sensory information, e.g. deafness or inattention, leading to difficulty in recall. Many older adults have devised lists as means of overcoming this difficulty. Routines support role performance in tasks which rely upon memory.

Problem-solving ability with regard to everyday life situations is probably better than in younger people, as the older adult uses tried and tested formulas. Older people tend to take longer to solve new or novel problems, and this had led to the misconception that problem-solving ability declines with age.

Environment

The environment with which the older person is in constant interaction appears to shrink. This is caused by a decrease in energy and mobility and loss of social contacts through illness and death. Older people will attempt to improve the quality of their environment in order to compensate for the changes and to ensure positive reinforcement to maintain self-esteem, roles and routines. Objects become more meaningful as a person grows older because these are associated with the past and provide a sense of security and orientating clues.

Tasks are attached to routines, and these can become limited if the older person becomes frail.

Disability

Disabling conditions disrupt normal function. There can be little to compare with the personal devastation caused by dementia. The consequences are numerous and complex, they may involve cognitive, behavioural, emotional, physical and social disability. Consequences are devastating for the individual and are equally cata-strophic for the relatives. For the person with dementia, the normal developmental process and the disruption of that process by dementia will determine abilities, limits and behaviour. Knowledge of the disease process can assist in understand-ing the areas of function which may be affected and those which may remain intact throughout the progress of the disease. It is important that the expectations of the client are not mistakenly set too high or too low.

The major features of dementia can be defined as amnesia, agnosia, apraxia and neurophysical changes. These changes initially affect the performance subsystem, with consequent changes to both the habituation and volitional subsystems to cause occupational dysfunction. Changes to the performance subsystem will be considered first.

Performance and disability
In the early stages of dementia changes may occur in the cognitive component that can result in short-term memory impairment. The client may experience difficulties in performing life skills, e.g. shopping, as he/she is unable to recall what to buy, or cooking, when food is left to burn on the stove as the person has forgotten.

Table 6.2 (pp. 104–5) illustrates the major features of dementia in relation to this subsystem.

Effects of disability on the other subsystems
In the early stages of dementia, changes initially occurring in the performance subsystem have a minimal effect upon the habituation and volitional subsys-tems, especially to those clients with rigid habits and a constant balance of roles, that is, the client is able to continue to carry out a balance of regular activ-ities.

However, should environmental factors alter this delicate balance – a room is redecorated and furniture relocated, there is a temporary loss of support struc-tures (carer, spouse) or the client becomes ill – rapid changes in the habituation and volitional subsystems occur, that is, the person will experience difficulties in performing once 'automatic' activities of self-care. The person is unable to readdress their normal balance of occupations, and it is at this point that many people with dementia first come into contact with health and social services.

Activity analysis and synthesis

Activity analysis is the process of identifying the various components of an activity. It considers the steps involved in the activity and the skills required for each step.

In order to understand the effect an activity will have on a client, the therapist needs to break it down into the performance skills areas and look at each one in detail. Skill in activity analysis is essential.

Activity analysis enables the therapist to choose activities which will afford the client the optimum chance of success. Analysis of an activity will provide the therapist with:

- an understanding of the activity;
- knowledge of the skiils required for its successful performance;
- a knowledge base for instruction/presentation of the activity (justification for using the activity with clients by detailing the therapeutic benefits of the activity);
- the ability to determine whether or not an activity is within a client's present capabilities; and
- the ability to determine which of the client's needs the activity may satisfy.

A framework for analysing activity is necessary to enable the therapist to gain competence in using activity.

Framework for analysing activity

The framework presented is a generic one currently used in clinical practice. It is recommended that the reader completes the process with at least one activity, perhaps most usefully one that has not been successful, as it may help to explain why it failed.

Identifying stages of activity

The specific actions of an activity need to be identified as separate stages and listed in sequential order. To place limits upon this task a maximum of ten steps is useful.

Stage breakdown

Each stage can be further broken down into subskills required to complete the stage. These subskills require precise description; each step is described by identifying the action to what? and how?; for example:

Action	**What?**	**How?**
Pick up	pen	quickly, carefully

Each of these is significant to allowing the therapist to use this information to give the client precise and specific instructions. The how or descriptor is

Table 6.2 Major features of Alzheimer's type dementia in relation to the performance subsystem

Cognitive	Sensory motor	Psychosocial
Amnesia – occurs in a total of 92% of sufferers. Main presenting features:	In the early stages of the disease the client is often physically well	Social behaviour initially intact
Generally presents as mild forgetfulness, that is: • immediate recall and registration intact • long-term memory intact • deficit of new learning abilities, i.e. recalling new information after few minutes delay	Agnosia for faces (prosopagnosia), i.e. client is unable to recognize faces	Reduced spontaneity
	Unable to recognize own face – may converse with self in mirror	Anxiety frequently present, an understandable response to the insight into failing cognition
		Some clients develop depression
• increasing dependence on visual cues • if attention is diverted unable to complete task • client seeks constant reassurance unaware that has asked before, especially in stressful situations; new learning abilities declining rapidly • long-term memory remains generally intact	Apraxia – the apraxias are 'somatospatial', i.e. secondary to disorders of visuo-spatial perception and disorders of body awareness: • disorder of location • difficulties locating objects in space; once located have difficulty letting go; attention directed inappropriately • client has difficulty with the relationship between different objects in environment, i.e. if asked to copy a drawing on separate sheet, often start by attaching own to original, known as "closing in phenomena" (also seen when clients follow spouse or carer around)	Social withdrawal or avoidance (as client tries to maintain functional equilibrium) Restlessness, wandering *Speech* Aphasia – initially mild and increasing in severity, frequently alongside deficits in comprehension Speech remains fluent but less rich in content Social utterances present for early and middle stages, i.e. "How are you" – in later stages, language becomes incomprehensible, client uses less and less speech
Long-term memory becomes affected; client lives in past, i.e. names of children not recognized; client believes self to be younger	• difficulties experienced with relationship between self and other objects – generally seen when getting dressed (dressing	Mute

than is; talks about dead parents as alive; mis-recognizes relatives; may deny marriage

Concentration becomes increasingly impaired; client is unable to focus on a task which further compounds impairment of new learning

Attention span decreases; difficulties are experienced in focusing attention

Orientation – difficulties with memory concentration and attention cause a decrease in ability to comprehend and define the environment leading to orientation for time, person and place

Cognitive integration – induces the individual's abilities to integrate cognitive skills and diminishes the abilities reliant upon their integration, e.g. problem-solving skills, i.e. ability to plan behaviour and successfully monitor the execution of that plan

apraxia); feeding remains intact until later stages
- perception of height becomes impaired
- difficulty in negotiating steps; changes in floor colour or covering misapprehended as step or barrier
- difficulties in walking – gait apraxia; muscle wasting is common in later stages

Speech difficulties and other failing abilities lead to change in social behaviour, i.e. agitation and wandering, or misinterpreting non-verbal communication leading to aggressive outbursts frequently overlooked, but is necessary as it identifies the quality of the action. The how is determined by the therapist to allow adaptation of the activity to meet the individual client's needs.

The following is an example of the major stages and stage breakdown of an activity used in treatment. The descriptors have been omitted as these are decided to meet individual client needs.

ACTIVITY: 'GRASS HEADS'

1. Prepare the stocking bag
1.1 If the stocking piece being used has both ends open, knot one end.
1.2 Decide whether it is preferred to have the knots or ridges on the inside.
1.3 If it is preferred, turn the bag inside out.
1.4 If the material is stiff, to slacken the bag, place a hand inside and spread out the fingers.
1.5 Take the hand out of the bag.

2. Add grass seed to the stocking bag
2.1 Using all fingers of one hand pick up a large pinch of grass seed.
2.2 Place this pinch of seed in the stocking bag.
2.3 If fingers are small, and the amount now in the stocking bag is less than a level tablespoonful, repeat steps 2.1 and 2.2.
2.4 Place the stocking bag on the table with the open end uppermost.

3. Part-filling the stocking bag with sawdust
3.1 Ensure the stocking bag has open end uppermost.
3.2 Scoop up sawdust with the cup.
3.3 Pour sawdust into the open end of stocking bag.
3.4 Repeat steps 3.1 and 3.2.

4. Making a ball shape out of the stocking bag
4.1 Gather the material together at the open end of the stocking bag.
4.2 Hold the gathered material firmly.
4.3 Gently tap the bag on the table.
4.4 Gather the material more tightly.
4.5 Inspect to see if the bag is similar in shape to a ball.
4.6 If it is like a ball, tie a knot in the gathered material and move to stage 5.
4.7 If it is not like a ball, repeat steps 4.2 to 4.5 before tying a knot in the gathered material.
4.8 Move to stage 5.

5. Preparing the head for putting on facial features
5.1 Check the location of the seed below the surface of the nylon on the ball.
5.2 Stand the ball on the table with the seed uppermost.
5.3 For the rest of this task, regard the end with the seed as the top of the head and the opposite side as the base.

5.4 Observe the junction where the seed ends and the sawdust begins.
5.5 Regard this junction as the 'hairline' for the rest of the task.
5.6 Decide which half of the sphere of the ball will be the face and which will be the back of the head.

6. Making the nose
6.1 On the face, choose the central point.
6.2 Grasp the nylon around this central point with the fingertips.
6.3 Enclose a portion of the sawdust, making a prominence which is to be a nose.
6.4 Tie a thread around the nose to partially close its sawdust off from that in the head.
6.5 Tie a knot in the thread.
6.6 Trim the thread.

7. Making the eyes
7.1 Choose two matching buttons to be eyes, or choose two matching felt discs and eyeballs.
7.2 Choose two places for the eyes which must be **all** of the following:

    on the face side
    below the hairline
    above the nose
    about an inch apart.

7.3 Sew the buttons on to these chosen places, or glue the discs on to the chosen places.
7.4 If using felt eyes, glue on felt eyeballs.

8. Making the mouth
8.1 Dip the brush in the waterproof paint or varnish.
8.2 Wipe excess on edge of bottle.
8.3 Paint a mouth shape on the face below the nose and above the base.

Identification of performance components
Examination of the performance components required to complete the activity is the next logical step. Each activity is considered according to which skill components are required to complete the activity.

Cognitive
Perceptual
Sensory   Sensory motor
Motor

Psychological
Emotional   Psychosocial
Social

The dysfunction experienced by a client affects the degree of relevance of various components. In the following clinical example, a client was requested to cross a road.

The client with whom this activity was analysed demonstrated a prerequisite of strong need for independence to cope with the pressure of a fear of crossing roads. The road to be crossed is a busy dual carriageway. It is a demanding activity, and this client had a history of depression and stroke without major physical damage. The client wanted to master this activity to be able to visit friends and reduce the burden on the family.

For this client, the psychosocial performance components were the most important.

Table 6.3 Identification of performance components: psychosocial

Psychological	Emotional	Social
Control of feelings	Gratification	Responsibility
Coping with pressure	Structured	In practice with therapist:
Gratification of needs	Allows control	interaction
Tolerate risk	Allows success/failure	cooperation
Trust	Handle feelings	negotiation
Independence	Impulse control	lead/follow
Explore feelings and motives	In practice with therapist:	Rules/structures
Responsibility	dependence/independence	Individual activity
Self-image		
Real experience		

When broken down this activity displays the need to integrate a vast range of components due to the need to plan, perceive, make decisions whether to act, move or place oneself appropriately to complete the task safely. Its performance can provide independence and control as well as access to other activities and interactions.

The component groups in Table 6.4 also interlink very closely with each other and, to a degree, with the psychosocial element.

Grading activity
Grading activity is always individualized to the client's needs. It may involve a gradual change in the nature of the activity by changing one or two components. In the person with dementia, the disorganization of skills is such that for the client to achieve success a greater number of specific stages may have to be identified. Knowledge of the individual client will assist in knowing when and

Table 6.4 Identification of performance components: interlinking component groups

Cognitive	Perceptual	Sensory	Motor
Attention	Differentiation (e.g. colour and auditory perception)	Visual	Gross
Concentration	Object constancy	Auditory	Fine
Discrimination	Proprioception	Tactile (e.g. button press	Bilateral
Use of symbols	Tactile integration	appropriate pressure)	Unilateral
Perceive cause/effect	Bilateral integration	Sensory integration	Manual dexterity
Choice	Motor planning		Repetition
Following directions	Tactile integration		Endurance
Reading	Vestibular function		Static work
Orientation	Body schema		
Memory			
Planning			
Organization			
Logic			
Problem solving			

(Information reproduced by permission of Mary Mayio.)

where in the task this will be required; for example a client who has difficulty identifying objects may require additional steps to be included when the task requires object identification for successful completion.

The gradability of the activity relates to the manner in which the physical and psychological characteristics of activities can be gradually modified to meet therapeutic requirements. Many aspects of the activity can be graded. Consider the following methods currently employed when working with clients who have dementia.

- Increase or decrease the complexity of the task.
  The client is asked to identify an object from its verbal description (skill comprehension), starting with a concrete description: 'It is an animal and it barks' – answer: 'dog'.
  - Increase complexity by presenting an abstract description: 'You will find these at Crufts'.
  - Decrease complexity by presenting a personal description: 'Mary, you have one called Fido'.
- Change the steps within the activity.
  Example: with this pencil draw two lines on the paper; draw one line with the pencil, and draw one line with the pen. In both cases the end product is two lines on a piece of paper.
- Change the method of giving instructions.
  Example:
  - therapist demonstrates the activity;
  - therapist gives verbal instructions;
  - therapist gives written instructions.
- Change the amount of cueing given to the client.
  The therapist may decrease the amount of cueing provided as the individual becomes more proficient, or increase the amount if the client is struggling to ensure the client succeeds.
- Use the natural sequence of skill to upgrade.
  Example: problem-solving activity may be increased from trial and error to planning, sequencing and initiation.
- Change the amount of X to complete the activity.
  Example: the amount of concentration and attention span required for an activity may be increased.
  This may be achieved by increasing the number of repetitions required by the activity and/or the length of time spent performing the activity.

As a general rule, an activity should be graded up when the client is able to accomplish the task and further progress is desired, and graded down when the client is having difficulty with performance. The therapist must decide when change is indicated.

Activities may be adapted by modifying or changing the sequence of the activity or both, such as the position of the client, the position of the material, the size, shape, weight or texture of the material, the procedures and the nature and degree of interpersonal contact. Adaptation involves the process of continually modifying an activity to meet the specific needs of the client.

Backward chaining

The client is first assisted to do the last step independently and as competence develops works backwards through the steps, e.g. in throwing a ball, the last step is to release the ball, and the person is physically guided to do this step. Clients report greater intrinsic reward when working in this fashion.

Other methods of modifying an activity include using alternative equipment, changing the environment, both human and non-human, where the activity would occur, by altering the method and by involving the client in related activities.

Throughout the activity, therapists should modify their method of personal interaction to achieve the desired results of the activity.

Environment in activity synthesis

The environment is defined 'as a composite of all external forces and influences affecting the development and maintenance of the individual' (Hopkins and Smith, 1988).

The environment is the site of performance of skills, the maintenance of roles and routines and is the source of positive reinforcement of the volitional subsystem.

Man has a basic drive; to have an effect on and/or mastery of his environment. For an activity to be beneficial it must allow this need to be satisfied. This drive is illustrated by some people with advanced dementia when they can be observed collecting and rearranging objects, such as ornaments and furniture. The observer may perceive little purpose to the activity, whilst the client may express that 'it needs to be done'.

Clients need to be encouraged and allowed, to the extent possible, to decide the nature of the activity and how they will participate. They need to see that they have an effect on the quality of their own lives.

When considering how to use activities, the therapist must consider the individual's environment. The environment possesses two dimensions, the physical and the social, that affect the development of the individual.

The therapist alters, adjusts and adapts the physical and social environment to place the achievement of an activity within the ability range of the client. This process is facilitated by the therapist's knowledge and understanding of the client's deficits and how these interact with environmental factors. It is, therefore, important to match the complexity of the environment to the functional ability of the client.

Physical environment

This refers to the site in which the individual functions, for example town, street, public house, hospital and his/her home. Within a building, it is the building design and layout of the interior and furnishings.

In clinical practice, most clients participate in planned activities within a hospital environment. In relation to the physical environment, the abilities of a client to function and engage in activity are improved when:

- the room used is not too large, so that clients can see the walls, fixtures and fittings – smaller rooms help clients feel more relaxed, large rooms threaten;
- furniture and decor are appropriate for client needs and thus assist performance, e.g. walls and doors are contrasting colours, as this helps when visual activity is diminished;
- chairs are of suitable height and styles;
- furnishings are homely and comfortable – clients should be encouraged to participate in activities which facilitate this;
- environmental noise is minimalized;
- lighting and heating are appropriate for the activity – low lighting and warmth (80°F) promote relaxation and often sleep, whilst brightness and cooler conditions (70°F) enhance concentration;
- within the total environment a variety of smaller environments can be created, using a combination of sensory stimuli to enhance the activity and the clients' opportunity to succeed.

Norms for behaviour are influenced by the physical environment and need to be considered when planning activities enabling appropriate action to be taken to maximize their benefits and/or minimalize their negative features.

When working with clients with dementia, it is necessary to carry out activities in the environment in which they would expect them to occur. The environment frequently provides cues to appropriate behaviour; for example, a client who is asked, in a kitchen, to collect those ingredients and equipment to make a cup of tea will find it easier than if asked to perform the same task in a bedroom (even if the items are available within the bedroom).

Social environment

This refers to the people with whom the client interacts. The abilities of the client to function and participate in an activity (within a hospital) are improved when:

- clients work with others who have similar functional, social and cognitive abilities – observation suggests that when a client is placed with a group of others who are less able than himself/herself, that client's performance will drop to the level of the other group members; conversely, when a client is placed with a group of clients who are more able, the client's performance may improve.

- group size is correctly matched to activity requirements – activities requiring clients to performs 'skills' are better in groups of 2 to 7, whilst 'social' groups require 6 to 30;
- the number of people within the total environment does not exceed 30, including staff and clients – clinical observation of clients with dementia suggests that individuals are more able to function in activities when this number is not surpassed (perhaps because the staff and clients feel that they are responsible for events occurring within the environment); otherwise they are encouraged to disengage from the environment, thus making participation in activity difficult, an observation which remains constant even with fluctuating staff:client ratios;
- clients are allowed and encouraged to function socially within individual norms for social behaviour, and the social environment enables them to engage in behaviour which meets their role needs and enhances their volition;
- the attitude of therapists and other staff involved in activities with clients is positive; for example, clients are not precluded from staff conversations.

Behavioural norms exist within a social environment, and these may be positive or negative – a 'do nothing' attitude is an example of a negative attitude. If such a constraining attitude prevails, it is difficult to organize purposeful activities.

In many cases, activities may have to be graded below the level of ability of the client to compensate for this environmental effect. The 'do nothing' attitude can originate from the client, but more usually comes from the carers who encourage this behaviour to ensure greater efficiency in their own lives. The therapist may have to remove the client from this environment before the client will be 'allowed' to participate in any planned activity.

Attitude and approach of the therapist

Attitude

Therapists working with older people with mental health problems face a number of challenges, both on a personal and professional level. The denial, anxiety and frustration of the family of the carer(s) and the scepticism of other professionals complicate the therapist's feelings. These feelings can raise the question whether or not it is worthwhile to engage the client in activities which may only produce immediate but transitory benefits to the client. It is important for the therapist to confront negative attitudes, such as 'It's not worthwhile' or 'It makes no difference'.

We need to develop a positive attitude to confront common misconceptions, like 'They have forgotten all about it by the time they have left the room'. Clinical observations of clients with dementia demonstrate that clients behave differently when engaged in purposeful activity, and the change is frequently positive and heartening to observe, as in the following example.

When Albert Smith is not engaged in activity, he will wander within the unit becoming increasingly perplexed and agitated, and this can escalate into displays of aggressive behaviour. However, when engaged in planned activity his behaviour is very different. During a cognitive function group he is presented with several exercises to challenge his existing cognitive skills; he is able to concentrate, and his attention is diverted to solving stated problems.

By providing a structured focus he is able to process and use information presented, he becomes calmer and states he enjoys solving problems.

Following the activity, Albert is unable to recall that he has participated, but he is noticeably calmer and he continues to interact appropriately with others.

The immediate benefits to Albert of this activity are:

- ability to concentrate;
- reinforcement of existing cognitive skills;
- reduction in anxiety;
- enjoyment;
- challenge and success;
- ability to work and socialize with others, and after group activity;
- continued reduction of anxiety and continued socialization with others.

It is these positive benefits, however short term, upon which therapists should concentrate if they are to believe in the value of what they are doing. When concentrating upon the benefits of activities with clients, therapists may observe that they view clients from a different perspective, that clients cease to be old persons with dementia who are unable to, and become Joe or Betty who is able to.

Approach

Positive attitudes need to be channelled into an appropriate approach which ensure required responses from the client to the activity. Clinical experience suggests the following approaches be considered:

- therapist should select activity in the ability range of client to ensure best possibility of success;
- responsibility for the outcome of an activity remains with client;
- client should retain the right to participate in any activity;
- actions required by the activity should hold a social value;
- graded activities to maintain motivation;
- develop client's feeling of efficiency by:
  - starting with playful exploration
  - giving time to develop and practise skills
  - providing opportunities to use skills realistically;

- give client respectful attention when performing an activity;
- expose client to appropriate role models;
- provide opportunities for client to succeed by giving clear instructions;
- avoid ridiculing client (laughing when client makes a mistake);
- activities should have novelty value, but not so much that failure is feared;
- retain faith in client's potential to succeed;
- choose type and frequency of external reinforcers for each client.

These approaches will influence therapists' behaviour towards clients whilst they are participating in a planned activity. Choosing the correct approach is dependent upon knowledge of the clients and the activity to be performed.

CATEGORIES OF ACTIVITIES

A number of activities may be used therapeutically. The following categories are not exhaustive but provide a framework for generating activities:

- life skills
- crafts
- creative expressions
- self-discovery
- social interaction
- cognitive abilities.

In working with an older client population, I have employed the principles of reminiscence, reality orientation, sensory stimulation and behaviouralism, their features being incorporated according to client need in specific activities.

Life skills

These involve practical activities of self-care, of the physical environment and participation in the social environment. Participation in these activities provides an opportunity to maintain former roles, skills and values.

Deficits associated with dementia have a progressive negative effect on the performance of activities of daily living. In the early stages a person may forget a hair appointment; as the disease progresses the person may be unable to initiate hair combing. The following activities, which assist in maintaining function, may be used, and consideration should be given to such factors as the time of day when the activity is normally performed:

- food/eating: including all aspects of obtaining, preparing, serving, eating and clearing up after same – can be performed individually or as part of a group;
- grooming: including washing, shaving, hair care, application and removal of make-up, dressing and undressing – usually carried out in private, although some aspects are suitable for group format;

- community: going out, using various methods of transport, crossing roads, etc.

Other activities include domestic management and gardening.

Crafts

Crafts involve participation in the creative process. Craft activities have an end product upon which the client is able to measure his effectiveness against a known standard, i.e. what the product should be. This can serve as a motivator and enhance self-esteem. Crafts exercise a number of performance skills components.

It is unfortunately the case that in order to simplify craft activities to match the skill level of the individual with dementia, activities intended for children are used. These are an insult to adult dignity and should be avoided. Simple activities must have an adult format.

It should be considered that many older people had little time in their working lives for purely leisure activities. Crafts were done as a gift for someone or because they were needed. Incorporate the above purpose into craft activities: work towards making an item for a specific individual or towards a specific event, such as a fund-raising fair.

This client group is willing to attempt most familiar clean crafts and, with the correct choice of activity, clients are able to achieve outstanding results, especially when working as a group.

Creative expression

Clients determine the finished product, materials and the procedures used. They are allowed to be more able and can increase the level of self-awareness, contributing to feelings of achievement, competence and self-worth.

These activities may involve drama, music, movement and writing.

Self-discovery

These activities are frequently group based and allow individuals to recount and discuss their own lives, past, present and future.

Reminiscence therapy and validation therapies may be employed within this category. Self-discovery can facilitate cognitive and emotional functioning and allow individuals to review their values. The activities can assist clients to gain insight into their mental health problem and improve self-esteem.

Social activities

These have particular value for clients with dementia; carers in the community will compensate for loss of practical life skills, such as dressing, but not for the loss of social skills. Loss of these skills frequently results in isolation, reduction in belief of self, values and interests and, as a consequence, further loss of functional skills.

Maintaining social interactive skills may allow clients to continue to function within the community, so these activities can promote communication, cooperation, negotiation, sharing reality testing and comprehension skills.

Cognitive abilities

In clinical practice, many clients have dementia which is characterized by the decline in cognitive functioning abilities. Specific activities are required to improve, maintain and support deterioration of these skills. It is for this reason that cognitive skills have been given a separate category.

Activities may be structured to use one or several cognitive skills and to integrate the skills into functional performance. These activities allow clients to use their existing skills to best effect and the benefits of the practice and successful completion of cognitive activity lead to increased self-esteem.

CONCLUSION

Purposeful activities have characteristics which make them a significant intervention strategy in working with the older mentally ill client. The process which has been described enables therapists, through their own philosophical beliefs, knowledge of normal ageing, disability, individual clients, activity analysis and the environment, and their own attitude and approach, to find the format by which activities become therapeutic for a client.

REFERENCES

Hopkins, H. and Smith, H. (eds) (1988) *Occupational Therapy*, Willard and Spackman, Philadelphia.
Keilhofner, G. and Nicol, M. (1989) The model of human occupation – a developing conceptual tool for clinicians. *British Journal of Occupational Therapy*, June.

FURTHER READING

Burton, J.E. (1989) The model of human occupation and occupational therapy practice with elderly patients, Part I. *British Journal of Occupational Therapy*, June.
Creek, J. (ed.) (1990) *Occupation Therapy and Mental Health*, Churchill Livingstone, London.

Foster, P.M. (ed.) *Therapeutic Activities with the Impaired Elderly*, Haworth Press, New York and London.

Hinojosa, J., Sabori, J. and Rosenfield, M.S. (1983) *Purposeful Activity*. A position paper. Adopted April 1983 by the American Occupational Therapy Association Inc., American Occupational Therapy Association.

Kirkland, D.V. (1986) *The Role of Occupational Therapy with the Elderly*, The American Occupational Therapy Association,

Mosey, A.C. (1973) *Activities Therapy*, Rowan Press, New York.

Oakley, F. (1988) Clinical applications of the model of human occupation in dementia of the Alzheimer's type. *Occupational Therapy Mental Health.*

Pedretti, L.W. (1981) *Occupational Therapy: Practice Skills for Physical Dysfunction*, St Louis.

Pitt, B. (ed.) (1987) *Dementia*, Churchill Livingstone, London.

Stokes, G., Goudie, F. et al (1990) *Working with Dementia*, Winslow Press.

Dance movement therapy: a group therapy approach for older people with mental health problems

7

Bonnie Meekums

INTRODUCTION

The context

This chapter describes a pilot dance movement therapy group for people over the age of 65 who were suffering from a range of mental health problems, and whose status ranged from in-patient to day-patient to living independently in the community.

The dance movement therapy post

In November 1990, Tameside and Glossop Health Authority (now Tameside and Glossop Community and Priority Services NHS Trust) employed its first full-time, permanent dance movement therapist, believed to be the first such appointment in the region. The post formed part of a new team of arts therapists. Dramatherapy and art therapy had already been represented in the health authority for several years, although this was the first time that the arts therapists were sufficient in number to form a distinct team, with the creation of a new Head Arts Therapist post, making Tameside and Glossop one of very few areas in the country to be so well served by the arts therapies.

LITERATURE REVIEW: DANCE MOVEMENT THERAPY

Definition and description

Dance movement therapy (DMT) can be defined thus: 'The use of expressive movement and dance to communicate and evaluate feelings, attitudes, experiences and relationships, whether consciously or unconsciously, and to develop towards more spontaneous and adaptive functioning' (Meekums, 1990).

The content of a DMT group session can vary considerably, being largely determined by the themes brought by the group to that session and by the therapist's reflections on the previous session.

However, it is possible to identify the following potential stages:

1. Check in
   Group members sit in a circular formation and tell each other about their important thoughts and events since the last session. The therapist often observes common themes which evolve from this, for example loss, betrayal or trust, and may reflect these themes verbally to the group.
2. Warm-up
   This may take place on chairs, or moving into a larger space but still often in the circle formation. Typical warm-ups include repeating a familiar dance form as a group, to re-establish the group as a moving entity; follow-my-leader to a piece of music; or a movement game which is non-competitive, such as passing a hand squeeze around the circle.
3. Thematic exploration
   This may arise from a movement theme which has evolved during the warm-up, for example dancing in pairs, or from a symbolic theme. An example of the latter might be for each person to explore the room as if it were a swimming pool with a deep end, shallow end and so on, choosing a place where they feel comfortable.
4. Verbal processing
   Each person's insights and reactions to the thematic exploration are explored whilst sitting on the circle of chairs.
5. Closing ritual
   Again, this is conducted in a circular formation to re-emphasize the group and the idea of containment. It is important to note that not all of the stages outlined above will necessarily be present in every session.

Research

The literature on DMT is growing. Some of the research in this country makes use of what may be referred to as 'emerging paradigm' methodologies (Meekums and Payne, 1993). The aim is not so much to prove that DMT is effective, but to describe one aspect of DMT in a particular context. The reasons for using such a methodology are explained in Meekums and Payne (1993).

Briefly, the more established experimental approach, in which matching groups are sought and subjected either to the therapy in question or to a control, is often not appropriate for DMT. One reason for this is that DMT is still quite new; samples are often small and matching groups impossible to find. Moreover, for clinical trials of drug treatments, it is possible to use 'double blinds', in which neither doctor or patient knows whether the drug or placebo is being administered. In the case of DMT, it would be difficult to pretend to be engaged in the therapy without actually being so! The therapy is not a set of actions done to someone but an interactive process and, as such, is affected greatly by the personality of the therapist. It is not a repeatable experience.

The emerging paradigm also raises epistemological questions about who can be a 'knower'. It takes as its starting point the assumption that the 'subjects' and researchers know best about their own experience, and can contribute actively to the research (Reason, 1988) as well as being affected by it. Thus, researchers and subjects become co-researchers and co-subjects.

This author has made use of an emerging paradigm methodology to study DMT with mothers and young children at risk of abuse (Meekums 1989, 1990, 1991), and is currently engaged in research using a similar methodology to study groupwork (combined arts therapies) with women who were sexually abused as children. Using a cooperative enquiry approach (Reason, 1988), both group members and therapists examine their perceptions of the developmental and therapeutic process. In such research, the researcher uses 'critical subjectivity' (Reason, 1988) to raise to consciousness personal impressions and experience, rather than hiding behind the pretence of objectivity. In raising such experience to consciousness, it can be examined and taken into account in the research.

The limitation of such research is that the information gleaned is largely relevant to the context studied; generalizations are very tentative, if present in the conclusions at all. To be able to predict the usefulness of DMT in the mental health context *per se*, it is necessary to look wider, including those studies which make use of a more traditional methodology. However, in doing so it must always be remembered that the design is likely to be flawed in the ways outlined above.

One study which uses conventional 'scientific' methods to study the effect of dance, though not of DMT, on anxiety levels is that by Lesté and Rust (1984). The researchers used the Spielberger State-Trait Anxiety Inventory, a valid and reliable test, to assess anxiety states before and after a three-month programme of either modern dance (the 'experimental group'), physical education (controlling for the effects of exercise), music (controlling for the effects of music) or mathematics (controlling, presumably, for the effects of maturation and group learning activity). All of the 114 subjects were from further education colleges and of similar ages (mean age 19.9 years). The largest drop in anxiety scores was for the dance group, the only result which was statistically significant. The study did not measure long-term effects of dance on anxiety.

Two seminal papers attempt to measure affective change in dance therapy. The first of these, Kuettel (1982), reports two experiments. In experiment one, 17 female psychiatric nursing students with a mean age of 21.8 years were randomly divided into two groups, the experimental group receiving a one-hour dance therapy session and the control group participating in their usual student functions. A Feelings Questionnaire, modified from a Therapy Session Report, was administered both before and after the hour for both groups. The dance therapy group showed a significant reduction in anxiety and depression and an increase in 'eroticized affection' (Kuettel does not define this term). There was also an insignificant increase in confidence. In the second experiment, 46 occupational therapy students participated in either dance therapy or a T-group (Kuettel does not define this term, but this is generally assumed to indicate verbal group therapy). Again, there was a reduction in anxiety and depression and an increase in 'eroticized affection' and confidence for the dance therapy participants, although the result for depression was insignificant.

The second paper (Brooks and Stark, 1989) concerns itself with changes in affect in hospitalized psychiatric patients. Twenty hospitalized people and 20 non-hospitalized people of ages between 18 and 60 years were divided into four groups, two experimental groups receiving a dance movement therapy session and two control groups relaxing in the hospital lounge. A Multiple Affect Adjective Check List was administered before and after this period. All participants in the DMT sessions showed a decrease in depression and anxiety scores, although there was no significant difference between hospitalized and non-hospitalized groups. A major shortcoming of both of these papers is that no attempt was made to measure permanence of change.

Puretz (1978) compared the effects of dance and physical education on the self-concept of 150 disadvantaged girls, divided equally into experimental and control groups. The experimental group received daily half-hour modern dance instruction for one term, and the control group received daily physical education instruction for the same length of time. The term 'disadvantaged' was defined socio-economically. All of the girls were aged between 10 and 12 years, and dance had not previously been offered in the school. The Lipsitt Self-Concept Scale was used as a measurement, both pre-test in September and post-test in January, and again three and a half years later when the numbers had dropped to 63 in the experimental group and 59 in the control group. Puretz found a statistically insignificant increase in self-concept for the girls who had engaged in the dance programme.

May et al. (1978) carried out research with 38 subjects who had a diagnosis of schizophrenia, 18 women and 20 men, all of whom were given a 'difficult' or 'hopeless' prognosis. The subjects were assigned randomly to either individual dance therapy, group dance therapy or music therapy (the control). (One assumes that music therapy was chosen in order to control for music, which is often one component of a DMT session. However, just as there is more to DMT than dance, there is more to music therapy than music. The two professions are quite distinct and, though related as arts therapies, each has its own theory and practice. The outcome of any therapeutic intervention, it could be argued, is determined by many factors, including the investment of the therapist. As one of the authors is an eminent dance therapist, this could easily have biased the results. These should therefore be treated with extreme caution.)

All subjects were examined 'blind' by a psychiatrist at the beginning and end of therapy, which lasted six months. Three rating scales were used to assess body and self-image: the Ann Arbor Mental Status Scale, the Jenkins Symptom Rating Scale and the Camarillo Dynamic Assessment Scale. The results apparently showed that the greatest improvement in body image occurred in the group having individual dance therapy, followed by those having group dance therapy, then lastly those receiving music therapy.

Christrup (1962) looked at the effect of dance therapy on the concept of body image in hospitalized subjects who had a diagnosis of chronic schizophrenia, using projective drawings to measure change. The subjects, aged between 20 and 50 years, and receiving no other therapies than drugs, were organized into two groups of 12 women each and two groups of 15 men each, matched as closely as possible for Goodenough score, length of hospitalization and age. The experimental groups (one of men, one of women) were then placed in dance therapy for 21 sessions over 13 weeks. The drawings prior to and at the end of the experimental period were rated on Goodenough and Swenson scales. It was found that significant positive changes did occur among the female subjects (whose mean length of hospitalization was shorter than that for the men by four and a half years), and that, for both women and men, those who had participated most actively in the sessions (as measured by an activity rating by two recorders with good inter-rater reliability) showed significant improvement.

Work with older people

Stockley (1992) writes specifically about DMT with older people in a descriptive account of her work with a group of Afro-Caribbean people, mainly women. She makes the point that very little has been written either about dance or DMT with older people, and no in-depth research studies have been published on the topic. This situation exists despite the fact that Marian Chace, who is generally accepted as the mother of DMT, began working with this client group in the USA as early as 1942 (Sandel, 1987a; Stockley, 1992). Sandel (Sandel and Kelleher, 1987) found the following elements of DMT to be beneficial from her clinical experience:

- use of a circular formation at the beginning and end of the session – Sandel suggests that circles aid group unity, increase opportunities for eye contact, facilitate mutual touch and provide opportunities for those with hearing difficulties to stand opposite the therapist or other helper and for those with visual difficulties to stand next to someone who can help;

- mutual touch, which is really orientating and contrasts with the experience of physical care, in which the person may be a passive recipient;
- music, especially if there is a clear rhythmic beat, which aids organization;
- vocalization, stimulating central body involvement and breathing – Sandel welcomes any vocalization from participants;
- props, which can provide a focus for the group and a means of stimulation;
- empathic movement (by the therapist), which is one of the main ways in which dance movement therapists guide and develop movement material;
- imagery arising from the movement, rather than vice versa – the therapist may develop the imagery provided by the group and ask questions to facilitate exploration; for example while stamping, the therapist might ask what the members imagine they are stamping on;
- reminiscence, again arising from movement – Sandel (1987a, 1987b) suggests that movement can remind the participant of former pleasures and competencies, bringing alertness and mastery into the present, or it can allow for the expression of painful memories.

The very real physical limitations of the ageing body cannot be ignored. Stockley (1992) discusses a paradox for some older people; what was once pleasurable may now be painful, yet is necessary if mobility is to be maintained. Yet, Stockley suggests, being confronted with movement restrictions which may be the result of chronically held postures and body attitudes provides a fresh opportunity for change. However, it must never be assumed that older people are a homogeneous group: they may be 65 years old, or 90, with as many somatic and emotional issues as any group of individuals under that age; some will still be fit, perhaps even fitter than the group therapist; some will have suffered abuse as children, others will be suffering from a diagnosed mental illness. The possibilities are endless.

Loss is often a very present issue as people age. Friends and family members or spouses may die, but also there is the loss of bodily functions to face and this may include loss of range of movement, or fear of it. However, Stockley suggests that the most difficult loss may be that of sensation, including the loss of skin sensation. She suggests the use of specific sensory stimulation in the DMT session, to assist spatial orientation, self-awareness and awareness of the here-and-now. She also discusses the need for physical contact which is caring, respectful and non-invasive.

Samberg (1988, p.233) claims that dance has a 'medicinal effect'; a rather boggling phrase given that DMT by its very nature is different from the concept of medicine, being a largely interactive event which is not measurable in terms of dosage. Sadly, her language is also open to interpretation as judgemental, as she talks of older people who are 'overcome by self-pity' (p. 235), engaged in a 'constantly complaining and demanding style of interaction' (p. 238) or displaying 'argumentative, sluggish, irrational or unresponsive behaviour' (p. 240). She makes wild and unsubstantiated claims for DMT which do nothing to further the credibility of a profession which, even in America, is often marginalized. However, Samberg does make some useful suggestions about the therapist's role, and reports that social workers state that clients are more likely to participate in other activities following a DMT session and to be more responsive at meal times and social events. Samberg claims that it is the 'joy of the moment' which is important in working with older clients, and it is those moments which might carry over into relationships with others.

By contrast, Pasch (1982) was one of the first British practitioners to write about work with older people. Her work concerns movement sessions which she describes as 'classes', but in which relationship-building is seen as vital. Her approach, she states, 'is one of validation and support' (p. 2). Her descriptive account demonstrates great sensitivity to the population she works with and an informed attitude.

Fersch (1981) also writes with this sensitivity, describing DMT as a holistic approach to working with older people. In her opening paragraph she states that 'Growth and maturation occur throughout the entire course of a lifetime'. Fersch gives many suggestions for activities to include in a DMT sessions for older people. She identifies some of these as particularly useful, one presumes from her clinical experience, for special populations. These include those with physical disabilities, cognitive dysfunctions and emotional disturbances including paranoid states, hypochondriacal states and mania. The reader is referred to her writing for further information concerning her suggestions.

THE DANCE MOVEMENT THERAPY GROUP

Setting up the group

The idea of a DMT group with older clients arose out of discussion between Bonnie Meekums (a dance movement therapist) and Laraine Chaisty (a community psychiatric nurse) who writes elsewhere in this volume. Since this was to be an innovative provision, it was necessary to discuss the potentially complex issue of how the two workers from very different professions might co-work as equals.

The group ran in a general purpose room, some distance from the wards. The room was carpeted and housed long tables and chairs which had to be moved before each session. There was no lock and no engaged sign for the door. The windows, though having blinds, were at ground level on two sides and single glazed. It was less than ideal, but just large enough for the purpose. There was no specialist equipment in the room; everything, including a large and heavy 'ghetto blaster', had to be transported to and from the room, across car parks, each week.

Due to administrative delays beyond the control of the therapists, it was only possible to schedule nine sessions before summer holidays would interrupt. It was decided that this would also be the end of the group since any such interruption might mean a fall in attendance thus jeopardizing a clear ending.

Only four of the seven people present at the first session were referred in sufficient time to be assessed prior to the group and no one could be seen more than once beforehand. One of the seven expressed uncertainty at interview but was invited to attend the group anyway. She did so, but subsequently left. An eighth person joined at session three, although the group therapists felt that she was never fully 'engaged' and the group eventually settled into a reliable six people.

The clients

All of the six clients (five women and one man) who attended the group regularly have agreed to their work being written about anonymously for this chapter. They did so, in writing, after the purpose and nature of the publication was carefully explained to them. Because of the failure of the referral system, it is difficult to present a breakdown of diagnoses. However, it is possible to say that all presented with functional illness or emotional difficulties. During the group's life, the group therapists recommended that one of the members, who seemed to be presenting with early symptoms of dementia, be investigated for organic illness; this was later confirmed. All of the group participants were white and ambulant and all but one were women; these limitations must be borne in mind when reading the conclusions to this study.

Methods used

Each week, the session began in a circle with a brief 'check in', during which each member of the group had the opportunity to share something of themselves and to be heard. This aspect of the session became increasingly important to group members as they began to trust each other and to share more of themselves. On some occasions, members brought objects to share with others, for example a poem, or a photograph of themselves dancing or of a child who had since died.

There followed a dance movement activity, planned in response to themes which emerged in the group. These included:

- fingertip dances, in pairs;
- group improvisations, using a prop, such as a circular piece of broad elastic, held by the whole group and moved rhythmically to the music;
- ballroom dancing movements;
- arm movements synchronized to breathing patterns;
- mime;
- paired improvisation using a prop, such as fans, as the focus of movement;
- movement as an expression of feeling/emotional states;

- follow-my-leader structures, using creative dance movements in which each person's contribution was valued and validated by the participation of others, the dance movement therapist empathically mirroring each change in the movement;
- a song called the 'I love me' song, to which the group set actions:

> I love me, whether I know it or not,
> I love me, whether I show it or not,
> There are so many things I haven't said inside my heart,
> And now is a good time to start.
> (from a Universal Peace Dance)

- circle dances, with set steps originating in folk dance from all over the world, often with some symbolic significance, e.g. greeting dances – the dances being performed in a circle, they affirmed the group relationship and provided an opportunity for non-threatening contact.

Memories, feelings and associations often developed from the movement (see Issues and themes below). Following the movement section, each session ended, again in a circle formation, with a feedback period, when group members could say how they had experienced the session.

Issues and themes

In the first session, movement experiences centred around 'getting to know you', for example by throwing a ball around the group and calling out the names of the person to whom it was thrown. The circle of elastic was also introduced, as a focus for movement to which the whole group could connect by holding on or moving against or within it. In the discussion which followed, the group members began to talk spontaneously about the war and comradeship and caring. The practice of 'leaving one's door open', a metaphor for and expression of trust, was also remembered with fondness.

Movement experience in pairs, and with the group, provided many opportunities for both verbal and non-verbal interaction. Following dance movement improvisation which offered the chance of gentle physical contact, for example hand dances, several of the group members began to talk freely about their losses, in particular of spouses.

In the fifth session, when the membership of the group was established, the group was named by its participants. Various suggestions were made, but the group members eventually settled on the name of the 'Social Group'.

Reminiscence played a part in some of the activities; one week photographs of Blackpool ballroom were passed around, for example, and the music used for dance movement was largely taken from the 30s and 40s. Through the reminiscence work, present concerns, in particular the need for friendship and belonging, were frequently addressed.

Dance movement therapy is usually conducted with clear time boundaries, as one would expect in a psychotherapy session. However, the group therapists found that it was less appropriate to exert strict time boundaries with this group than with groups of younger people. Participants would arrive early and chat as the therapists set up their equipment. Some would continue chatting after the group had ended or while others were talking. In acknowledgement of their need for social contact, the group therapists offered the chance for a cup of tea after each session but, surprisingly, this was refused.

Many of the props and movements, whether set or improvised, acquired metaphorical significance for the group; for example, through hand dances members were able to address the need for intimacy. The circle of elastic, which bound the group together in movement and provided a focus for improvisation, came to represent the group itself, to which each member was attached, some more strongly than others. Individuals took turns to 'show off' by dancing within the circle and were rewarded by the enthusiastic attention of the group. As each person 'took the floor' they were held and contained by the group in its secure yet flexible form. The group (elastic) moved out to give space, new partnerships were tried, and several people tested the strength of the group by leaning on the elastic or pulling at it. When, in the last session, the time came for the last dance together to end, the elastic was placed down with great care and reverence.

RITA: A CASE STUDY

Rita (not her real name) was referred to the group during her stay on the ward. The referral was made too late for her to be assessed and so she was taken directly into the group following a brief discussion with ward staff. A failure of communication meant that she was discharged from the ward following the second session without prior knowledge of the group therapists, resulting in a two-week absence. Eventually, transport was arranged for her and she rejoined at session five.

Initially, Rita appeared confused and agitated in the group, interrupting when others were speaking and clearly anxious to be discharged from the ward. However, in the second session she was able to contribute more creatively, and during the 'I Love Me' song she engaged in a debate about whether it was wrong (her expressed view) or right to love oneself. She also became self-limiting to the extent that she was able to stop herself from interrupting others, and consequently engaged more with the group. As the session ended, she mentioned her son who had broken his back 17 years previously.

Despite her absence for two sessions, Rita integrated into the group when she returned. She was very talkative, though she claimed she had gone deaf and denied missing people from the ward despite frequently asking after them.

Rita's personal appearance changed considerably as the group wore on; though never unkempt, she began to dress more smartly and in brighter colours. In the penultimate session, when asked to mime taking a very special piece of clothing from a rail, wearing it 'on the catwalk' to applause from the rest of the group then placing it back, Rita chose a low-backed, brightly coloured sundress with no bra. She walked with obvious delight in her own attractiveness, swinging her hips and 'performing' for her audience.

Rita participated enthusiastically in both the dance movement and discussion aspects of the group, often continuing to dance after others had stopped and contributing readily in improvisations. Initially, when the ending was discussed in session seven, Rita denied her impending loss, questioning why the group had to end and saying she hoped it wouldn't. However, by the time she performed the clothing mime she was beginning to think about how she might fill Monday mornings with her ironing. She presented with a cough and was anxious she might become 'low'; she recalled one other occasion when she had become 'low' following a cough. She was also feeling anxious about alterations which her son was planning to make to her house, fearing that she might be pushed out.

It is often (in the clinical experience of this author) in the penultimate session that anxieties about ending reveal themselves as mini-crises for group participants, and Rita's response appears to have been demonstrative of this trend. Although still expressing sadness during the final session, she seemed much better. The feelings Rita expressed about her son 'pushing her out' may have been an expression of her resentment at having to lose the group, which she regarded as a place for her. Her willingness to dance and her response to the clothing mime demonstrate just how much Rita blossomed in the group; if the clothing she imagined was a symbol for what the group meant to her, it was clearly an opportunity to be valued, to feel attractive and sensual, a way of feeling fully herself.

There is support for this interpretation in Rita's comments at her review interview after the group therapy had ended, when she said that the group offered a chance to get out alone in a taxi, without her husband. About this, she said, 'I feel myself – it's just my body that won't behave', and went on to describe her tendency to overstep boundaries when out walking, for example to walk into walls and off the pavement. Interestingly, this tendency was never observed by the group therapists in sessions, when Rita appeared to be averagely well coordinated in her movements, expressive but not without control. Rita's husband tended to drive her everywhere and may have been a little overprotective. It is possible that Rita did overstep boundaries when she was out with him, but the limitations of nine sessions did not provide the opportunity to explore this further in movement. Rita identified the group as being 'very helpful'. One important aspect of this help was the attitude of the therapists, which she described as 'friendly': 'Being friendly, accepting how we are, makes a difference. We might never get completely better, but it helps'. However, she also volunteered: 'I think the music part is better than any of it – it makes you move, doesn't it?...It (dancing) brought a lot of depression off my shoulders'.

Pondering on her loss of the group, Rita began to reminisce about the day she left work, which was a painful experience for her. On that occasion she could bring herself to say nothing, but described how she simply changed her shoes and said 'Tarrah' as she walked out the door. At least this time it was different. Although she left quickly at the end of the last session, she had been able to acknowledge the end, participating in the ritual of moving for the last time together and placing the elastic circle, which had come to symbolize the group, carefully down. She had also been able to symbolically give and receive something and complete with each member of the group.

DISCUSSION AND CONCLUSIONS

One of the major problems encountered was in the referral process. Lack of clarity about who was, in fact, going to be in the group may have meant that some of the group members felt unsafe initially; it was felt by the therapists and their supervisor that this must be a potent issue for this particular group as so many of the group members had suffered losses. The co-workers distributed information sheets to colleagues several weeks prior to the group's start, giving information about the nature of the group, starting date and so on, yet there was little take-up until the last minute, which meant that the assessment process was rushed and inadequate as preparation for the clients, group workers and care coordinators. This led to one 'inappropriate' referral of someone who (it was later discovered) had an organic illness in addition to schizophrenia and was unable to follow verbal dialogue. Given the last minute rush of referrals, it was also not possible to ensure an even gender balance.

It is not clear why take-up was so slow. One reason may have been that groupwork was, at that time, relatively new within this service for community clients over the age of 65. But this would not explain the apparent reluctance of ward staff to refer and to communicate about discharge and so on. Another possible reason here is that ward routines and groupwork timetables are so vastly different, they require completely different ways of thinking about the needs of a client, particularly in the time-scale of planning involved. Thirdly, DMT is still very new in this Trust. Attitudes may be more widely represented by the one care coordinator who admitted to being sceptical. Dance has a frivolous image in society and is not generally associated with the kind of professionalism needed in the mental health services. In fact, DMT has been in existence as a modern profession since the 1940s and has its roots in psychiatry. Training courses (all postgraduate) exist in Britain, there is a professional association and all practitioners adhere to a code of conduct. But no one could be blamed for being sceptical about DMT before they have had exposure to it, either through direct experience, indirect experience (e.g. clients appearing to benefit) or reading.

Social interaction is often a goal of DMT with older people (Sandel and Kelleher, 1987). Dance movement is potentially a social activity *par excellence*, particularly for people who matured in an age when dancing was a favourite pastime, a place in which beaus were met and courted and group identities reinforced. It provides an accessible route to socialization for many people in the over 65 age group. There is likely to be a reminiscence factor in any dance activity for people over the age of 65. But DMT is not just about reminiscence, nor simply about socializing and having a good time. It is also about using movement to explore and express feelings, attitudes, memories and relationships, through the power of the 'movement metaphor', so that these can be processed and resolved. It is not necessary for such symbols to become explicit in words; in fact they often seem to hold more power at the level of metaphor.

The issue of boundaries, as viewed in therapy, had to be re-examined by this author. Being less experienced than her co-worker in working with older clients, there was much to learn. Indeed, both co-workers learned a lot, because of the unique blend of their skills and because each group is different. Rather than drawing any firm conclusions about 'work with older clients', as if there was a uniformity in people who are over 65 years of age, it is preferable to simply make observations from this limited experience and test them in each new situation as it arises. It was apparent that the group members valued friendliness, approachability and acceptance more than the traditionally professional boundaries employed by therapists. This challenged the co-workers, who were forced to find new ways of approaching the work which were flexible and did not alienate the people they were seeking to help, whilst not compromising therapeutic objectives.

Potential benefits

It is difficult to assess the potential benefits of DMT for people over the age of 65 from one brief experience. The number of sessions meant that any benefits were likely to be short term anyway and might be confined to in-session change, reported by the therapists' subjective impressions.

The therapists' impressions of Rita are reported above, along with her own account at interview. In this one case, and despite a short group and a confused referral period, the changes appear to have been dramatic. What is clear is that Rita was able partially to confront a loss which she had been hitherto unable to face up to.

Other associated changes reported by some of the group members at follow-up included growing independence, self-confidence and self-esteem, improved relating and, in Rita's case, alleviated depression which appears to have been maintained. Rita herself attributes this to the dance, a view supported by the papers reviewed earlier in this chapter by Kuettel (1982) and Brooks and Stark

(1989). One might expect that some temporary euphoria might result, either from the endogenous opiates released during exercise and/or from the reminiscence factor, associating movement with youth and good times. But these would be unlikely to be permanent. For permanent change of this kind to result from DMT, one must postulate some other mechanism, for example a shift in perception resulting from the group process or from the exploration of significant themes through movement (Sandel, 1987b). Not all group members reported an improvement, and for two other women who appeared to make some progress in the group (by the therapists' clinical judgement) the change was very short-lived. The possibility of undiagnosed organic disease could not be ruled out and may have been a complicating factor here.

It behoves anyone working with older clients to examine their own attitudes to older people (MacLennan, 1988; Tross and Blum, 1988). To this end, supervision from an external source was particularly useful, enabling a frank, honest discussion. The format of dance movement therapy provided an acceptable framework for the clients and one which was familiar to most of them, having had a personal history of social dancing. Yet some aspects of the therapy were challenging and might have been viewed by some of the participants as 'silly'. These were largely the more playful aspects of the therapy; it cannot be overstated that, whilst play is important whatever the age of the individual, opportunities to play must be offered with great sensitivity. Initially, one of the group therapists was concerned that older people might reject opportunities to engage in creative explorations such as 'clothing' mime (see Rita's case study above). However, these perceptions quickly changed on witnessing the creativity in the group.

The group therapists used supervision to examine their role in relation to the clients. Both therapists were in their late thirties/early forties and, as such, were of an age to be seen as potential daughters by the group members as opposed to the more usual transference of parent in a therapeutic relationship. Support for this view is to be found in Meerloo (1955), Berezin (1969), Fersch (1981), MacLennan (1988) and Lakin (1988). This may account for the fact that the dance movement therapist was chided by one of the group members for not being 'kind' to a member of catering staff with a drinks machine who wanted to come in during a session. This is complicated, however, by the view expressed by MacLennan (1988) who claims that therapists of this age will tend to be seen by older clients as they might view their own offspring, within a generational role reversal, as they become more dependent on younger people for care. Lothstein (1988) writes of a third stage of separation/individuation, in which the task is for the older person to maintain a sense of self amid increasing dependency on others. Whilst DMT provides opportunities to explore sexuality issues (Sandel, 1987c) it is also possible for some therapists to be shaken by displays of overt sexuality in their clients, such as Rita's imagined low-cut dress with no bra; many people find it difficult to acknowledge their own parents' sexuality and this can extend to the transference/counter-transference relationship (Berezin, 1969; Sandel, 1987c).

Apart from any change that may or may not have been assisted by the DMT group experience, the dance movement therapist was able to give valuable feedback to the care coordinator of one participant concerning her observations of the client's movement and the particular difficulties faced by that person. Interestingly, the difficulties noted included an inability to direct hand movements accurately in throwing a ball to other group members, and the client reported dizziness in turning. As well-being increased these difficulties subsided, and the client became very coordinated, was able to turn, unbidden, with a clear smile and without any report of dizziness, and movements were focused.

Recommendations for future practice

Closer collaboration with the care coordinator to include the joint setting of goals at an earlier stage might maximize the therapeutic effect for clients and allow for a freer flow of information. Movement observations, a particular skill of the dance movement therapist, might be of particular relevance here.

The co-worker combination of a qualified psychiatric nurse and a dance movement therapist allowed a rich exchange of ideas and experience. In future, different co-worker combinations might be tried, for example an occupational therapist and a dance movement therapist. Through co-work, informal training opportunities arise and it may be possible to build a pool of workers who can offer, if not dance movement therapy as such, groups which employ dance movement structures within a generally therapeutic framework. This has at least two major advantages: DMT becomes demystified and accessible at the same time as reaching more potential clients. The disadvantage of co-work is that DMT, whilst being more widely employed in one sense, may, paradoxically, become marginalized and relegated to the ranks of a 'technique' to be used as only one facet of more accepted, established forms of therapy.

This author's previous clinical experience had tended to be that 20 sessions is most likely to be optimal. However, to maximize the therapeutic effects for the client, it would be important in future groups to engage the care coordinator at an earlier stage. The referral procedure needs to take into account the needs for information, for personal contact between therapists and referrers and for clear guidelines on who might be appropriate for the group, time schedules for assessments, etc.

The revelations to the dance movement therapist in this study concerning appropriate boundaries with this particular group need to be tested in future groups. Finally, in order to maximize the therapeutic effect for the clients, it is desirable to use a purpose-built or adapted studio in which a full complement of equipment is available and privacy is maintained.

Research possibilities

There is s need for a systematic research study including follow-up of group members six months after the end of the group,a larger sample, more DMT sessions, more than one location and a more thorough exploration of the perceptions of both therapists and group members. It should also be possible to look in a more focused way at certain questions: what is an appropriate referral to DMT in this age group (which factors do clients have in common who make some progress following DMT); what issues and themes are explored through the 'movement metaphor' in such a group; what is the nature of the transference/ counter-transference relationship between clients and workers of various ages? It might also be interesting to use creative media in the evaluative process for both therapists and clients, for example using drawings to express feelings about the therapy.

SUMMARY

This chapter has described a pilot dance movement therapy group at Tameside and Glossop Mental Health Services. A case study was presented to illustrate the process. Whilst it is fully acknowledged that such work is in its infancy and suffers from a paucity of research, the method is offered as one potential form of adjunctive group therapy for this client group which may have particular relevance to a way of exploring specific concerns of people over the age of 65 who are experiencing certain mental health problems, in particular those arising from loss of intimacy. Although DMT groups can only be run when a qualified dance movement therapist is present, the potential training and service development opportunities for other parts of the mental health service in incorporating DMT are worthy of further exploration.

REFERENCES

Berezin, M. (1969) Sex and old age: a review of the literature. *Journal of Geriatric Psychiatry*, **2**, 123–8.

Brooks, D. and Stark, A. (1989) The effect of dance/movement therapy on affect: a pilot study. *American Journal of Dance Therapy*, **11**(2), 101–12.

Christrup, H. (1962) The effect of dance therapy on the concept of body image. *Psychiatric Quarterly Supplement*, **2**(36), 196–303.

Fersch, I. (1981) Dance/movement therapy: a holistic approach to working with the elderly. *Activities, Adaptation and Ageing*, **2**(1), 21–30.

Kuettel, T. (1982) Affective change in dance therapy. *American Journal of Dance Therapy*, **5**, 56–64.

Lakin, M. (1988) Group therapies with the elderly: issues and prospects, in *Group Psychotherapies for the Elderly*, (eds B.W. MacLennan, S. Saul and M.B. Weiner),

Monograph 5, American Group Psychotherapy Association Monograph Series, International Universities Press, Madison, Connecticut, Chapter 3, pp. 43–55.

Lesté, A. and Rust, J. (1984) Effects of dance on anxiety. *Perceptual and Motor Skills*, **58**, 767–72.

Lothstein, L. (1988) Psychodynamic group therapy with the active elderly: a preliminary investigation, in *Group Psychotherapies for the Elderly*, (eds B.W. MacLennan, S. Saul and M.B. Weiner), Monograph 5, American Group Psychotherapy Association Monograph Series, International Universities Press, Madison, Connecticut, Chapter 5, pp. 67–87.

MacLennan, B.W. (1988) Introduction, in *Group Psychotherapy for the Elderly*, (eds B.W. MacLennan, S. Saul and M.B. Weiner), Monograph 5, American Group Psychotherapy Association Monograph Series, International Universities Press, Madison, Connecticut, pp. xiii–xxii.

May, P., Wexler, M., Salkin, J. and Schoop, T. (1978) Nonverbal techniques in the re-establishment of body image and self-identity – a report, in *Therapy in Motion*, (ed. M.N. Costonis), University of Illinois Press, Chicago, Illinois, pp. 135–52.

Meekums, B. (1989) *Dance Movement Therapy and the Development of Mother-Child Interaction – A Pilot Study*. Proceedings of Dance and the Child International Conference, Roehampton Institute, London.

Meekums, B. (1990) Dance movement therapy and the development of mother–child interaction. Unpublished MPhil thesis. Victoria University of Manchester.

Meekums, B. (1991) Dance/movement therapy with mothers and young children at risk of abuse. *The Arts of Psychotherapy*, **18**(3), 223–30.

Meekums, B. and Payne, H. (1993) Emerging paradigm methodology in dance movement therapy research, in *A Handbook of Inquiry in the Arts Therapies: One River, Many Currents*, (ed. H. Payne), Jessica Kingsley, London, Chapter 12, pp. 62–174.

Meerloo, J. (1955) Transference and resistance in geriatric psychotherapy. *Psychoanalytic Review*, **42**, 72–82

Pasch, K. (1982) *Movement of Old People*, The Association for Dance Movement Therapy, London.

Puretz (1978) A comparison of the effects of dance and physical education on the self-concept of selected disadvantaged girls, in *Dance Research Annual*, (ed. R. Priddle), Vol. 11, *Psychological Perspectives on Dance*, CORD (Congress on Research in Dance), New York.

Reason, P. (1988) Introduction, in *Human Inquiry in Action*, (ed. P. Reason), Saga, London, pp. 1–17.

Samberg, S. (1988) Dance therapy groups for the elderly, in *Group Psychotherapies for the Elderly*, (eds B.W. MacLennan, S. Saul and M.B. Weiner), Monograph 5, American Group Psychotherapy Association Monograph Series, International Universities Press, Madison, Connecticut, Chapter 16, pp. 211–22.

Sandel, S. (1987a) Developing a movement therapy programme for geriatric patients, in *Waiting at the Gate: Creativity and Hope in the Nursing Home*, (eds S.L. Sandel and D.R. Johnson), Haworth Press, London, Chapter 4, pp. 41–7.

Sandel, S. (1987b) Reminiscence in movement therapy, in *Waiting at the Gate: Creativity and Hope in the Nursing Home*, (eds S.L. Sandel and D.R. Johnson), Haworth Press, London, Chapter 6, pp. 81–9.

Sandel, S. (1987c) Exploring sexual issues through movement therapy, in *Waiting at the Gate: Creativity and Hope in the Nursing Home*, (eds S.L. Sandel and D.R. Johnson), Haworth Press, London, Chapter 7, pp. 91–9.

Sandel, S.L. and Kelleher, M. (1987) A psychosocial approach to dance-movement therapy, in *Waiting at the Gate: Creativity and Hope in the Nursing Home*, (eds S.L. Sandel and D.R. Johnson), Haworth Press, London, Chapter 3, pp. 25–40.

Stockley, S. (1992) Older lives, older dances: dance movement therapy with older people, in *Dance Movement Therapy: Theory and Practice*, (ed. H. Payne), Routledge, London, Chapter 4, pp. 81–101.

Tross, S. and Blum, J. (1988) A review of group therapy with the older adult: practice and research, in *Group Psychotherapies for the Elderly*, (eds B.W. MacLennan, S. Saul and M.B. Weiner), Monograph 5, American Group Psychotherapy Association Monograph Series, International Universities Press, Madison, Connecticut, Chapter 1, pp. 3–29.

ACKNOWLEDGEMENTS

My thanks to Laraine Chaisty, my co-worker; Liz Matthew and Alan Slater for supporting the work as our managers; Roland Javanaud, our supervisor; Liz Matthew, Laraine Chaisty, Roland Javanaud and Philip Spence for their insightful comments on this manuscript; Rachel Ecclestone, music therapist, for discussing my remarks concerning music therapy.

Group grief therapy

8

Bob Spall and Hazel Smith

This chapter describes an attempt to get older people to work through grief by sharing their experiences. The underlying assumption is that they are capable of regaining a sense of mastery and can be empowered to do so.

Older people grew up with a pre-psychological world view and are less likely to view problems as psychological. This is reflected in some of the issues raised in this chapter, e.g. being unclear about the purpose and potential benefit of a therapeutic group, lack of motivation and dropping out. The importance of multiple losses is highlighted; for some people the prospect of facing up to multiple losses may be too much.

The two people who initially had the most positive views about joining the group attended regularly and benefited. However, even they could have been better prepared for what to expect. Lessons to be learnt are discussed.

Working with older people with mental health problems who have experienced multiple losses (including bereavements and chronic illness) is not easy. However, it is important not to adopt an ageist attitude which implies that older people's distress associated with loss is less important than that of younger people. Rather, we should continue to explore ways of helping older people to help themselves. Group approaches could usefully be developed and improved.

The authors wished to pilot a small group in a day hospital setting for older people experiencing grief problems. The day hospital was part of the psychiatric services for older people, so many attenders would have a history of mental health problems and be under the care of a consultant psychiatrist. At the time this groupwork was carried out, the service setting could be described as traditional, including psychiatric diagnosis, medical treatment and customary occupational therapy. No previous groupwork in relation to grief problems had been carried out in the day hospital.

In addition to helping people to work through their emotional reactions, the aim of the group was practical, involving trying out different ways of coping, homework tasks, problem solving and confronting and dealing with triggers of unpleasant emotions. In adopting this approach, it was hoped that group members would be empowered to work through and make a satisfactory adjustment to their grief.

Reference will be made to research on grief in older people and the theoretical background to the group run by the authors. The measures used to evaluate the usefulness of the group and the selection of group members will be described. A brief outline of a typical group session will be given and the reader will gain an insight into the nature of the group in the section headed 'The group sessions'. This gives examples of the work done and describes the progress of group members.

GRIEF IN OLDER PEOPLE

Several investigators have claimed that the elderly suffer less from grief than their younger counterparts and that the risk to mental health is correspondingly reduced (e.g. Parkes, 1964, Maddison and Walker, 1967). In their study of the elderly widowed, Bowling and Cartwright (1982) found that younger widows and widowers were more likely to find loneliness a problem and to have more problems in adjustment (although their measure of adjustment was somewhat crude, consisting of five questions including whether the widowed felt they had come to terms with the death of their husband/wife or whether they felt apart or remote even among friends). The notion of timeliness is often quoted; if something is seen as appropriate for that point in the life cycle, for example the death of an elderly spouse, then it is felt that it will be easier to cope with. By comparison, the death of a grown child is not timely and is reported to be most distressing (Osterweis, 1985). Lopata (1971) has suggested that younger widowed feel their widowhood more acutely as they have been bereaved before their friends. It is also probable that younger people are less comfortable with thinking about death. Kalish (1976), for example, found that older people talk and think more about death than younger people.

Although many studies have indicated the relatively good adjustment of the older compared to the younger widowed, as Stroebe and Stroebe (1987) point out, 'this does not imply that the older do not suffer detriments to their health and symptoms of distress following bereavement'. In one study (Sanders, 1981), there is an indication that older people may have more persisting problems in adjustment than younger people. After 18 to 24 months of bereavement, the older widowed scored higher on the denial sub-scale of the Grief Experience Inventory (Sanders, Mauger and Strong, 1979). This was related to the persistence of extreme loneliness and deprivation and to minimal social support.

In the light of some of this research, it would be easy to unwittingly adopt an ageist attitude towards bereavement in old age – the elderly do not have to earn a living or support dependants; it is natural to die at that age so they must find it easier to cope with than younger people – and attitudes along the lines 'they've lived their lives', which imply that the problems of the younger bereaved are more important. It is essential that a therapist working with older people should have worked through any such attitudes and also thought about his or her own ageing. Ideally, some thought should also have been given to one's own attitudes towards death and personal ways of coping with bereavement. Unresolved issues for the therapist in these areas would not be helpful to elderly people in therapy (psychoanalysts would refer to this as counter-transference).

The form that grieving takes may well differ for older people; extreme outbursts of despair and rage seem to be less common. The effect of the duration of the deceased's illness also seems to be affected by age. Evidence suggests that the younger widowed find it most difficult when their spouse dies suddenly and the older widowed find it most difficult when the spouse dies a lingering death (Vachon, 1976; Clayton *et al.*, 1973). It may be even less likely that older people will fit neatly into a 'stage' model of bereavement. A common pattern is for there to be gradual adjustment with occasional lapses into more severe grief (Parkes, 1972; Brink, 1985).

In one study (Parkes, 1964), those widowed over the age of 65 years, in Britain, were found to have consulted their general practitioners less often for psychological symptoms, and to have received fewer prescriptions of tranquillizers during the first 18 months after bereavement compared with a group of the younger widowed registered with the same GPs. These elderly widowed, however, were more likely than the younger ones to have consulted their GPs with physical complaints. One interpretation of this is that the elderly are more vulnerable than younger people to the physical effects of bereavement. It is also possible though that older people are less able or willing to 'psychologize' what is wrong with them. Much of the high incidence of depression and of suicide in old age may well be attributable to bereavement (Kay, Roth and Hopkins, 1955; Richards and McCallum, 1979).

In a study by Gerber *et al.* (1975), emotional support was provided to a sample of elderly bereaved people in New York by trained psychiatric workers for the first six months after bereavement. During this time companionship support was also organized, plus help with legal and financial matters and household chores. Follow-up assessments were made until 15 months after bereavement. For these older people there was a positive impact on medical outcome when compared with a no-treatment control group. They received fewer drug prescriptions, consulted with doctors less frequently and reported feeling ill without consultation less often.

There are reports of group therapy with the elderly in the literature (Altholz, 1986). Some of these focus on loss issues and on depressed individuals. Solomon and Zinke (1991) describe psychotherapy groups for elderly people with various problems, mainly depression and anxiety, but including other problems such as chronic schizophrenia and mania. The paper did not claim to examine therapeutic success or failure, but made the rather glib statement that the majority of group members experienced remission of their presenting symptoms. It would appear that group leaders had great difficulty in getting members to express their feelings.

Sorensen (1986) refers to the importance of regaining a sense of mastery and provides a good description of the goal of an older adult group: 'An older adults' group strives to provide an environment where the patients may consolidate once again an awareness of themselves as having been, and as capable of being, individuals able to affect change in their world' (p. 543).

Often elderly people seen in clinical contexts will have become preoccupied with the deficits in their lives and ignore the evidence that they have accomplished much that they can take pride in. Talking about past achievements helps to build up self- esteem.

THEORETICAL BACKGROUND TO GROUP RUN BY AUTHORS

It was assumed that many of the emotions experienced by the bereaved – shock, denial, anger, guilt, depression and anxiety – would be relevant topics for discussion. No assumptions were made about the order in which such feelings would occur.

The task of coping with bereavement can be viewed as similar to the task of coping with any major transition. Adams, Hayes and Hopson (1976) view a transition as a discontinuity in a person's life space and describe transition phases representing a cycle of experiencing a disruption; gradually acknowledging its reality, testing oneself, understanding oneself and incorporating changes in one's behaviour. Addressing these issues practically involves asking questions, such as 'What important changes in my life have I coped with up to now and how did I cope with them?'; 'Am I proactive or do I usually sit back and wait for things to happen?'; 'Do I know my personal 'anchor points' (things that remain unchanged in the face of other major change)?'; 'If I feel under stress do I know what I can do to help myself?'

Elderly people who are bereaved may often feel depressed and helpless, for example in relation to 'first time tasks' (such as having to deal with household finances which a spouse may have dealt with before) or going out socially without a partner. (For a brief description of learned helplessness and ideas relating to social reinforcement and bereavement, see Ramsay and Happee, 1977.)

Learning how to take a problem-solving approach can be a useful skill to acquire. D'Zurilla and Goldfried (1971) define problem solving as 'a behavioural process, whether overt or cognitive in nature, which (a) makes available a variety of potentially effective response alternatives for dealing with the problematic situation, and (b) increases the probability of selecting the most effective response from among these various alternatives'. Steps include defining the problem, generating alternatives, decision making and evaluating the effectiveness of the solution. The approach will include breaking a problem down into its component parts and sorting out parts which cannot be controlled. For the parts that are left, solutions will be brainstormed (a process whereby any solution that comes to mind will be written down however offbeat it may seem). For each solution its consequences will be judged and maybe its practicality and chances of success. The most appropriate solution will be selected and targets set for achieving it. (Goldfried and Goldfried, 1975, describe how to apply the approach.)

The approach of confronting things that trigger off an emotional reaction derives from a behavioural formulation of grief as being similar to phobias (Ramsay, 1977). In phobic reactions there is anxiety and avoidance of an objectively harmless situation. In bereavement certain situations and reminders may be avoided; for example, linking objects may be put away and never looked at because this would lead to people feeling upset. The behavioural approaches to dealing with phobias involve confronting the feared situation until the emotional responses are reduced.

MEASURES USED TO EVALUATE USEFULNESS OF GROUP

Various questionnaires were used and these are described below. Faschingbaurer, Devaul and Zisook (1977) describe a short Texas Inventory of Grief. It includes statements, such as 'At times I still feel the need to cry for the person who died', 'I have pain in the same area of my body as the person who died'. Items are rated on a five-point scale (completely false, mostly false, partly true and partly false, mostly true and completely true) as to whether they have applied over the past few weeks. This questionnaire was slightly modified to include some of the original items from the Expanded Texas Inventory of Grief (Zisook, Devaul and Click, 1982), such as 'I feel he/she is still with me at times', 'I get angry when I think of him/her'. The modified questionnaire consisted of only six items.

Horowitz, Wilner and Alvarez (1979) developed an Impact of Event Scale. It is a measure of subjective stress, and includes items like 'I thought about it when I didn't mean to', 'I had trouble falling asleep or staying asleep because of pictures or thoughts about it that came into my mind' and 'I stayed away from reminders of it'. Items are rated on a frequency scale for the past seven days (not at all, rarely, sometimes and often).

The Beck Depression Inventory (Beck *et al.*, 1961) consists of items relating to mood, sense of failure, guilt, crying and sleep disturbance. Items are rated on four- or five-point scales. For mood, it is 'I do not feel sad' (0), 'I feel blue or sad' (1), 'I am blue or sad all the time and I can't snap out of it' (2a), 'I am so sad or unhappy that it is very painful' (2b) and 'I am so sad or unhappy that I can't stand it' (3). This is a well-researched scale, although for older people it may overestimate the incidence of depression because physical symptoms occur more frequently amongst older people. For the current study, the level of depression was of less interest than changes in depressive symptoms over time.

Goldberg and Hillier (1979) developed a scaled 28-item version of the General Health Questionnaire. It consists of four sub-scales relating to somatic symptoms ('been getting a feeling of tightness or pressure in your head'), anxiety and insomnia ('found everything getting on top of you'), social dysfunction ('felt capable of making decisions about things') and severe depression ('been thinking of yourself as a worthless person'). Each item is rated on a four-point scale – not at all, no more than usual, rather more than usual and much more than usual. For the question about making decisions, the ratings are more so than usual, same as usual, less so than usual and much less capable. All items are rated according to how people have been over the past few weeks. The General Health Questionnaire was designed as a screening questionnaire for use in consulting settings to detect people with probable psychiatric disorder and each version has a threshold score. However, in the present study the main interest was in changes in scores over time.

GROUP PHILOSOPHY

The approach is as taken by Sorensen (1986), i.e. that elderly people are capable of making change in their lives. Describing the bereavement process may help group members to realize that to a large extent their emotional experience following bereavement is normal. By looking at the ways previous major life events have been coped with, elderly people can identify their own strengths and resources. Also, it is never too late to learn, for example how to apply problem-solving approaches to real life situations.

The aim is to empower people to help themselves. Also, built into the group is an understanding that evaluating its usefulness is important, both for the individuals concerned and for elderly people who may be involved in similar groups in the future.

A MULTI-DISCIPLINARY APPROACH

The authors, a clinical psychologist and a drama therapist/counsellor, had not worked together before and, prior to the group, there was a willingness to use whatever techniques were felt appropriate.

The use of drama therapy techniques was not pursued because of some limitations, such as the small size of the room available for the meetings and the physical condition of some of the group members (including one who could not walk very well). This would have made the use of theatre, perhaps for reliving an event, very difficult. For the reader interested in this area, refer to Langley (1987).

The multi-disciplinary approach was further extended in one of the later sessions, when an Age Concern worker attended to talk about local opportunities for volunteering and other activities.

The service setting

The group was run in a small meeting room in a day hospital for the elderly sick and mentally infirm. (This unit also consists of two wards above the day hospital.) The day hospital caters for people with dementia and for people with other problems such as depression and anxiety. It is situated in an urban area, surrounded by houses and quite close to a town centre.

SELECTING THE GROUP MEMBERS

People attending the day hospital were referred to the group, usually by their consultant psychiatrist and, in one case, a local general practitioner who had heard about the proposed group referred someone. Each person was then interviewed by the two authors; information was collected on current health problems, medication, support network, degree of dependence on the deceased (both practically and emotionally), details relating to the bereavement (sudden or expected), details relating to previous bereavements and information on how each coped with past losses. Current crises other than bereavement and the nature of the relationship with the deceased were also taken into account.

People were given an explanation about the proposed group (e.g. that it would involve talking about their feelings), and then asked how helpful they felt it would be to them. A four-point scale was used: not really helpful at all, a little helpful, fairly helpful and very helpful. It was felt important to try to measure motivation regarding joining the group.

An assessment was also made of the experience of grief so far by discussing the common components of grief – shock, denial, depression, guilt, anxiety and aggression. People were also asked how they felt about their ability to cope with the future.

Exclusions from the group

Four people were interviewed regarding the possibility of joining the group who were excluded for various reasons. One of them, Mrs J. (age 71 years), was clearly ambivalent, and after a relatively short interview stated that she did not wish to join the group. She was, therefore, not asked the various questions mentioned above and not given any questionnaires to complete. Mrs J.'s husband had died over five years previously and she had been very demanding of relatives, friends and neighbours, not wanting to be left alone. She was taking minor tranquillizers. The other three people excluded are described below.

Mrs G. (age 72 years) had been married for 52 years and her husband died suddenly three years previously from a myocardial infarction. They had both run a newsagent's. The husband had dealt with all practical matters and Mrs G. now relied on her son and daughter-in-law for help. Apart from her parents and two friends, her previous bereavements included her 17-year-old grandson four years previously; he was killed in a car crash, having just passed his driving test. Mrs G. developed asthma soon after her husband died and felt anxious, especially about being alone. She reported seeing Mr G. everywhere and said that she often cried, particularly at night. Regarding her ability to cope in the future she felt it was hard to say: 'I'm hoping I will be able to cope before so long'. She felt that she had coped with past losses to a certain extent, but when asked whether she thought the group would be helpful to her, she replied that she did not know. It was felt that Mrs G. was not sufficiently motivated to be able to benefit from the group.

Mrs S. (age 76 years) had been married for 20 years and her husband had died 29 years previously from cancer of the stomach. She had been a machinist and her husband had done office work. Their relationship had been strong. Amongst her previous bereavements was the death of a son at age two years, 44 years before. She suffered from arthritis, chronic obstructive pulmonary disease and was also depressed, for which she was taking medication. She never cried at Mr S.'s funeral and did not cry for years afterwards. One year previously she had seen a shape on the stairs and felt the presence of her husband. She regretted that she did not discuss his illness with him before his death. There was some anger with staff at one hospital, who at one point had said there was nothing wrong with Mr S. When asked how she felt about her ability to cope with the future, Mrs S. said she did not know and she felt the future would be dismal. Regarding motivation to attend the group, Mrs S. felt it would be between a little and fairly helpful. One week later Mrs S. reported that she had been very upset by the previous session, that she could not sleep for several nights and had to take sleeping tablets. Consequently it was agreed that she would not join the group.

Mrs K. (age 73 years) had been married for 50 years and her husband died one year previously of cancer of the liver. She had worked in a mill when younger and her husband had been involved in making batteries. He had handled all household finances and she was finding it difficult to cope with these. Amongst her previous bereavements was the death of a son at 12 days old, 45 years before. She had experienced a period of depression about 10 years previously and at the time she was interviewed was taking medication for anxiety and depression, after a period of hospitalization.

Mrs K. said that she had no feelings, just like when she was told her husband was dying of cancer. She made comments like, 'What am I going to do? Am I going to get better?' Her son and daughter were seeing her less often because they were finding it difficult to cope with her. When asked whether she felt she would benefit from the group, her reply was that she did not know. The interview and completing the questionnaire took a long time as Mrs K. was very slow and deliberate and it was sometimes difficult for her to answer questions. She was not felt to be appropriate for the group.

The initial scores on the questionnaires for the people who were excluded from the group are given in Table 8.1 (this does not include Mrs J. who, as mentioned above, was not given the questionnaires).

Table 8.1 Initial total scores on questionnaires for people excluded from group (higher scores = worse scores)

	Mrs G.	Mrs S.	Mrs K.
Impact of Event Scale	27	22	10
Texas Grief Inventory (modified)	19	10	10
Beck Depression Inventory	28	19	17
General Health Questionnaire	27	26	29

The group members

Four people were included in the group and brief information on them is given below.

Mrs R. (age 73 years) had been married for 47 years and her husband had died of a stroke three and a half years previously. She had worked in a cotton mill up to the age of 23 and her husband had done general clerical work. Her son had also died almost five years previously from a myocardial infarction at age 42. Mrs R. and her husband were very close and hardly ever went out without one another. Following the death of her son, she developed a problem with dizziness associated with various anxiety symptoms; this restricted her going out and the problem was apparently getting worse. About a year after her son died she spent five weeks in a psychiatric hospital and at the time she was interviewed she was taking minor tranquillizers. When comparing herself with other widows, she felt that they coped better than herself. She had thoughts of suicide on several occasions, often felt that life was not worth living and kept thinking she was never going to get better. She was anxious about being lonely and having nobody to confide in. There was still some anger towards hospital staff for what she felt was inadequate treatment of her husband, for example not being fed properly, developing bed sores, being sent home without his teeth. Regarding her ability to cope with the future she felt it would be very difficult, but it would be a great help if she could get rid of her dizziness. She was interested in joining the group and hoped that it would be fairly helpful to her.

Mrs H. (age 77 years) had been married for 52 years and her husband, who had a problem with his heart, died suddenly just under two years previously. They had worked in the hotel business. She had developed diabetes three years previously and also had heart disease. Apart from her parents her previous bereavements included two brothers and a sister. Her social network consisted of a good lady friend, a niece and a home help, but she did not really feel that she had a confidant. She talked to her husband every night, and there seemed to be some guilt associated with her 'straying once or twice' (previous affairs?). One of her worries was being taken bad in the night and not being able to get hold of anybody. She said she would try to cope with the future but really she felt there was no future for her. She was interested in joining the group and felt it might be fairly helpful to her, commenting that it 'may be the answer' and it was worth 'having a go'.

Mrs B. (age 66 years) was referred by her general practitioner so was not actually attending the day hospital. She had been married for 42 years and her husband had died suddenly after a myocardial infarction 15 months previously. She had worked as a hand finisher/inspector in a mill and her husband had been a headmaster. Mrs B. reported that their relationship had been good, but she relied on her husband more than she thought and she hated dealing with practical things. She had to look after her daughter who suffered from Crohn's disease and various problems associated with inflammation of her joints. Her social network consisted of a few friends and neighbours whom she saw about once a week. She viewed herself as a coper (for example she had cared for her mother and mother-in-law prior to their deaths) and was annoyed that she was not coping very well currently and was having to take tranquillizers and sleeping tablets. She felt lacking in confidence and guilty that she had sexual intercourse with her husband just prior to his death. Mrs B. was keen on joining the group although she did not really know how helpful it would be to her.

Mrs M. (age 72 years) had been married for 25 years and her husband had died of cancer of the bowel 18 months previously (about 18 months after she was first given the diagnosis). She had worked as an assistant matron in an elderly persons home and her husband had been a dustman. Their relationship had been good and they had confided in each other. She felt that she had not coped very well with her parents' death, who both died in the same year 33 years previously, and that she had not coped very well with the menopause. About five years prior to her husband's death, she had suffered from depression requiring just under four months in hospital.

Mrs M. lived in an elderly persons home and had a close friend there. At the time of first being interviewed she was worried about her sister who had cancer of the breast and lived 50 miles away. Also, she was taking antidepressants and sleeping tablets. She reported 'seeing him' on a number of occasions and feeling his presence. Several people she had known had died of cancer and she felt that they were all leaving her, leading to her feeling alone even though she lived in an elderly persons home. There were some general guilt feelings that she could have done more for her husband, and that being a religious person she felt she should have talked to him more about God. Mrs M. felt the group would be very helpful to her; in particular she felt it would be a relief to be able to talk about things, as she could not always confide in her close friend.

The initial scores on the questionnaires for people included in the group are given in Table 8.2.

Table 8.2 Initial total scores on questionnaires for people included in group

	Mrs M.	Mrs B.	Mrs H.	Mrs R.
Impact of Event Scale	19	20	23	11
Texas Grief Inventory (modified)	16.5	18	15	15
Beck Depression Inventory	22	21	19	19
General Health Questionnaire	33	28	32	58

A TYPICAL GROUP SESSION

A session would start with a discussion of how people had been since the last meeting and then a report on any homework tasks attempted – making notes on things that triggered an emotional reaction, facing up to an avoided trigger, trying to replace negative depressive thinking in certain situations with more positive helpful thinking.

Then a theme or topic might be focused on, for example brainstorming and writing on a board any feelings of guilt or completing a coping skills questionnaire and discussing members' various ways of coping. A discussion of problem solving was spread over two sessions.

Sometimes issues had to be addressed for individuals, such as resistance to discussing certain things or not completing a homework task. On occasions, feelings were put into perspective by discussing them in the framework of a normal grief process.

Before the end of a session, members would agree on any homework tasks they would tackle before the next meeting.

THE GROUP SESSIONS

The group met most weeks for a period of three months, each session lasting about an hour (on four occasions there was a gap of two weeks). At the beginning of the first session the importance of regular attendance was stressed and the group philosophy and approach were restated. Any discussion in the group would be confidential to group members, and it was agreed that group members and therapists would refer to each other using first names.

Early in the first session, all group members noted two things they had in common: they were all taking sleeping tablets and had all experienced the comment 'Pull yourself together'. Each group member was asked to talk briefly about significant deaths, and it was noted that Mrs H. could not do this, having just passed the second anniversary of her husband's death. A two-page handout covering common experiences in grief was given at the end of the first session and the homework was to read this handout before the next session. Two members commented to staff not connected with the group that they thought the first session was good.

Within the first few meetings it became apparent to the therapists that two group members would probably be dropping out for different reasons. Mrs R. only attended two of the first four meetings (on two occasions she had been attending an out-patient appointment at another hospital). She was able to talk about her loneliness and guilt related to going into hospital when her husband was ill. However, she felt that she was getting worse, commenting, 'If only they were here' (her son and her husband). After the fourth session Mrs R. stopped attending the day hospital. She told staff that she could find better things to do at home than attending the day hospital and that she was not benefiting from the grief therapy group. Consequently Mrs R. attended no further group sessions.

As mentioned above, Mrs H. could not talk about her husband's death in the first session. During the second session she was saying, 'I can't talk about these sort of things', and it was noted that she had not read the handout given out at the end of the first session. She was anxious that the session should finish in case she missed her coffee in the day hospital. In subsequent meetings, Mrs H. was making comments, such as 'You want attention when you're on your own, that's why I like coming here'. She felt guilty that on the day her husband died she was not at the hospital, and again asked the rhetorical question 'Have I done the right thing in years gone by?'. One homework task after one of the sessions was to make notes regarding any guilty feelings, and Mrs H. did not do this. By the sixth meeting she reported thinking more and getting upset after the meetings. She did not feel the group was helping and really wanted to be excused from the sixth meeting, although she stayed. Guilt related to her 'straying' was mentioned again. She commented, 'I don't want to talk about bereavement stuff, it churns me up inside'. Mrs H. arrived late for the seventh session and stated that she did not want to continue discussing this 'bereavement stuff' and that she would prefer to do painting in the day hospital. Therefore, she left the group before the meeting started.

Between her sixth and last session Mrs H. was interviewed to complete the questionnaires again, and she commented that she could not see the point of them. During this interview she claimed that she had nothing to feel guilty about during the war; she drove men about in an ambulance and had friendships with men, but not affairs. She also commented, 'If I did feel guilty about something, I wouldn't talk about it – it's something you've got to sort out yourself, inside you'. At the end of this interview Mrs H. said she would continue attending the group, but she had obviously changed her mind about this by the next meeting.

The halfway stage

By this stage the group was about half way through its planned number of meetings, and it was agreed with the two remaining group members (Mrs B. and Mrs M.) that we would continue with the further six meetings. It was interesting to note that these two people, for example, had been more able to talk about guilt feelings, such as not having physical contact with her husband when he died (Mrs M.) and making love with her husband just before he died (Mrs B.).

By the fifth session, Mrs M. reported not being able to stop crying at times and feeling that she should be getting over it more. Mrs B. felt inadequate and that she was letting her husband down; she was not coping very well with household tasks and was taking a long time to make decisions. Jealousy was experienced by both members – both felt that other women should not be out with their husbands. Unfortunately, these kind of thoughts then made them feel guilty. It was discussed in the group that such feelings of jealousy/envy are normal in the sense that many bereaved people experience them.

At the sixth session, Mrs M. had been able to make notes relating to her guilt feelings (something she had not been able to do before this point) and felt she was getting things into better perspective. Mrs B. commented at the beginning of the session, 'I wish I could change, I'm not getting any better'. However, she had made a vow with herself that when she was out shopping she would not look at families out together and be envious, she would try to be happy for them. She had also done some clearing up in the garden for 30 minutes and got some pleasure out of it.

As the group progressed, Mrs M. reported that she had been able to go past the flat where she used to live with her husband (something she had always avoided doing). This had been upsetting, but she felt it helped her in coming to terms with his death. There had also been a positive element in that certain flowers were in blossom in the garden and Mrs M. felt her husband would have been pleased. She lived in an elderly persons home and at times felt unwanted. This would lead to thoughts of 'I wish he was here, he understood me'. Although she reported bursting into tears now and again, she usually felt better afterwards. She found she began to concentrate better and so was able to do more reading.

Mrs M. started talking about when she did various jobs in Canada and when she worked in an elderly persons home. She had also survived a period of illness in hospital. This led to her making comments like, 'I've always come up' and 'Sometimes we've got more power that we think we have'. In a discussion about learning from the past, Mrs M. identified that she had determination. After quite a long period thinking about it, she bought a radio and reported that it cheered her up.

Examples of her answers to a coping skills questionnaire (Hopson, 1981) include that she was learning to let go of the past and trying to make the best of things now. Her personal anchor point was mixing with other residents in the home where she lived. In a section on knowing other people who can help, her answer to the questions 'Who can make me feel competent and valued?', 'Who can give me important information?', 'Who will challenge me to sit up and take a good look at myself?' and 'Who will give me constructive feedback?' was 'the two therapists in the group'. She did not feel that anyone else could help her in these ways.

Unfortunately, just before the penultimate group session Mrs M.'s friend died. She had been planning to visit her sister (who lived about 250 miles away) with this friend. Some time was spent talking about this in the remaining session. The Age Concern worker attended the penultimate session and talked about possibilities for volunteering and various activities, and Mrs M. was very interested in the possibilities raised.

As the group progressed, Mrs B. still reported examples of negative things, such as feeling sorry for herself, that others had more ability to do things than herself and that she was not doing what she should be doing. She was encouraged to think more positively, especially in response to triggers such as seeing families out (mentioned previously). Another trigger was when she was waiting for an ambulance or taxi with her daughter (previously her husband would have transported them by car). She was annoyed that she could not drive. She reported that she was not looking at other people, for example in a restaurant, and thinking, 'If only he was here...'. She had not been able to cry much, but at one of the sessions commented that she had been able to cry with her daughter recently. She really needed to move to a bungalow and was beginning to think about this.

As a homework exercise, Mrs B. obtained some information on a flat and a bungalow and said that she would probably view them. She asked a friend for help in completing a tax form (previously her husband would have dealt with this). Examples of her responses to the coping skills questionnaire included that what she wanted from her new situation was to come to terms with it and try to find a new life. She wanted to feel in command. Her daughter could make her feel competent and valued and she could share good news and good feelings with her daughter. Mrs B. felt that home was her anchor point and that she was trying to let go of the past, but it was still difficult. She thought she would have been a better coper and felt that she must have used her husband as a prop. Having said this, she felt that she had coped well with her financial affairs though.

Mrs B. felt that she wanted new interests in life. She attended one session of a Yoga class, but she felt it was not suitable and joined a course on general exercise for fitness instead. Also, she booked to go on a craft course which was once a week for 10 weeks. She had made a decision to get some work done on the house and was still considering moving. She still had days when she felt down and had some good cries. However, in the last session she commented, 'We could go on moaning for ages'.

Both Mrs M. and Mrs B. had been interested in the sessions on problem solving. The process had been illustrated by taking the example of developing a new interest, brainstorming the possibilities, or developing an old interest, and finding out what was going on locally from the library. The distance to travel to pursue the interest may be a limiting factor. Mrs B. appeared to find applying the approach easier than Mrs M. (although Mrs M. was reading more and doing some painting at home).

OUTCOME MEASURES

Apart from the questionnaires, Mrs M. and Mrs B. were asked to complete a short form after the last session, giving feedback on how they found the group. Mrs M. placed a lot of importance on being able to talk frankly about herself and sharing her feelings with someone in a similar situation. She felt it helped her to let go slowly of the past because she did not feel sad so often, she was learning to know herself, take things one day at a time and accept the situation. The group helped her work through her guilt feelings, not to feel sorry for herself and to face the future better. She noted again how helpful it had been to walk past the flat where she lived with her husband. There were still some beautiful flowers that her husband had planted in the garden and she thought how pleased he would have been to see them.

Mrs B. felt that the group had helped her to be more positive and not to feel so sorry for herself; 'I know when a situation comes up I have the courage to sort things out'. She still felt she did not have the strength she had in the past, but the group had helped her to do positive things, such as jobs around the house. Talking through guilt feelings was felt to be very helpful, as was talking about and confronting things which trigger off emotions. Being given permission not to be ashamed of crying and sharing hidden feelings was also felt to be beneficial. Mrs B. had found the systematic approach to problem solving helpful; apart from the new interests mentioned above, she had also joined a historical society. She had some work done on the paths round the house without waiting a week to make the decision, but she was still not very confident about making the decision to move. She had found the handout on bereavement (given out at the end of the first session) very helpful; it summarized her own feelings and made her think that they (the therapists) understood what she was going through.

Both Mrs M. and Mrs B. would have liked the group to have been larger, so there was a wider scope in hearing other people's opinions and sharing experiences.

Questionnaires were completed by Mrs M. and Mrs B. before the group started, halfway through (between the sixth and seventh sessions), at the end of the group, three months after the end of the group and at six months after the end of the group. The scores on the questionnaires are presented in Table 8.3.

Scores are also available for Mrs H. halfway through the group as she did not leave the group until after this point. Her halfway scores together with the pre-group scores are presented in Table 8.4.

DISCUSSION

It can be seen from the pattern of Mrs B.'s scores on the questionnaires that she appeared to get worse halfway through the group course. Her depression score increased from mild to moderate, for example her mood, guilt feelings and

Table 8.3 Total scores for Mrs M. and Mrs B. – pre-, mid-, post-group and follow-up

	Pre-group	Mid-group	Post-group	Follow-up (3 months)	Follow-up (6 months)
Mrs M.					
Impact of Event Scale	19	17	9	11	7
Texas Grief Inventory (modified)	16.5	14	11	14	13
Beck Depression Inventory	22	19	12	11	11
General Health Questionnaire	33	23	18	24	27
Mrs B.					
Impact of Event Scale	20	27	24	15	10
Texas Grief Inventory (modified)	18	18	14	14	14
Beck Depression Inventory	21	27	16	9	5
General Health Questionnaire	28	62	36	20	17

Table 8.4 Pre- and mid-group total scores for Mrs H.

	Pre-group	Mid-group
Impact of Event Scale	23	16
Texas Grief Inventory (modified)	15	15
Beck Depression Inventory	19	19
General Health Questionnaire	32	20

somatic preoccupation all became worse. On the Impact of Event Scale, for example, she experienced waves of strong feelings more often and was more frequently aware that she still had a lot of feelings that she did not deal with. Her scores on all four sub-scales of the General Health Questionnaire increased quite considerably. Her total score on the Grief Inventory remained the same. At the end of the group and at both follow-ups, her scores progressively improved. This would suggest that the group stirred up a lot of difficult feelings for Mrs B. and she had to get worse before she could get better. These findings from the questionnaires are consistent with her progress through the group reported above. At the follow-up sessions she reported that her jealous thoughts were less frequent, she was getting better at letting go of the past and had extended her range of social activities. She was thinking more positively and generally felt that she was coping a lot better.

The pattern of Mrs M.'s scores on the questionnaires indicated that she gradually improved during the group and this improvement was mostly maintained at follow-up. The exception to this was her score on the General Health Questionnaire at follow-up, in particular an increase in the severe depression scale six months after the end of the group. This appeared to be related to her feeling excluded in the elderly persons home where she lived, especially over Christmas when her friend was away. She had also been discharged from the day hospital and viewed this as a wrench. At follow-up she felt she was letting go more and although she still got upset at times, this happened less frequently. Making decisions had improved; for example, she had decided to have a telephone installed and had made a will. Mrs M. also commented that realizing that bereavement was a natural process had helped her, and she became aware that the group was helping her in the last few meetings.

Although Mrs B. and Mrs M. benefited from the group, an important issue is that of careful selection of group members, thereby preventing people dropping out. The questionnaire scores for those people who were excluded from the group before it started were similar to those who were included, but the scores of Mrs G. (excluded) tended to be higher, for example her depression and Impact of Event Scale scores. Also, the initial General Health Questionnaire scores tended to be higher amongst people included in the group.

Multiple losses may be an important issue in selection. It is interesting to note that the three people who were excluded from the group after completing the initial questionnaires had all experienced multiple losses. In Mrs G.'s case she had lost her husband and grandson and had developed asthma; Mrs S. had lost her husband and a son when he was young, suffered from arthritis and had a chronic obstructive pulmonary disease; and Mrs K. had lost her husband and a son when he was a baby. Also, Mrs R., who dropped out of the group early on, had lost her husband and son when he was 42 years old and had a severe problem with dizziness. It may be that for these people the death of their husbands brought back unresolved feelings related to the deaths of their sons or grandson which were too difficult to face. It is also interesting to note that Mrs H., who dropped out of the group midway through the course, had diabetes and heart disease to cope with as well as the death of her husband.

The four people who were excluded clearly lacked motivation. The two people who stopped attending appeared to be motivated to attend initially. Of these, it was interesting to note that Mrs R.'s initial scores on the General Health Questionnaire were very high. She was clearly disenchanted with the day hospital and stopped attending before she had given the group a chance. Mrs H.'s negative attitude towards the group was unexpected. Her scores on the questionnaires from pre- to mid-group either remained the same or improved. However, her attitude would have prevented her from acknowledging that the group may be able to help her.

One possible reason for Mrs H. dropping out may have been connected with her expectations. She clearly was not able to discuss her feelings as she found it too upsetting, so she may have thought that the group would be more social in nature and not involve in-depth discussions. For the two people who attended the whole group course it also became apparent that they really did not have a clear idea of what the group would involve, apart from being a discussion group. Similar observations have been made by Altholz (1986), who noted that the concept of group therapy is alien to many older people, and so at the beginning they are often unclear about the purpose of the group. This would suggest that for future similar groups more time should be spent explaining what will be involved, perhaps backing this up with written information. This would apply for professionals who might refer to the group and to potential group members. As mentioned in the introduction, elderly people may find it difficult to view their problems as psychological and so find it hard to 'tune in' to talking about feelings and different ways of coping. Therefore, the more explanation about any therapy the better.

Another issue is the size of the group; Mrs B. and Mrs M. both commented that it would have been better if there had been more people with whom to share experiences. Providing clearer explanations about the group (as mentioned above) and starting off with more people (perhaps about eight) would help to ensure a group with several members throughout.

Better ways of measuring changes in grief would also be helpful. There are problems in using some items from the Texas Inventory of Grief; for example, the item 'I feel he/she is still with me at times' can be interpreted as a pleasant reassuring feeling and so need not indicate poor adjustment. When applying the Impact of Event Scale to grief, there are problems with some items, such as 'other things kept making me think about it', 'any reminder brought back feelings about it' and 'pictures about it popped into my mind'. It is possible that some of these thoughts/feelings could be pleasant and so a high score may not necessarily indicate poor adjustment.

Clearly Mrs B. and Mrs M. had quite strong grief reactions but it would appear that the group helped them to help themselves and that this improvement was largely maintained or developed six months after the group had stopped meeting. When the group started they had both been bereaved for between one and two years and it is unlikely that they would have made the same progress had they not attended the group. A larger scale study with a matched control group would be needed to establish whether the passage of time or non-specific therapy could have brought about the same improvements as the grief therapy group.

Parkes (1985) met an old man during the course of making a television documentary, *The Life That's Left*. At that time, two years after his wife's death, this man had been depressed and negativistic, refusing offers of help and without hope for the future. Eight years later when Parkes met him again, he appeared suntanned and smiling, slightly plumper and was engaging in a wide range of hobbies and other activities. In the film he had asked for euthanasia, and when asked what he thought about that now his reply was, 'It would have been such a waste'. This presents a positive view of adjustment to bereavement in old age and is consistent with the authors' philosophy (as mentioned in the introduction) that elderly people can make change in their lives and they can be empowered to help themselves. Hopefully, developing and improving the group therapy approach described in this chapter will help more elderly people who are having problems in adjusting to bereavement to regain a sense of mastery. As Sorensen (1986) describes it, 'to consolidate once again an awareness of themselves as having been, and as capable of being, individuals able to affect change in their world'.

REFERENCES

Adams, J.D., Hayes, J. and Hopson, B. (1976) *Transition: Understanding and Managing Personal Change*, Martin Robertson, London.

Altholz, J.A.S. (1986) Group psychotherapy with the elderly, in *Working with the Elderly: Group Process and Techniques*, (ed. I. Burnside), Jones and Bartlett, Boston, pp. 248–58.

Beck, A.T., Ward, C.H., Mendelson, M. *et al.* (1961) An inventory for measuring depression. *Archives of General Psychiatry*, **4**, 561–71.

Bowling, A. and Cartwright, A. (1982) *Life After A Death: A Study of the Elderly Widowed*, Tavistock, London.

Brink, T. L. (1985) The grieving patient in later life. *Psychotherapy – Patient*, **2**(1), 117–27.

Clayton, P.J., Halikas, J., Maurice, W. and Robins, E. (1973) Anticipatory grief and widowhood. *British Journal of Psychiatry*, **122**, 47–51.

D'Zurilla, T.J. and Goldfried, M.R. (1971) Problem solving and behaviour modification. *Journal of Abnormal Psychology*, **78**, 107–26.

Faschingbaurer, T.R., Devaul, R.A. and Zisook, S. (1977) Development of the Texas Inventory of Grief. *American Journal of Psychiatry*, **134**, 696–8.

Gerber, I., Wiener, A., Battin, D., and Arkin, A.M. (1975) *Grief Therapy to the Aged Bereaved in Bereavement: Its Psychosocial Aspects*, (eds B. Schoenberg, A.C. Carr, A.H. Kutscher *et al.*), Columbia University Press, New York.

Goldberg, D.P. and Hillier, V.F. (1979) A scaled version of the General Health Questionnaire. *Psychological Medicine*, **9**, 139–45.

Goldfried, M.R. and Goldfried, A.P. (1975) Cognitive change methods, in *Helping People Change*, (eds F.H. Kanfer and A.P. Goldstein), Pergamon, New York, pp. 89–116.

Hopson, B. (1981) Transition: understanding and managing personal change, in *Psychology and Medicine*, (ed. D. Griffiths), The British Psychological Society and Macmillan, London, pp. 323–48.

Horowitz, M., Wilner, N. and Alvarez, W. (1979) Impact of Event Scale: a measure of subjective stress. *Psychosomatic Medicine*, **41**, 209–18.

Kalish, R. (1976) Death and dying in a social context, in *Handbook of Ageing and the Social Sciences*, (eds R. Binstock and E. Sharas), Van Nostrand Reinhold, New York.

Kay, D.W., Roth, M. and Hopkins, B. (1955) Aetiological factors in the causation of affective disorders in old age. *British Journal of Mental Science*, **101**, 302.

Langley, D. (1987) Dramatherapy with elderly people, in *Dramatherapy: Theory and Practice for Teachers and Clinicians*, (ed. S. Jennings), Croom Helm, London, pp. 233–56.

Lopata, H. (1971) Widows as a minority group. *Gerontologist*, **11**(1), 67–77.

Maddison, D.C. and Walker, W.L. (1967) Factors affecting the outcome of conjugal bereavement. *British Journal of Psychiatry*, **113**, 1057–67.

Osterweis, M. (1985) Bereavement and the elderly. *Ageing*, **348**, 5–41.

Parkes, C.M. (1964) The effects of bereavement on physical and mental health: a study of the medical records of widows. *British Medical Journal*, **2**, 274–9.

Parkes, C.M. (1972) *Bereavement: Studies of Adult Grief*, International Universities Press, New York.

Parkes, C.M. (1985) Bereavement in the elderly. *Geriatric Medicine Today*, **4**, 55–64.

Ramsay, R.W. (1977) Behavioural approaches to bereavement. *Behaviour Research and Therapy*, **15**, 131–5.

Ramsay, R.W. and Happee, J.A. (1977) The stress of bereavement: components and treatment, in *Stress and Anxiety*, Vol. 4, (eds C.D. Spielberger and I.G. Sarason), Wiley, London, pp. 53–64.

Richards, J.G. and McCallum, J. (1979) Bereavement in the elderly. *New Zealand Medical Journal*, **89**, 201–4.

Sanders, C. (1981) Comparison of younger and older spouses in bereavement outcome. *Omega*, **11**, 217–32.

Sanders, C., Mauger, P.A. and Strong, P.N. (1979) *A Manual for the Grief Experience Inventory* Loss and Bereavement Resource Centre, University of South Florida.

Solomon, K. and Zinke, M.R. (1991) Group psychotherapy with the depressed elderly. *Journal of Gerontological Social Work*, **17**(1–2), 47–57.

Sorensen, M.H. (1986) Narcissism and loss in the elderly: strategies for an in-patient older adults group. *International Journal of Group Psychotherapy*, **36**(4), 533–47.

Stroebe, W. and Stroebe, M.S. (1987) *Bereavement and Health. The Psychological and Physical Consequences of Partner Loss*, Cambridge University Press, Cambridge.

Vachon, M.L.S. (1976) Grief and bereavement following the death of a spouse. *Canadian Psychiatric Association Journal*, **21**, 35–44.

Zisook, S., Devaul, R.A. and Click, M.A. (1982) Measuring symptoms of grief and bereavement. *American Journal of Psychiatry*, **139**, 1590–3.

9

Sexuality and the older adult

Andrew Yates

> There is every reason to believe that maintained regularity of sexual expression coupled with adequate physical well being and mental health orientation to the ageing process combine to provide a sexually stimulative climate ... This climate will, in turn, improve sexual tension and provide a capacity for sexual performance that frequently may extend to and beyond the 80 year level.
>
> *(Masters and Johnson, 1981)*

INTRODUCTION

There is no escaping one's sexuality. It is the one thread which is woven through our very existence, and perhaps the most constant and reliable element. There cannot be many for whom embracing their sexuality has not been anything but a small part of life, for others it has been an overriding 'genre' which has been ever present.

If I were to ask you to sit down now and determine the period in your life which would herald the cessation of your sex life or sexual expression in general, you would probably have difficulty. However, this is the position the vast majority of older adults find themselves in, due to a variety of mechanisms, biological, sociological or psychological. For some it may be a happy state, knowing that all that 'messy business' is over. For many people, sex within the marriage may have been less than joyous, in fact, it could well have been a harrowing and thoroughly unpleasant duty, based on satisfying a partner or purely for the bearing of children. It is, therefore, hardly surprising that, as

Eliopoulos (1989) iterates, the menopause and advancing age may have provided the opportunity for sex to be put aside and left in the realms of the younger and fertile generations, though for many, being desexualized may be an externally imposed and totally interminable state in which gender has been placed in a state of splendid isolation.

Most nursing and related health models either explicitly or implicitly indicate the consideration of the person's sexuality, thus incorporating this information into care planning. But do health care workers necessarily have a good enough understanding of sexuality as a global phenomenon, or is it from a perspective which is comfortable and therefore unchallenging? Even if an understanding is present, is the desire or the skill to look outside taken on in a non-judgemental way which does not impinge upon the quality and quantity of care relationships between themselves and the client (Lief and Payne, 1975)?

The broad aims of this chapter are to consider sexuality from an older person's perspective, and from a non-traditional stance, thereby examining various forms in which a person's sexuality may be expressed.

DECONSTRUCTING THE MYTHS OF SEXUAL AGEING

The myths about sexuality and ageing are worthy of inclusion because of their sheer fallacy and broad misassumptions. What the myths actually do achieve is the reinforcement of what Kuhn (1976) regards as the self-fulfilling prophecy which is bedevilling to the self-concept of older adults. Older people are relentlessly bombarded with messages which indicate loss of productivity, unattractiveness and social and economic burden. The work of Comfort (1990) illustrates where the locus of disability lies. It is shown that 25% of disability experienced by older people is biogenic, i.e. pertaining to the living organism and reliant upon medicine to palliate or cure. However, the remaining 75% of those disabilities are sociogenic, and for mitigation depend on changed attitudes on the part of society and those who have dealings with older adults (Comfort, 1990). According to Hite (1990, p. 863), the typical stereotype of the older man or woman is that they 'should not fall in love – they should not feel passionate or romantic about their partners, whether new or long term, and that they should not develop new attachments'. This, linked with other widely held stereotypes, brings about an internalization resulting in a negative self-view due to a damaged self-concept (Weg, 1983).

The myths

Let us now examine the myths in Table 9.1.

1. As far as it can be seen there does not appear to be any link between intercourse and the emission of semen and mortality. Bancroft (1990) notes that

Table 9.1 Myths about sexuality and ageing

1. Intercourse and emission of semen are debilitating and will tend to hasten old age and death.

2. One's sex life can be prolonged by abstinence in earlier years and activities in later years.

3. Masturbation is a childish activity that is put aside when one reaches adulthood, and is carried out by older persons only if they are seriously disturbed.

4. Coital satisfaction decreases considerably after menopause.

5. Older men are particularly subject to sexual deviations, for example exhibitionism and child molesting.

6. Older women who still enjoy sex were probably nymphomaniacs when they were younger.

7. Most older men lose their ability to have sex.

8. Sexual abilities and performances remain the same throughout life.

9. If older individuals go without sex for several years, they will not be able to have sex at a future time.

10. Older people with chronic illness or physical disabilities should cease sex activity completely.

(Source: Croft (1992)).

there is a reduction of semen and ejaculatory power (see Sexuality, ageing and the male below); however, he does not conclude that there are any directly detrimental physiological effects. Penetrative intercourse may not always be in the desirable form of lovemaking, thus orgasm may not always be reached.

2. I am unable to find any evidence to support the notion that sexual longevity can be achieved through sexual abstinence in earlier years. In the words of T. Gibson (1992), 'this is simply rubbish'.

3. There is an overabundance of research to support the fact that masturbation is not cast aside on entering adult life. Masturbation either in youth or older adults, whether male or female, is perfectly natural and healthy and a good way of relieving sexual tension.

4. There is no evidence to suggest that coital satisfaction decreases as a result of age (Bancroft, 1990). Some postmenopausal women do experience a dryness of the vagina due to a reduction of the hormone oestrogen and painful vaginal contractions during orgasm. A visit to the GP for possible hormone replacement therapy, topical oestrogen creams or the use of water based lubricants, for example KY Jelly, during intercourse may help (remember older adults are not exempt from practising safer sex).

5. Older men are no more susceptible to developing sexual deviations or antisocial aberrations as a direct result of their ageing.

6. Older women who still enjoy sex in later life have probably always had the

same level of desire from youth. Women are, unfortunately, faced with greater difficulties in finding a suitable partner than are older men.

7. Older men can experience and maintain an erection, but this myth is based on the assumption that sex is always penetrative.

8. No one can expect to escape the physiological process of ageing, and sexual performance is no exception. Changes in sexual performance ensue very slowly and give ample time to adjust to a new and more creative approach to sex. Hite (1990) reports people over 80 years saying their sex lives have improved.

9. This is not so at all. What is damaging here is the creation of a self-fulfilling prophecy and its effects on self-concept.

10. This is like saying that those with nervous dispositions should stay indoors. Physical illness is no reason for giving up sex.

SOCIETY AND THE OLDER ADULT

Although society's attitudes towards 'sexually active older people' have begun to become more realistic and honest, there is still the feeling that if any sexual expression is to occur it will undoubtedly be heterosexual. Lawler (1991), in her book *Behind the Screens*, illustrates how sexuality and sexual behaviours 'have generally been accepted as androcentric, phallocentric, essentially copulatory in nature, and heterosexuality is taken as the norm' (p. 87). This provides us with a glowing testimony illustrating the accepted model of living, and what tool is drawn upon to measure those who do not share this form of sexual expression. Unfortunately, attitudes towards men and women who are older engaging in any form of sexual expression which is not totally traditional, that is heterosexual, are slow to change.

Any open interest or discussion around sex by the older person is still generally received with a gulp. This illustrates the construction of life continuum which had certain socially predetermined sexual cut-off points. For older people themselves, there is a reluctance to enter into any discourse regarding their sexual feelings due to fear of being defined as depraved or lecherous, therefore the myths about their sexuality become further internalized. One hears such labels, such as 'playboys' and 'studs', being applied to younger sexually active males, but at the other end of the continuum, with age against them, they could easily be described as 'dirty old men' and labelled as lecherous. Webb (1991) poses that within an already age-discriminating society, there are inter-shades of discrimination; rather like the Orwellian ideology that all people are equal, but some are more equal than others. From a feminist perspective, Webb (1991) identifies how society views various age-related bodily changes, and either adds its sanction by charging them with qualities that society holds with reverence, i.e. beauty, sensuality or productivity, or disregards them as less than acceptable and something to be hidden. Balding in men is one such example of this process offered for illustration by Webb (1991). Words such as 'virile' and 'distinguished', which are positively laden with ideas of continued sexuality and desirability, are often offered to men. Webb, however, asks us to attempt to find similar positive words to describe such a presentation in the older woman and consider what consequences this has on her sexuality.

So, what is this thing sexuality? Can it be so simple as bringing about the physiological state of orgasm as a result of orthodox penetration of a woman by a man, or is it more complex than it first appears? Certainly, there are wider issues to consider when attempting to define this fundamental concept. Sexuality is a core within each person which weaves through every action, interaction and reaction, making us anthropologically unique and individual. Just imagine the scenario where the shop assistant who is asked to describe the elderly person he/she has served just two minutes earlier. It would typically run along the descriptive line of grey hair, glasses and a walking stick. The truth of the matter is that we live in a society which either consciously or unconsciously operates an ageist paradigm, which reflects Webb's (1991) observations of youth, beauty and productivity. For the older man, sexuality is directly linked to his continued levels of productivity and how socially valued he is. Kuhn (1976) reminds us that when a man's social function is considered to be no longer necessary, his retirement from occupation occurs; this is also regarded as heralding a decline and probable cessation of his sex life. There is a need to look beyond the greying hair and flawless complexions which we hold in such reverence, and see people for what they are and have been, and not for what we think they ought to be when using a stereotype based on the chronology of ageing.

Sexuality is not like a fashion accessory which is superficially worn, it is much more. It is the capacity to love and be loved, however fleetingly or transiently expressed. Human qualities, such as caring, warmth and sharing between people, feeling important and valued socially, and the investment in security, either shared or maintained individually, are all intricacies of human sexuality.

Individuality, being free and able to express oneself and be perceived as a man or a woman, may stem from fundamental biology or the creation of the characteristics of the preferred sex, i.e. transvestism or transsexualism.

AVAILABILITY OF A PARTNER

Whatever the chosen sexual expression, there is no escaping the fact that the older adult, even though sexually active and willing, undoubtedly faces difficulty in finding an appropriate sexual partner. The fact that both partners are alive does not necessarily equate to being fit and healthy and engaging in intercourse. One may be too infirm and has renounced sex in the face of illness, or, worse, they could have been separated due to one requiring specialized care in an institutional setting. This is particularly so since men, on the whole, marry younger women. Corbin and Solnick (1980) identify this tendency, noting that 'available partners for a woman of any age can be described as all single men, older than she. For a man, available partners would be all single women younger than he'. Women not only face the situation of having few, if any, available men older than themselves; with the passage of time their available choice is reduced sharply. In fact, Eliopoulos (1989) estimates that by the age of 65 there are only seven males to every ten females, and, if this is not bad enough, by the time she is 85 years of age the ratio will be a lean 5:1.

Those reaching the golden years of marriage may naturally assume that everything will continue to remain the same. Projected figures (Wicks and Henwood, 1988) on divorce in the over 65 age group show that the trend traditionally located in the younger age group is set to rise. Wicks and Henwood (1988) illustrate that in 1981 1.6% of elderly males and 2.2% of females over 65 years of age were divorced, with the expected projection by 2019 set at 3.6% and 7.2% respectively.

It would seem, therefore, that one of the major reasons why older adults cease active sex may be due to 'partner availability' (Stokes, 1992). Again, stacked against the older woman is the fact that on average she lives seven years longer than her male counterpart. Bretschneider and McCoy (1988) suggest from the findings of their study that this is the reason why sexual activity ceases; in fact 74% of men and 75% of women found themselves with no partner. In the Corbin and Solnick (1980) study, 48% of women gave having no partner as the reason for terminating their sex lives, as opposed to only 10% of men.

Such difficulties are further magnified for gay men and women who find themselves bereft of available partners. Weg (1983) suggests that the needs of gay people are not that much different from those of older heterosexuals. However, I would suggest that they are different. First, the chance of finding another gay partner is reduced by virtue of the very percentage of gay people per population, and this is again diminished by longevity. Secondly, gay people are subject to accepting a heterosexual culture, and this is worsened by the enforced sterility and castration of the elderly.

Webb (1991) claims that older gay men are damaged by the construction of stereotypes which are based on a 'youth orientated perspective'. This is particularly so, and one of the most bedevilling and pejorative assumptions made about gay men is that of promiscuity. With the misguided notion of promiscuity comes some rather odd value judgements and assumptions. First, it is generally regarded that promiscuous sex in gay men occurs because of an inability to form and maintain lasting relationships. Coleman (1982) attempts to offer an explanation of promiscuous behaviour based on gay men being 'at a disadvantage of learning intimacy and relationship skills because they have few role models to follow'. What Coleman is attempting is to pathologise a behaviour which is based on many factors other than relationships and role models and locate it within the realms of heterosexual solidarity. If judgements about what is regarded as promiscuous behaviour are to be made, then let them be based on Bentham's (1984) sentiments, 'judge by the criteria of pleasure'.

THE AGEING PROCESS AND SEXUALITY

Like all biological processes, human sexual response and effectiveness do not remain unaffected by ageing, but this does not mean to say that a cessation is necessary. It should be borne in mind that these biological changes occur gradually over a long period of time and, therefore, provide ample opportunity for the older adult to adapt to them. Kinsey, Pomeroy and Martin (1948, p. 227) in their study of human loving conclude that 'from early and middle years the decline in sexual activity is remarkably steady and there is no point at which old age suddenly enters the picture'. Although this pattern is generally the same for men and women, it is suggested (Kinsey *et al.*, 1953) that, for the female, sexual capacity remains unchallenged until very much later in life.

Sexuality, ageing and the male

For the male, the major difficulties which can be attributed to ageing lie in erection, orgasm and ejaculation. Martin (1977) and Hegler and Mortensen (1978) note a slight reduction in sexual interest (when interviewing men aged 50 to over 80) and a decline in spontaneous morning erections. They illustrate that there is a reduction in the frequency of coitus (penetrative sex) and that it is more marked than the reduction of masturbation. They conclude that masturbation is probably the most frequent form of sexual expression in this age group.

The evidence so far could lead to the conclusion that age-linked physiological processes could naturally result in a reduction in sexual activity. The fact is that this is pure presumption, as Martin (1981) has shown that only a minimal correlation can be demonstrated between ageing and sexual decline compared with younger adult life. It is a truism (Martin, 1981) that those people with the highest levels of sexual activity when younger demonstrated proportionately the least amount of decline when older. The findings of the Martin (1981) study were reflected in the work of Bretcher (1984) when studying older married couples over the age of 70. It was shown that 81% of the participants were still sexually active; however, only 59% were engaging in sex with their spouse, thus leading to the conclusion that masturbation featured highly in a large proportion.

The impact of ageing upon the sexual response cycle means that older men take longer to develop full erection and may require more tactile stimulation as purely psychic stimulus becomes less effective (Bancroft, 1990). Once erection has been achieved, the length of time it can be sustained lessens – the duration could be only minutes for those over 70 (Bancroft, 1990). There is a reduction in pre-ejaculatory mucus and ejaculation is less powerful, with fewer contractions and a reduced volume of semen (Bancroft, 1990).

In the refractory phase, i.e. post-ejaculation, Bancroft (1990) notes that older men may find themselves unable to gain a further erection for 24 hours or more. In a sample of 2402 older men, Bretcher (1984) reports that 65% self-identified a second erection and 44% found their erections less rigid, if achieved, with 32% experiencing a loss of tumescence during sex.

Sexuality, ageing and the female

There has been the suggestion (Pfeiffer and Davis, 1972) that loss of interest in sex is disparate as between men and women in that women are noted for showing a greater decline in libido than men. In a study of 241 women, Pfeiffer and Davis (1972) identified that the most dramatic changes relating to interest in sex took place within the 50–60 age group, with 50% of the women studied reporting a cessation of sexual activity, as opposed to 10% of the 260 men in the male sample. An explanation of why women note a reduction in sex could be erectile dysfunction in males (Bretcher, 1984) and a considerably reduced opportunity to find a partner (Stokes, 1992). Although the work of Pfeiffer and Davis (1972) does not adequately address non-penetrative sex when attempting to explain women's loss of libido, they do posit that women who had masturbated throughout youth do not appear to show any change with ageing.

Older women frequently reported vaginal dryness which is due to a reduction in oestrogen. Bretcher (1984) surveyed many older women and asked whether or not they experienced insufficient vaginal lubrication during arousal. He concluded that reduced vaginal lubrication was problematic in sexually active women, based on the findings that 48% of 50 year olds, 35% of 60 year olds and 23% of over 75 year olds noted this to be an issue.

Shrinkage and loss of elasticity of the vaginal barrel were also features of the Bretcher (1984) study and were more pronounced in those women who had ceased vaginal intercourse. There is the suggestion that frequency of orgasm does not alter proportionately in older women (Bretcher, 1984) but there is an association with a reduction in contractions, which may be painful in older women. The female refractory stage is faster than in men, thus coupled orgasm may still be achieved.

DEPRESSION

Depression is something which everyone will suffer to some degree in the course of their lifetime. However, the degree and intensity with associated debility will vary greatly, and in some people result in the necessity for treatment and possible hospitalization. It is hardly surprising that many older people have experienced this unpleasant phenomenon due to the many losses and transitions which they have traversed in the course of their lives. Certainly the effects of bereavement, of retirement with temporary loss of role or financial crisis and so on, linked with society's ageist attitudes towards the older adult, highlight the need for depressive illness not to be underestimated.

Notwithstanding, depression remains the commonest illness seen by general practitioners (Wright, 1993). The incidence of depressive illness is extremely difficult to determine: what age group to study, the numbers of people undetected by GPs or those who do not present for treatment are only a few of the variables which make accurate statistical recording difficult. It has been estimated that 5% of people who consult their GP show major depression, a further 5% have a mild depression and 10% show some depressive symptoms (Wright, 1993). Considering this incidence, Wright suggests that one depressed patient will be seen at every clinic session.

Sleep disturbance, loss of appetite and feeling generally low and apathetic are some of the symptoms of depression. One symptom which is generally underestimated in the older adult, whether as a consequence of a patchy grasp of the pathology of depression, not recognizing depression as a common illness experienced by older people; or the view that all older people are asexual, is the temporary reduction of libido and impaired sexual functioning. Mathew and Weinman's (1982) study of the sexual responses of men and women with a depressive illness very clearly illustrates that there was a definite reduction in sexual interest within the group. This is further reinforced by the work of Sanders *et al.* (1983) which draws a direct correlation between self-ratings, particularly in women, and general feelings of well-being and interest in sex.

One of the most favoured treatments for depressive illness is the use of antidepressants in an attempt to bring about an upturn in mood. However, such drugs, and in particular the tricyclic group, are renowned for inducing temporary states of reduced libido, impotence, erectile dysfunction and delayed or absent orgasm (de Leo and Magni, 1983). The sensitive nature of such sexual changes may often result in them not being reported to health care staff; this may be due to the person not recognizing them as a consequence of treatment or attributing them to another episode of illness. There is, therefore, the need for those people receiving antidepressant therapy to be made fully aware of their temporary side-effects when commencing treatment and given full opportunity to discuss concerns with a member of the medical team. It has been suggested by Pollack and Rosenbaum (1987) that such sexual effects may be one of the reasons for non-compliance with treatment.

OVERCOMING OBSTACLES

There is no reason why older adults should not, as Masters and Johnson (1981) suggest, maintain a healthy sex life indefinitely. However, some basic mechanical and situational considerations may have to be borne in mind (Table 9.2).

Many older people suffer from arthritis, resulting in painful joints, restricted mobility and the unreliability of limbs or joints which give way at inopportune moments. The stiffness and discomfort which ensue from such conditions may

Table 9.2 Some dos and don'ts for maintaining a happy sex life into old age

Dos	*Don'ts*
Modify positions if pain is experienced during sex due to physical problems.	Don't assume that you are past it.
	Don't attempt to hurry sex.
If vaginal dryness is experienced try using a water-based lubricant.	Don't always base good sex on having an orgasm.
Try sex in the morning when you are more relaxed.	Avoid excessive alcohol prior to sex.
Ensure adequate privacy.	Avoid having sex after a heavy meal.
Use touch, massage and other creative techniques.	Don't always assume that because libido and sexual functioning are impaired it is due to age. It may be due to medication.
Take painkillers before foreplay commences if you are prescribed them.	Don't be frightened to masturbate.
Use pillows or rolled up blankets to support lumbar spine.	Don't stick to regular days and times: be spontaneous – anywhere, any time.
Have sex in the warmth or stay under the covers.	Don't be afraid to seek help.
Be creative, penetration is not the only way to sexual fulfilment.	
Ensure that you have enough time without the risk of interruptions.	

have the consequence of making sex both painful and uncomfortable. For the woman adopting the traditional missionary position, with her partner on top of her, the unpleasantness of the pain may far outweigh the pleasure.

The key to surviving such mechanical problems may lie either in changing position from the ones traditionally adopted or utilizing pillows to support limbs. Greengross and Greengross (1989) in their book, *Living, Loving and Ageing*, recommend a change in position, with the woman lying on her side with her partner behind her 'like a pair of spoons'. Apart from not being squashed by her partner, the risk of weight-bearing joints giving way at an inopportune moment is reduced. If the missionary position is particularly desired, strategies which can be used successfully in attempting to minimize pain and discomfort are suggested by Greengross and Greengross (1989). Placing a pillow under the lumbar spine may add support, and painful limbs may be supported by cushions or a rolled up blanket to reduce unnecessary movement.

As previously noted, post-menopausal women may experience a dryness of the vagina, thus rendering intercourse painful and unpleasant. This could easily be remedied by use of a water-soluble lubricating jelly during sex. The use of a lubricant, such as KY Jelly, is particularly important in not breaching safer sex guidance, from which older adults are not exempt.

Linked with vaginal dryness may be painful uterine contractions during orgasm (Birchenall and Streight, 1993). Approaching the general practitioner for a topical oestrogen cream could be beneficial. The old adage 'use it or lose it' is particularly apt. Bretcher (1984) posits that a more proactive approach to maintaining vaginal health is needed. He recommends that regular intercourse keeps the vaginal barrel healthy and prevents shrinkage, as opposed to the accelerated rate found in celibate women.

Apart from vaginal dryness, painful intercourse may stem from other underlying pathologies. Simple cystitis or urinary tract infections could be the causative factor in the discomfort. In such cases, as with any form of vaginal tenderness, medical opinion should be sought and measures taken to correct it, rather than the attribution being made to the consequences of ageing.

One of the golden rules for successful sex, whether younger or older, must be to allow sufficient time and not be hurried. Feeling relaxed and taking time to enjoy physical closeness and tenderness cannot be overestimated. What may be regarded as foreplay, such as touch and massage and digital stimulation, may be equally as satisfying as penetration. Rather than engaging in sex at night time when the stresses and strains of the day have taken their toll, wait until the morning when feeling more relaxed and possibly more energetic.

Linked with having enough time comes the question of privacy. There is nothing more restricting and off-putting than the fear that one's intimacy could be invaded at any time. This is particularly troublesome for older people who either share the house with their children or live in a residential setting. What is required is the pursuance of pure selfish luxury, where time should be found to be alone together and feeling secure in the knowledge that other family members are unlikely to return home unexpectedly. A simple way of ensuring privacy may be by reminding others of the common courtesy of knocking prior to entering or installing a means of locking the door.

The problems associated with incontinence should not be dismissed. As Suthurst and Brown (1980) illustrated in their study of 208 older women, 73 identified that urinary incontinence was the major factor responsible for their reduced intercourse, and 17 had ceased sex altogether because of it. During intercourse it may be necessary for older men to void the bladder and, as a result, they may experience difficulty in regaining erection afterwards (although the sensation of a partially full bladder may help maintain erection (Garrett, 1991)). For women, stress incontinence could result in urine being leaked due to pressure being applied to the abdomen during penetrative sex, particularly if the traditional missionary position is adopted. Voiding the bladder prior to engaging in intercourse and a change of position is the simple and effective answer to this very surmountable difficulty.

Many people believe in the natural aphrodisiac qualities of alcohol. There is no doubt that a small quantity will have a pleasantly relaxing effect and may result in less inhibition. Masters, Johnson and Kolodny (1986) suggest that alcohol can quite easily result in erectile dysfunction in men. This, linked to an already reduced erectile efficiency (Bretschneider and McCoy, 1988), could result in a most frustrating and irritating conclusion. Usually alcohol and food go hand in hand, and it is worthy of note that the effects of a heavy meal could also be problematic.

A set routine for sex should be avoided, i.e. predetermined days or times, as this only results in a lack of spontaneity and a sense of frustration if one partner is exhausted or simply does not feel like it. The expectation of performance and fear of failure can be extremely anxiety provoking, and in some men can lead to impotence. Bretschneider and McCoy (1988) note that fear of failure in 61% of men over 80 years of age led to problems with either achieving or maintaining erection.

MASTURBATION AS SEXUAL EXPRESSION

For many health care workers, masturbation remains one of the most problematic forms of sexual expression encountered and yet this practice is as old as the hills. The history of masturbation is too lengthy to begin to chronicle here; however, it suffices to say that it has been scorned from the beginning of recorded time. Genesis 38; 8–10 talks of using one's 'seed' for procreative sex only and warns of the perils of 'spilling it on the ground'. Henceforth masturbation has been seen as a sign of possession, insanity or immorality, and those who indulged in this practice were subjected to many forms of 'corrective' treatments (Bullough, 1976, p211). It is hardly surprising that being raised with such strong moral and religious codes of behaviour, many older people view masturbation as something of a taboo.

Throughout history female masturbation has received little attention or discourse due to strong Victorian and Edwardian codes of moral behaviour, which, in turn, may be a mechanism of patriarchal oppression. Women were taught from an early age not to touch their genitals (Ladas, Whipple and Perry, 1983). Indeed, the idea of wanting or enjoying genital stimulation represented a sharp decline in moral fibre.

Only now, due to the widespread growth and strength of the feminist movement, is female masturbation receiving the consideration and recognition which it deserves. But attitudes are slow to change, and this is no exception. There remains the impression that masturbation in men is far more widely acceptable than in women, perhaps due to the unfounded belief that it is a means by which masculinity and virility is reasserted. What may be the uncomfortable challenge to such a patriarchal analysis of masturbation is the realization that a woman's sexual pleasure and satisfaction is not dependent solely upon the actions of a male partner.

Older people who masturbate are regarded negatively, in that they are either believed to be mentally ill or lecherous, and all too frequently one hears the use of such terms as 'dirty old man' applied by society. The attribution of such terms probably stems from a lack of understanding that older people remain sexual beings, thus providing a manner in which the behaviour can be rationalized and managed. Catania and White's (1982) study of older people living in the community addresses the cognitive domain of masturbation and its locus of control. They conclude that masturbation is not solely a result of the lack of a partner, but the frequency of masturbation is strongly related to an internal locus of control. This indicates that a more psychic/cognitive phenomenon is in operation, and the wealth of past events and experiences act as stimuli for arousal. Catania and White (1982) offer a discussion which firmly locates masturbation within the general framework of sexuality and not as a rogue pathology. They see masturbation as a means of sexual regulation and the demonstration of a high degree of individuality. Perhaps the most pertinent element of their discourse is that it is a way in which older adults can maintain a sexual identity, i.e. proof of continuing sexuality when bombarded with negative and damaging societal attitudes.

Nursing has adopted an asexual role, where neither the care worker nor the patient's sexuality is regarded as significant to the care task in hand. We should be now accepting, as Lawler (1991) states, that nursing has to come to terms with its own sexuality, and how, as sexual beings, we interact and therefore react. But it is the way we interact and how we maintain our self-esteem and that of the older adults with whom we are working that is of prime importance. Perhaps overt masturbation in old age, in particular, for those who reside in residential or institutional settings, is a way of reasserting a sexual identity in an all too frequently sterile environment.

Kaas (1978) interviewed residents and staff in a residential area and asked the general question whether masturbation was an acceptable behaviour. He concluded that it was generally regarded by all as an unacceptable expression of sexuality, but it was regarded as a means of attaining sexual relief, as a pleasurable experience and a way of maintaining sexual function, particularly in the absence of a partner. From the study one can detect that there is a degree of cognitive dissonance in that, although people expressed a lack of tolerance of masturbation, there is the suggestion that it is part of life for many of the study.

NORMALIZING MASTURBATION

Over the past few years there has been a major emphasis placed on delivering care in a more humanistic and holistic way. Most models have the person's sexuality as one of the fundamental underpinning principles. An example of an early system of care which included the person's sexuality was Roper, Logan and Tierney's (1984) Activities of Daily Living. Although much emphasis is placed on sexuality, masturbation and how the health care worker reacts to it is still misunderstood. Strategies to manage this in a way which does not deter the person from expressing their sexuality may be difficult for many health care workers. So, how can those involved in the delivery of care use their skills to enable people to express their sexuality through masturbation which does not bring with it denigrating stereotypes?

Health care workers may react to masturbation either positively or negatively, depending upon their personal beliefs. What is clear is that health care workers are required to manage their own feelings of embarrassment whilst attempting to maintain their own and the client's self-esteem. Ways in which embarrassment may be managed in a non-productive way are discussed by Lawler (1991) in her book, *Behind The Screens*, and include such tactics as avoiding eye contact, being professional, matter of fact or using humour. If the situation is not handled sensitively for all concerned, the older person's behaviour may very well be regarded as aberrant. Instead of trying to manage masturbation *per se*, it is more desirable to promote an attitude by care staff which provides the opportunity for masturbation to be accepted through all aspects of daily living in a spontaneous way.

Strategies by which this attitude may be encouraged reside in good practice. One golden rule must be to provide adequate privacy for people to retire to, whether it is a curtained bed area, a side room or even a bathroom or toilet cubicle. Wherever the place, it is of prime importance that interruption is minimized. It may mean the health care worker standing beyond the bed curtains or outside the bathroom door, ensuring that there is no breach of privacy. Without having to openly advocate masturbation, which may result in embarrassment for both patient and staff, it may be implied that whilst soaking in the bath there will be no interruptions. Through this process the normality of masturbation is conveyed and the staff attitude is accepting and non-judgemental. Inherent in this, the health care worker is engaging in the promotion of positive role modelling and not purveying wrongful stereotypes.

Without wishing to equate masturbation with sanitary processes, which generally creates a mind-set of dirty and unsavoury bodily functions (Douglas, 1984), certain ablutive equipment may be of help. Making a box of tissues available or providing a bowl of water and washing equipment, particularly for those whose ambulation is impaired, may be all that is necessary.

There may be a situation where some form of physical or mental incapacitation is evident which renders masturbation either difficult or impossible. It may be appropriate to assist the person in maintaining their sexuality, either by utilizing some of the suggestions above or by facilitating the continuance of intimacy and the possible role of a significant other person. This of course depends upon the attitude and skill of the person delivering the care. Health care workers entering into more intimate relationships with patients may quite easily find themselves in a situation which is inconsistent with that of their professional role and boundaries. Thus, it may be necessary to help patients understand that to participate in their masturbation directly is not appropriate. However, the facilitation of it in private and in a dignified way is something which can be entered into.

Remember, what may be regarded as a transmission of vital information at handovers may result in the manifestation of social lepers. Although it is accepted that talking amongst colleagues and the sharing of experiences is a way of managing embarrassing situations (Lawler, 1991), the avoidance of unnecessary and superfluous tittle-tattle about what has been observed or aided should be avoided. It should be borne in mind that a ready explanation of masturbation does not always lie in it being pathologized as abnormal behaviour.

DRUGS AND MEDICINE

There can be no denying that for many older adults the daily administration of medication is commonplace in the management of physical and psychological illnesses. Yet, how many people attribute their reduced interest in sex to ageing rather than to drugs?

For many older people taking such medications as antihypertensives and antidepressants which may be crucial in the management of their illness, unpleasant side-effects such as reduced libido, impotence and orgasmic dysfunction are commonplace. In themselves, the side-effects of such treatments are generally not viewed as life-threatening and may be regarded as a minor irritation and something to be endured. However, for the individual this 'minor irritation' could have momentous and distressing psychological repercussions.

It has already been illustrated in this chapter that a great many older people remain sexually active well into advanced years. It is, therefore, important that this fact is known when drugs which have side-effects affecting libido, erectile function or orgasm are being taken for the treatment of many common illnesses.

Without such vital information misconceptions may develop, with the attribution of such side-effects to either ageing or the onset of another episode of physical illness. This is not to say that medications which have such extra effects should not be taken; what is required is that physicians weigh up reasonable treatment and give proper insight into the effects of that treatment. Without question any health care worker should be aware of this and use mechanisms to begin to rectify it by giving sufficient advice. A list of some common drugs which are frequently taken by older adults is compiled in Table 9.3, but it is not all-inclusive.

Adequate drug awareness may mean that the person has a higher degree of control over the impairment which the medications bring to everyday living. With negotiation with the physician, drugs which are used in the management

Table 9.3 Some common drugs which may affect sexual functioning

Drugs	Interest	Arousal	Orgasm
Antidepressants			
Tricyclic group:			
Amitriptyline	Lowered	Erectile failure	Delayed or retarded
Clomipramine	Lowered	Erectile failure	ejaculation and orgasm
Trimipramine	Lowered	Erectile failure	with tricyclic group
Compound and other groups:			
Tryptophan	Lowered	Erectile failure	
Fluoxetine	Lowered	Erectile failure	
Paroxetine	Lowered	Erectile failure	
Antihypertensives			
Methyldopa	Lowered		Ejaculatory failure or
Guanethidine	Lowered		retrograde ejaculation
Labetalol	Lowered		
Propranolol	Lowered		
Diuretics			
Bendrofluazide	Lowered	Erectile failure	
Spironolactone	Lowered	Erectile failure	
Amiloride	Lowered	Erectile failure	
Hypnotics			
Nitrazepam	Lowered	Erectile failure	
Major tranquillizers			
Thioridazine	Lowered	Erectile failure	Delayed or absent
Chlorpromazine	Lowered	Erectile failure	
Haloperidol	Lowered		
Fluphenazine	Lowered		
Flupenthixol	Lowered	Erectile failure	Delayed or absent
Cardiac			
Digoxin	Lowered	Erectile failure	
Spironolactone	Lowered	Erectile failure	
Others			
Diclofenac sodium	Lowered	Erectile failure	Delayed or absent
Prochlorperazine		Erectile failure	

of less serious conditions could be reduced or temporarily omitted, thereby lessening the effects of the sexual impairment and thus maintaining unrestricted sexual activity.

RESIDENTIAL CARE

For many, residential care is the place where specific care needs are addressed which would be difficult or impossible with independent living. Its purpose is to 'enable residents to achieve their potential capacity – physical, intellectual, emotional and social ... by sensitive recognition of that potential in each individual and by an understanding that it may change over time' (Centre for Policy on Ageing, 1985, p. 15). The imposed separation due to specific care requirements is something which is frequently faced by many adults and, in many cases, accepted as part of growing older. After what may have been many years of sharing each other's company, and perhaps the same bed, it is hardly surprising that feelings of loss, isolation and loneliness, with possible depression, frequently ensue.

When one partner enters institutional care, messages which portray the cessation of sexual activity can quite easily be conveyed if staff are not sensitive and mindful of the fact that advancing years do not categorically result in asexuality. Recommendations for residential care found in *Home Life* (Centre for Policy on Ageing, 1985) expressly note that 'residents should have normal opportunities for emotional expression, in particular the freedom to have intimacy and personal relationships within, and outside the home', even though such recommendations raise an awareness of the issue of just how many people are allowed to express their sexuality in an unrestricted or monitored way in this setting.

Expression of the sexuality of older adults in a residential setting has been examined by Szasz (1983) who asked staff to identify behaviours which were sexual and 'causing problems'. The results fell into three broad areas: sex talk, sex acts and implied sexual behaviour. Sex talk comprised recounting past or current sexual experiences, including 'foul language' used to illustrate the account. The second category, sex acts, encompassed residents showing their genitalia, or touching and grabbing the 'private areas' of the staff. There was also identification of removing clothing at 'inappropriate times', public masturbation and, in one case, engaging in intercourse with a prostitute behind the resident's bed curtains. Finally, implied sexual behaviour was reported as reading of pornographic information with satisfaction, sexual comments relating to actors/actresses on the television and requesting physical care such as catheter changes and post rectal examination. In the light of what were viewed as problematic behaviours, staff did identify some 'acceptable sexual incidents', these being hugging and kissing on the cheek; however, a few staff did intimate that some residents possibly required 'more intimate touching and affection'.

If both partners were to move into residential care together there is no certainty that they would share the same room. It may be that one had greater care needs, thus requiring more specialized input which could only be available in another wing, or simply the fact that double beds did not feature as a priority when commissioning the home. Wherever possible older adults should be offered the choice of sharing a bedroom, but this is rather the exception than the rule.

As already noted, staff attitudes are of crucial significance in promoting optimum well-being and maintaining a healthy self-concept for those in care settings. Staff should not be so presumptuous as to consider themselves justified in sanctioning the continuance of sexuality in those in their charge, or offering it as a gift by allowing it to take place. There is no reason for staff to monitor it or oversee who is indulging in it, rather like making entries in residents' notes as to who has bathed that day. The only part that care staff have to play in this area is to ensure that basic courtesy and recognition of privacy and personal space are ensured, and everything will naturally fall into place.

When visitors come, staff should be cognizant of making a private place available to them, and not breach that privacy in the haste to undertake household tasks, such as putting laundry away. Those who seek privacy, for whatever reason, must not be made to feel guilty or infantile for their pursuit of sanctuary. Likewise, those who express their sexuality in whatever way, be it the choice of clothes, make-up or desired sexual object, should not be made to feel puerile or that their behaviour is inappropriate.

Staff must be aware that they are acting in a way which directly influences behaviour by proffering themselves as positive role models and not allowing themselves to project negative stereotypes which take an inordinate amount of time to correct when internalized by the elderly.

All too often residents have submitted to the belief that they are no longer sexual beings. Kaas (1978) illustrates that this appears to be the case and seeks to emphasize the impact which care staff can have on the exorcism of asexuality. As we have previously established, sexuality is more than the physical sex act, and is more far reaching than just the emotions which are experienced during a sexual relationship. The individual's self-concept holds the key to understanding the complex interrelationship of biological, psychological and social influences responsible for how we see ourselves. It can be clearly seen that those with a positive self-concept value themselves and believe in their worth, as opposed to people with rather more negative personal views. Using this basic psychology, older adults who have damaged self-esteem can be encouraged to take a more active part in self-care and develop a consciousness of projecting their personal appearance as an expression of their unique sexuality.

An assiduousness by care staff is required to begin to reverse the desexualized model which many older adults in care encounter. The choice of clothing and the appropriateness to the person who is to wear them requires mindfulness on the part of care staff when aiding choice. This is particularly so when clothing is purchased from one agency, such as a hospital shop or contract-holding boutique, as there is the tendency for everyone to look the same. Caution should also be exercised when clothing is used which is designed to aid those with physical problems as it tends to be rather asexual. Residents should be offered a choice of attendant to aid bathing. The denial of the resident's request for a particular gender of staff to give care or the ignoring of obvious cues to convey this is a negation of sexual reassertion. Likewise, not shaving men, leaving flies unfastened or exposing them to others when giving care is again part of this negative process. Men, like women, are generally unaccustomed to showing their bodies publicly, regardless of the notion of communal living and its consequential lack of privacy. It is worthy of note that some married men and women never saw each other undress or in a state of nakedness, so the assumption of 'all boys together' should be redefined.

A point worthy of recognition is that the vast majority of residential homes are based on a heterosexual model of living, therefore the culture which residents either adopt freely or by imposition is synonymous with heterosexual values. It is not beyond the bounds of chance that there will be a proportion, no matter how small, of gay men and women residing within the establishment who are having to adopt a style of living which may be somewhat alien. Derek Jarman (1993), in his book *At Your Own Risk: A Saint's Testament*, reminds us that 'heterosexuality isn't normal, it's just common'. It is, therefore, important to remember that language which reflects a heterosexual paradigm, such as the application of denigrating labels like 'pop' or 'gran', and the assumption of roles as husband or wife, should be avoided, as it brings into operation the agenda of the care giver, thus reflecting the milieu of the institution. In order for care staff to allow a convergence of the knowledge of what should constitute good wholesome humanistic care and what actually happens in practice, Webb (1987) exhorts a personal awareness of one's own sexuality and a coming to terms with it. This, according to Webb, will begin to bring about an enlightenment of how attitudes are transposed into behaviours and an awareness of the consequences on the care that is given.

OLDER GAY MEN

Throughout this chapter there has been a calculated avoidance of the term 'homosexual' or 'homosexuality' when describing men or women who are attracted to each other, either socially, psychologically or physically. During the passage of time, those who have shared a temporal or physical attraction to members of the same sex have been referred to by a gamut of terms, from sodomites to the more subtle Victorian anachronism of Inter Christianos Non Nominandum (not named amongst Christians).

The use of the word 'gay' was not stumbled upon by accident; in fact it emerged from America during the 1950s and 1960s as a self-description. The inception of this simple but powerful three letter word resulted in a turning point as far as gay men and lesbian women were concerned. This new chapter in sexual history came to address the politicized sexual identity of those men and women who previously had been viewed and judged by the antiquated patronage encapsulated in the word homosexual. Homosexual and homosexuality are terms of great power, loaded with the idea of unnaturalness and perversion, and relying heavily on Freudian analysis. It is undoubtedly better to use 'gay' when referring to people who prefer partners of the same sex, thereby minimizing Freudian attribution.

It can be seen that language frequently has an undertone of oppression however eloquently it is expressed and plays an important part in how people are regarded. The term 'natural' is frequently used to convey 'acceptable' or 'approved of' by an otherwise unrepresentative and frequently dominant majority (Weeks, 1991).

For older men, the word homosexual may evoke feelings of illegality, furtiveness and punishment either by imprisonment or compulsory psychological corrective treatment. Nor should the power of negative stereotypes, such as 'old queen' or 'auntie', be underestimated. This is, in part, due to consenting male–male sex being legalized and therefore not punishable under English law after 1967. As far as women were concerned, no legal emancipation was necessary as lesbianism has never been defined as an illegal act or warranting corrective interventions.

The idea that the needs of older gay men are not much different from those of heterosexuals of comparable ages (Weg, 1983) may be called into question. The legal position which many older gay men faced must have resulted in irrevocable psychological scarring. This group have been forced to hide or adopt a heterosexual facade, whilst seeking out consenting partners who were equally as well camouflaged as themselves due to the fear of legal sanctions or moralizing being brought to bear. The freedom and openness to develop relationships with members of the same sex is something which older gay men have been excluded from for the greater part of their formative years.

One problem that gay men face when growing older is the absence of family support. It is widely recognized that women in the role of wives or, typically, daughters or daughters-in-law play a crucial part in community care. For older gay men who, due to their sexuality, have remained unmarried or have not produced children, such support is somewhat limited or totally non-existent. A consequence of this lack of family network is that statutory services, such as home care agencies, are required to fill the gap. One possible outcome of this scenario may be that older gay men find themselves having to accept residential care at a much earlier stage in their lives than their heterosexual counterparts.

It sometimes feels like there is an extra-terrestrial force which is responsible for abducting gay men when they reach the age of 65. This phenomenon is touched upon by Berger (1980) in his survey of older gay men. Part of this stems from the fact that as far as society is concerned older gay men and women seem not to exist. This is surprising when one consults demographic data on ageing and sees the regularly tried and tested evidence of the incidence of gay men and women. The work of Kinsey, replicated by Kimmel (1975), continues to support the idea that 10% of the male population are gay, i.e. 1:10, and this in itself, when compared with current population figures, reiterates the theory of the invisibility of older gay men. H.B. Gibson (1992) notes that there are 4,000,000 men in England and Wales aged 60 years and over, therefore there must be 400,000 gay men in that group and, as Gibson highlights, some 300,000 of those must naturally be pensioners.

Perhaps the invisible nature of the older gay male population resides in the fact that most of their lives have been entrenched in illegality and, consequently, great social stigma. As a result, it must be assumed that a high degree of camouflage or a chameleon-like quality has been developed as a form of self-protection. Berger (1980), when interviewing a number of older gay men, concludes that there is a tendency to develop an over-masculinized facade which offers a heterosexual disguise.

THE LESBIAN ALTERNATIVE

It had been noted earlier in this chapter that women, when growing older, face a reduction in the availability of male partners and this has led to the development of the idea of the lesbian alternative.

For many feminists, lesbianism represents an alternative for women who do not wish to develop a sexual or cognitive relationship with members of the opposite sex and thus seek the company and camaraderie of another woman rather than that which is traditionally invested in men. As a consequence of this shortage of men in later life, many women who have been solidly heterosexual throughout their youth may adopt a lifestyle which is synonymous with lesbianism. It is not to presume that such relationships are purely sexual in their nature; frequently such bonds are located within the cognitive domain and involve sharing support, company and warmth amongst other things.

It is widely recognized that in exclusively single sex communities a same-sex alternative can be identified, however transient. This is frequently referred to as institutional homosexuality and noted to occur in prisons, boarding schools, nunneries or the armed forces for example. It is not too unrealistic to generalize this principle to older women who find themselves in communities predominantly made up of their own sex. For these women, adopting a bisexual or exclusively lesbian lifestyle may be a very realistic option.

CONCLUSION

Nurses, by virtue of their exposure to, and position of trust with patients, are in a favourable and almost unique position to challenge and educate older adults on issues of sexuality (Glass and Dalton, 1988). However, if this is to occur in a way which is positive and productive, nurses must be prepared to reflect upon and examine their own sexuality (Webb, 1987; Glass and Dalton, 1988).

Indeed, if those who work with older people and those who are responsible for educating them have negative attitudes about their own sexuality, then assisting the client to develop and maintain a positive self-identity will be impossible. In response to this, clinical nurses, teachers and other health care workers must begin to participate in exorcizing ageist beliefs and value judgements and invest in positivism. Only then will they begin to accept the realities of the older adult as a sexual being, capable of immersion in the complexities and pleasures of sexuality. For this to be facilitated, we must take a second and more honest look at the people whom we meet in our practice, and commit ourselves to working in a more creative and realistic way with them.

REFERENCES

Bancroft, J. (ed.) (1990) *Human Sexuality and its Problems*, Churchill Livingstone, London.

Bentham, J. (1984) Dentology, in *Homosexuality*, (ed. M. Ruse), Blackwell, Oxford.

Berger, R. (1980) *Gay and Gray: The Older Homosexual Man*, University of Illinois Press, Urbana.

Birchenall, J.M. and Streight, M.E. (1993) *Care of the Older Adult*, 2nd edn, J.B. Lippincott Company, Philadelphia.

Bretcher, E.M. (1984), Care, sex and ageing: a consumers union report, in *Human Sexuality and Its Problems*, (ed. J. Bancroft), Churchill Livingstone, London.

Bretschneider, J.G. and McCoy, N.L. (1988) Sexual interest and behaviours in healthy 80–120 year olds. *Archives of Sexual Behaviour*, **17**(2), 109–29.

Bullough, V.C. (1976) Sexual variance in society and history, in *Human Sexuality and Its Problems*, (ed. J. Bancroft), Churchill Livingstone, London.

Catania, J.A. and White, C.B. (1982) Sexuality in an aged sample: cognitive determinants of masturbation. *Archives of Sexual Behaviour*, **11**, 237–45.

Centre for Policy on Ageing (1985) *Home Life; A Code of Practice for Residential Care*, CPA, London.

Coleman, E. (1982) Developmental stages of the coming out process. *Journal of Homosexuality*, **7**(2–3), 31–43.

Comfort, A. (1990) *A Good Age*, Pan Books, London.

Corbin, N. and Solnick, R.L. (1980) Psychological and physiological influences on sexuality on the older adult, in *Masters and Johnson on Sex and Human Loving*, (eds W.H. Masters, V.E. Johnson and R.C. Kolodny), Macmillan, London.

Croft, L.H. (1992) Sexuality in later life, in *Love, Sex and Power in Later Life*, (ed. T. Gibson), Freedom Press, London.

de Leo, D. and Magni, G (1983) Sexual side-effects of antidepressant drugs. Psychosomatic, in *Long-Term Treatment of Depression*, (eds S. Montgomery and F. Rouillon), John Wiley & Sons, Chichester, Chapter 24, pp.1076–81.

Douglas, M. (1984) *Purity and Danger*, Ark Paperbacks, London.

Eliopoulos, C. (1989) *Geriatric Nursing*, J.B. Lippincott Company, New York, p. 117.

Garrett, G. (1991) *Relationships in Later Life*, Wolfe, London.

Gibson, H.B. (1992) *The Emotional and Sexual Lives of Older People*, Chapman & Hall, London.

Gibson, T. (1992) *Love, Sex and Power in Later Life*, Freedom Press, London.

Glass, J.C. and Dalton, J. (1988) Sexuality in older adults: a continuing education concern. *Journal of Continuing Education in Nursing*, **19**(1), 61–4.

Greengross, W. and Greengross, S. (1989) *Living, Loving and Ageing*, Age Concern, Surrey, England.

Hegler, S. and Mortensen, M. (1978) Sexuality and ageing. *British Journal of Sexual Medicine*, **5**(32), 16–19.

Hite, S. (1990) *The Report on Male Sexuality*, Optima, London.

Jarman, D. (1993) *At Your Own Risk: A Saint's Testament,* Vintage, London.

Kaas, M.J. (1978) Sexual expression of the elderly in nursing homes. *The Gerontologist*, **18**(4).

Kimmel, D.C. (1975) Adult development and ageing: a gay perspective. *Journal of Social Issues*, **34**, 113–30.

Kinsey, A.C., Pomeroy, W.B. and Martin, C.E. (1948) *Sexual Behaviour in the Human Male*, Saunders, Philadelphia.

Kinsey, A.C., Pomeroy, W.B., Martin, C.E. and Gebhard, P.H. (1953) *Sexual Behaviour in the Human Female*, Saunders, Philadelphia.

Kuhn, M.E. (1976) Sexual myths surrounding the ageing, in *Sex and the Life Cycle* (eds W.W.Oakes, G.A. Melchiode and I. Ficher), Grune and Stratton, New York.

Ladas, A.H., Whipple, B. and Perry, J.D. (1983) *The G Spot*, Corgi, London.

Lawler, J. (1991) *Behind the Screens*, Churchill Livingstone, London.

Lief, H.I. and Payne, T. (1975) Sexuality, knowledge and attitudes. *American Journal of Nursing*, **75**(11), 2026–9.

Martin, C.E. (1977) Sexual activity in the ageing male, in *Human Sexuality and its Problems*, (ed. J. Bancroft), Churchill Livingstone, London.

Martin, C.E. (1981) Factors affecting sexual functioning in 60–79 year-old married males. *Archives of Sexual Behaviour*, **10**, 399–420.

Masters, W.H., Johnson, V.E. and Kolodny, R.C. (1986) *Masters and Johnson on Sex and Human Loving*, Macmillan, London.

Mathew, R.J. and Weinman, M.L. (1982) Sexual dysfunction in depression. *Archives of Sexual Behaviour*, **11**, 323–8.

Pfeiffer, E. and Davis, G.C. (1972) Determinants of sexual behaviour in middle life. *Journal of The American Geriatric Society*, **20**, 151–8.

Pollack, H.M. and Rosenbaum, J.F. (1987) Management of antidepressant-induced side-effects: a practical guide for the clinician. *British Journal of Psychiatry*, **48**, 3–8.

Roper, N, Logan, W.W. and Tierney, A.J. (1984) *Elements of Nursing*, Churchill Livingstone, London.

Sanders, D., Warner, P., Backstorm, T. and Bancroft, J. (1983) Changes in moods and physical state: description of subjects and methods. *Psychosomatic Medicine*, **45**, 487–507.

Stokes, G. (1992) *On Being Old*, Palmer Press, Bristol.

Suthurst, J.R. and Brown, M. (1980) Sexual dysfunction associated with urinary incontinence. *Nursing Clinician North America*, **10**(3).

Szasz, G. (1983) Sexual incidents in an extended care unit for aged men. *Journal of The American Geriatric Society*, **31**(7), 407–11.

Webb, C. (1987) Nursing knowledge and attitudes about sexuality: a report of a study. *Nurse Education Today*, **7**, 209–14.

Webb, C. (1991) Expressing sexuality, in *Nursing Elderly People*, 2nd edn, (ed. S. Redfern), Churchill Livingstone, London, p. 294.

Weeks, J. (1991) *Sexuality*, Routledge, London.

Weg, P.B. (ed.) (1983) *Sexuality in the Later Years: Roles and Behaviours*, Academic Press, New York.

Wicks, M. and Henwood, M. (1988) Demographic and social circumstances of elderly people, in *Mental Health Problems in Old Age*, (eds B. Gearing, M. Johnson and T. Heler), Open University Press, Milton Keynes.

Wright, A. (1993) *Depression Recognition and Management in General Practice*, Royal College of Psychiatrists, London.

FURTHER READING

Birren, J.E. and Sloane, M.E. (eds) (1992) *Handbook of Mental Health and Ageing*, 2nd edn, Academic Press, New York.

Coslett, H.B. and Heilman, H.N. (1986) Male sex function: impairment after right hemisphere stroke. *Archives of Neurology*, **43**, 1036–9.

Roose, S.P., Glassman, A.H., Walsh, B.T. and Cullen, K. (1982) Reversible loss of nocturnal penile tumescence during depression: a preliminary report. *Neuropsychobiology*, **8**, 284–8.

Sherman, B. (1991) *Dementia With Dignity*, McGraw Hill, Australia.

Thomas, D. (1993) *Not Guilty : In Defence of the Modern Man*, Weidenfeld & Nicolson, London, p. 122.

Walker, G. (1993/94) *Data Sheet Compendium*, Datapharm Ltd, London.

10 | Cultural issues in the care of mentally ill Asian elders

Anupreeta Kumar

During the five years between 1986 and 1991, the population of Asians aged 60 or over increased by 106%.[1] The Asian elderly population is thus growing rather quickly, creating its own claims on the quality and quantity of professional care. However, not much literature is available on the various issues involved in the professional care of the mentally ill Asian elders. This chapter attempts to offer an overview of some of the issues which appear to be important in planning, developing and providing professional care for the mentally ill Asian elderly.

Considerations arising out of various dimensions of ethnicity are now the key issues for both the providers of health care services and the users from the Asian communities. Of particular concern are:

- difficulty in identifying mental illness;
- low uptake of existing services;
- diagnosis and treatment;
- assessment of social and health care needs;
- monitoring and reviewing of care packages;
- planning, developing and delivering appropriate services for ethnic clients.

The expression 'Asian' is used here to describe people from ethnic communities of Indian, Pakistani and Bangladeshi origin. According to the 1991 Census, these communities constituted nearly half (49%) of the total non-white ethnic groups in Great Britain.[2] Because they share a history of common problems of settling in this country, as well as some broad socio-cultural features, they have been treated here as a loosely homogeneous group – although, admittedly, various subgroups within Asian communities differ from each other in certain respects.[3] The expression 'carer or care provider' is used to include a whole range of carers in health and social services, whether statutory or voluntary. It may include medical professionals, health link workers, social workers and all others who come into contact with the mentally ill in the role of service provider.

ASIAN ELDERS AND MENTAL ILLNESS

Field research

It is interesting to explore the reasons underlying the relative scarcity of litera-ture pertaining to the issues involved in the professional care of the Asian mentally ill because the same set of reasons also seem to have implications for the relevant type of services. Similarly, the typology of mental diseases and the pattern of uptake of existing services are also characteristic in a way that facili-tates the discussion of race and culture.

Field studies and surveys constitute an important element in assessing care provision for various categories of users, both present and potential. They also serve to encourage improvement in the quality of the care being offered. Unfortunately there have not been many comprehensive studies pertaining to the mental health of the Asian elderly that might indicate the actual size of the incidence or identify a wide range of issues involved in the care interface. Certain studies have looked at some of the social care needs of the Asian elderly – AFOR study, Birmingham (Bhalla and Blakemore, 1981); Age Concern study, Manchester and London (Barker, 1984); Greenwich study (Turnbull, 1985); Coventry study (Holland and Lewando-Hundt, 1986) (cited by Patel, 1990, p. 17 and Norman, 1985, p. 68) – but these have not specifically addressed the issue of mental illness among Asian elders.

There are some probable reasons which may account for the paucity of mental health studies concerning the Asian elderly population. First, it was believed that the Asian elders did not form a viable group, comparable to that of the white elderly population in terms of size, for the purpose of policy studies. For example the average size of the population of people over 60 years of age within Asian communities in 1986 was just 2.66% of their total population as against 21% for the white population.[4] This will no longer be the case during the 1990s as the majority of Asian immigrants who came to this country in the 1960s and 1970s will be passing into the 'elderly' life stage. The percentage of people who are 50 years of age and above (elderly in the ethnic sense) has already become substantial. According to the 1991 Census, the percentage figures for persons over 50 years of age were 15.78%, 10.45% and 11.44% respectively for the Indian, Pakistani and Bangladeshi communities.[5] In addi-tion, the percentage figures for Asians who are 60 years of age and above has increased dramatically over just five years between 1986 and 1991: it has increased by 37% (from 5% to 6.87%) for the Indians; by 65% (from 2% to 3.53%) for the Pakistanis and by a staggering 216% (from 1% to 3.16%) for the

Bangladeshis.[6] In Figure 10.1 below, the 'elderly' population refers to people aged 60 years and above. The 1988 figures refer to populations in private households.

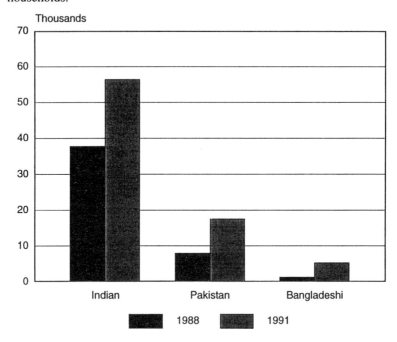

Figure 10.1 Growth of Asian elderly population 1988 to 1991

Secondly, there are some stereotypes held about the Asian elderly. Because they are not so visible, it is assumed that there must be few of them (Westwood and Bhachu, 1988). Similarly, it is widely believed that it is the 'family' that takes care and hence it is assumed Asian elders do not require services (Westwood and Bhachu, 1988; Jenkinson, 1987/1988).

Thirdly, there are difficulties in the collection of field data. The majority of elderly people will still be living with their families rather than in residential homes which makes identifying and accessing the target group more difficult. Furthermore, even if it is possible to contact older people or their families, they are not likely to report mental illness because they may simply not be aware of it. Even if they are, they still may not disclose it, because mental illness carries a social stigma of a nature that risks the social well-being of other members of the family, e.g. the matrimonial prospects of unmarried members, including grandchildren or great-grandchildren, may be adversely affected if the mental illness in the family becomes known within their community. Thus, the ideas, understanding and perception of mental illness within the Asian community

ideology, social organisation and the ways the people produce and distribute valued objects' that constitutes a cultural system, a perpetual lens, through which a particular version of reality is developed (Sokolovsky, 1990, p. 2).

The concept of 'old age' may have a different meaning in an ethnic cultural context. People above 50 years of age are most likely to be perceived as elderly within Asian communities, possibly due to the practice of early marriages and expectation of shorter life. The generally accepted notion of the ideal marriageable age is about 17–24 years of age for women and 22–28 years of age for men. Families coming from rural or orthodox backgrounds may prefer even younger thresholds. As a result, it is not unusual for women to find themselves grandmothers as early as 40 and for men to be grandfathers as early as 45 years of age.

In the Asian culture, there is a specific role model for the old people that focuses on paternalistic values – being advisers in all respects to the younger generation, mediating and reconciling family and community disputes, guiding socialization of grandchildren, withdrawing from usual leisure activities and involving themselves in religious practices, etc. This is a purposeful and productive role that society expects and values. The belief of having grown old may come from the fact they have become grandparents regardless of age. In a crosscultural setting, the care providers may be missing out on vital information related to delivering care, whether it is assessment, diagnosis, treatment or any kind of therapy. The care providers will need an adequate cultural insight to understand the cause of illness as it may be rooted in socio-cultural circumstances or categories not familiar to them. For example there is a sense of social purpose in old age in Asian communities, where old people are regarded as wisdom givers and valued as such and where, therefore, loss of social purpose may eventually lead to mental health problems.

Because ageing is likely to take place along the lines of cultural continuity, it would be useful to have a brief look at the general background of the experience of mental illness among the Asian community. This can be divided into sequential stages of experiences of settling down, coping with mental illness on their own and the care interface when they approach available services.

Roots of mental health problems

Many Asians came to this country in the 1960s and 1970s seeking work and better living conditions, but they found the process of adjustment to a new climate and new surroundings created its own pain and stress. As their second generation grew up in this country, they had to face a variety of new conflicts arising out of differences in perception of two sets of values – ethnic and native. It is common to see the 40–55 age group experiencing problems of stress and anxiety due to non-fulfilment of socio-cultural roles expected of their children (Kumar, 1992). For example British-born girls from the younger generation are reluctant to follow traditional roles and lifestyles and demand more freedom in every respect, including freedom of choice in career and marriage. Married sons tend to leave the parents and set up a new home and follow an independent life, breaking the extended family in the process.

The strain of adjusting to a new environment has created mental tensions which have affected the individual as well as relationships within the family. Added to this, there is a recognition of the widespread effect of racism. Racism has been recognized as a powerful factor affecting the mental health of the Asian community and has been the subject of much debate. Alibhai (1988) points out that racism itself has been seen as a causative factor in several kinds of depression in ethnic groups in this country. There is evidence that the effects of racism can result in a variety of symptoms through experience of rejection, frustration, loss, helplessness or depression, and through feelings of being inferior, hopelessness and inability to exercise any control over external forces. Racial discrimination is an obvious cause of stress in the lives of ethnic communities (Knight, 1981).

MacNaught (1987) documents racial discrimination that occurs in the health services. For example at patient reception, patients from ethnic minorities are kept waiting unnecessarily while racist comments are made within their earshot; during clinical consultation, poor or no explanations are offered of the treatment, assuming ethnic patients are faking illness or are hypochondriacs; with regard to patient consent, inadequate information is supplied on which to base the consent and they are put through unnecessary procedures; in nursing care, unnecessary medication is offered or medicine denied on the ground that they have low pain threshold; and for health surveillance, diagnosis parameters and behavioural models specific to white people are applied to ethnic minorities.

At the conference organized by the Mental Health Commission in 1987, it was noted that racism not only helps to provoke mental disorder but also permeates the professions empowered to define and control it and, as such, warrants a long and hard look (Tonkin, 1987). It was recently reported (Clark, 1993, p. 1) that The Racial Equality Commission has decided to investigate the racist practices in social services departments, and one of the important areas of services taken up for investigation is mental health services. The recent review of the research on the impact of community services on black people by the Social Policy Research Unit has led to the conclusion that racism is deeprooted in the delivery of the services (*Community Care*, 29.7.1993, p. 5).

The cultural roots of the Asian elderly have created a deeprooted tendency to conform to customs and traditions which, in turn, has resulted in a sense of loss brought about by intergenerational differences of values and attitudes. This observation is important from the carer's point of view. First, a substantial number of Asians come from traditional agrarian culture as opposed to a technological society and consequently have a lower receptivity for change. Secondly, those who immigrated into this country usually showed a tenacious tendency to cling to their traditional values and attitudes, probably born out of an anxiety to preserve their cultural identity. Thus one may understand that the

sense of loss is likely to be far greater and more acute than the one their counterparts suffer in the country of their origin where a general societal change is
taking place and is easier to accept. Thirdly, in their own society, their role as
elders is perceived in positive and productive terms as wisdom givers, as trans-
mitters of cultural heritage and as moral arbitrators. It is frustrating for them to
realize that they are no longer able to perform this role.

There is now a wide generation gap in values, and there are communication
difficulties within the family and economic circumstances which are forcing
them out of the extended family role. Perceptions within the family are also
changing, limiting the scope for the role of the older people. It is not uncommon
to find a young British born Asian mother who dislikes the influence of her
mother-in-law over her children, whilst the mother-in-law perceives it to be her
rightful place to be the moral guardian of the grandchildren. The young mother
brought up in this country may perceive the mother-in-law as a threat and fear
that her old-fashioned ideas may retard the child. Traditionally, family and
community disputes were referred to the elders; now that tradition seems to be
disappearing, partly because the importance of the extended family itself is on
the wane, and partly because other statutory services are being approached to
resolve the disputes.

Coping

Once a mental health problem is identified, the traditional methods of coping
normally sought in their country of origin are not available to Asian families,
such as community or kinship network, religious practices, native medicine, etc.
In this country there are no traditional temples or mosques and there are few
traditional healers. The network of relatives who counsel and provide emotional
support is either not adequate or simply absent. This is particularly true of
women who immigrated to this country as a result of marriage and whose relatives do not live here.

Mental health problems are frequently denied and not accepted by the family
out of fear of the stigma. I, myself, have seen many cases where marriage has
been seen as a remedy or a way of coping, in the belief that a marital relationship and responsibility would exert a stabilizing influence. It is also believed
that this socially conforming behaviour will improve the ill person's acceptance
within the community. It is expected that the newly wedded wife/husband will
assume or share the responsibility of the carer. However, in my experience, I
have noted that almost all of these marriages result in divorce or strained relationships. These circumstances, combined with the sense of stigma and family
disgrace often attached to mental illness, may have the consequence of drawing
the family in on itself, bringing an increased sense of isolation and risk of
further difficulties. Sometimes people try to fall back on traditional healers and
may be flown to their country of origin for native treatment at great expense.

The problems of coping are further exacerbated by the poor economic position of the elders. A recent survey by Jadeja and Sing (1993, pp. 12–13) distinguishes three main categories of Asian elders: those who were forced out of their homes elsewhere in the former British colonies, such as the Ugandan Asian refugees who came here in the early 1970s: the elderly parents who came to join their families settled in the UK: and economic immigrants who came to the UK in the 1950s and 1960s. The first two categories did not work in the UK for a sufficiently long time to earn any state or private pension. The contribution of elders in the last category was very low as they were in low-paid, semi-skilled jobs in the declining textile/machine tool sector. A sample survey of the Asian elders in Leicester showed that 70% of them never worked in the UK, only 14% of them had worked in the UK for more than 10 years, whilst just 4% of them worked for less than 10 years in the UK. Naturally, 85% of them were dependent on income support. This precarious economic position is under threat as social service budgets are decentralized, user charges are being introduced and care managers are invested with more discretion in the allotment of resources and decision making in individual cases. Economic burden is a major factor in the coping ability of the whole family, as the average Asian family is not at all well off.

THE CARE INTERFACE

Users

The care interface is characterized by the user's as well as care provider's attitudes. From the user point of view, there are two important considerations: the relevance of the service provision and accessibility to that provision.

The perception of the relevance of the services to their mental health needs on part of the Asian community is linked with their ideas, concepts and attitudes to mental illness. For instance any type of mental illness is likely to be understood in terms of superstition or religious beliefs, such as past karmas or the supernatural powers which are not recognized by the existing services, and, therefore, may be seen as irrelevant. Similarly, at the primary health care level, the role of the general practitioner in relation to mental illness is not well understood, because a general practitioner is regarded as someone who treats only physical illness. These beliefs, combined with the sense of stigma attached to mental illness, are the reason why many Asian families hesitate to approach existing care services for help until the problem becomes a crisis. This hesitation is reinforced by their past experiences of both the services and the whole process of passing through the mental health system.

Having approached the services, one of the first difficulties they encounter is communication. Where the patient does not speak English, interpreter services

are often seen as an answer, but there is a lack of trained professional interpreters which poses difficulties in clinical encounters.

Cultural differences manifest in the experience and presentation of the illness
further muddle the communication and may mislead the process of diagnosis
and treatment. An Asian woman, having heard of her mother's death, went into
shock and started trembling uncontrollably. She was thought to have gone
insane and was promptly brought into a psychiatric hospital. A young woman
who was trying to express symptoms of her physical illness for two years was
thought to be deluded and somatizing mental illness: she died of cancer at the
end of two years of fruitless effort to communicate.

Where the patient has been hospitalized, his or her experience is likely to be
frustrating. Accepting hospitalization without any physical illness is difficult to
come to terms with. The patient may encounter prejudiced and racist attitudes
among the staff. Further, they may find that the hospital routine has no regard
for their customs. For instance there may be a need to wash before eating food.
If they are Muslim, they will need to pray five times a day. Some Hindus are
strict vegetarians and would not consume even vegetarian food cooked in
kitchens used for cooking non-vegetarian foods. Muslims do not eat any other
meat than Halal meat.

Worst of all, many of them are not informed of the side-effects of the treatment, such as sedatives and tranquillizers that lead to heavy sedation.
Electroconvulsive treatment (ECT) may lead to loss of memory for a short
while and patients are left to deal with the side-effects on their own. This has
the consequence of inducing acute confusion, fear and anxiety, and many Asian
patients isolate themselves and lose their appetite.

These experiences, passed on by word of mouth, result in fortifying the
conviction of Asians that the services are, by and large, irrelevant to them.
Apart from the fact that existing services are not sensitive to their cultural
needs, the acceptable type of care to which they are culturally more receptive
may itself be absent. For example Asians do not appear to be getting the benefit
of socially meaningful care interventions such as counselling or various forms
of non-drug therapies. A recent survey (Kumar, 1992) reported overwhelming
response when a culturally sensitive service was offered in terms of counselling
and therapeutic approaches in the voluntary sector. The study reported that
during a 20-month period, 68 people used the newly introduced services, which
include dissemination of information and advice in their own language, counselling, some form of therapeutic interventions and support and advocacy. The
sample seeking help was twice this number, but the project did not have the
capacity to deal with them. This study shows that if socially meaningful interventions are offered in a culturally sensitive manner, Asian people do not hesitate to approach agencies for help.

Elsewhere, the failure of general practitioners to refer Asians to other appropriate mental health services, such as psychology, counselling or psychotherapy, has been observed and cited as one of the reasons why mental illness

among ethnic minorities is not reported until it becomes a crisis (Webb-Johnson, 1991, p. 15). Consequently, it is likely that the noticeable lack of Asian users in the mental health services is due to these reasons rather than relatively less incidence of mental illness among them.

Whilst the perceived lack of relevant services makes many Asians diffident to the take-up, consideration of accessibility is of no less significance. Many Asians speak poor or no English. As Qureshi (1988) estimates, about 80% of the Asian elderly cannot read or speak English, whereas almost all literature pertaining to available services is in English. Furthermore, there is very little awareness of mental health problems; for example depression or anxiety is not recognized as a mental health problem, and aggressive expression is linked to the supernatural. When a mental health problem occurs in the family, usually the first reaction is that of confusion, anxiety and denial of the problem. They do not feel the need to go to the GP since they do not recognize it as a problem relating to the health of the mind.

Asians are likely to undertake religious ritual or go to traditional healers. The family is likely to make persistent demands on the mentally ill member for a conforming behaviour. Similarly, Asian elders do not have any knowledge of available services. An AFOR study showed, for example, that over 80% of the Asian elders in Birmingham did not know about services like day centres, luncheon clubs, home helps, meals on wheels and night watch, while only 33% of them knew about old people's homes. This contrasts with Afro-Caribbeans, 80% of whom were informed of the services. The Coventry study (Holland and Levando-Hundt, 1986) confirmed the trend. Over 80% of Asian elders in Coventry were not aware of various services (barring day centres which 46% of the Asian elders knew of). By contrast, well over 80% of Afro-Caribbean elders in Coventry were aware of services (Patel, 1990, pp. 18–19). Finally, as mentioned earlier, mental illness in elders may have repercussions on the social well-being of other family members in Asian families and may result in being a barrier in accessing the services.

Providers

As regards care providers, racism is one of the most important factors in care interface. Webb-Johnson (1991, p. 10) has noted that conscious and overt racism is obvious in the service delivery and that it acts as a deterrent to Asian service users. She cites two studies: one by MacNaught (1984) reported racist comments in waiting rooms, longer waiting times and higher rates of prescription than whites in the delivery of health services; another study by Donovan (1986) documented instances where Asians were made to feel guilty about entitled health care they were receiving. There were also some instances where Asian patients were transferred without their knowledge to private treatment for which they had to pay and which should have been provided by the NHS.

The role of racism in mental health is also being acknowledged by official agencies. For example at the conference organized by the Mental Health Commission in 1987, it was noted that racism not only helps to provoke mental disorder but also permeates the professions empowered to define and control it and as such warrants a long and hard look (Tonkin, 1987). Similar concern is found in the recent announcement by the Racial Equality Commission that it has decided to investigate the racist practices in social services departments, and one of the important areas of services taken up for investigation is mental health services (Clark, 1993, p. 1). The recent review of the research on the impact of community services on black people by the Social Policy Research Unit confirms that racism is deeprooted in the delivery of the services (*Community Care*, 29.7.1993, p. 5). Racism assumes frightening proportions when it highlights the inequality between health giver and health receiver, a situation where people can be locked up at the stroke of a pen (Kareem quoted in Alibhai, 1988).

Stereotypes

People involved in providing services hold many stereotypical views about Asians. Popular images about Asian families are often selective and prejudiced. There are common myths such as the belief that Asian women are the victims of an oppressive family system. There is a belief that there must be a far smaller number of older people because they are not visible (Westwood and Bhachu, 1988). Yet another myth is that extended families are self-sufficient and, therefore, do not require the support of social services or voluntary organizations. There is also a fictitious view that in Asian culture experience of mental health problems is different and that it does not distress them in the same way as it does white people (Jenkinson, 1987/1988).

The institution of the extended family, which consists of grandparents, their married children and grandchildren, is not widely prevalent amongst Asians settled here. The extended family did offer care and support for all its members, but the present trend is towards nuclear families, driven by a number of economic and social compulsions of living in this country. In the sample of Beliappa's (1991) study of Asian mental health problems in Harringay, only 13% of respondents said that the family was a viable means of support (Webb-Johnson, 1991, p. 39)

A common fallacy suggests that Asian culture is homogeneous, while, in fact, even within the same language speakers coming from the same district in India, there may be significant differences, for example as between Gujarati Muslims and Gujarati Hindus. Yet other notions are that Asian culture is stifling and denies freedom to individuals; that it is characterized by men dominating submissive women; marriages are arranged by parents and forced upon their children; and that Asians are obsessed with religion and they want directive treatment.

Quite often these images are rooted in the fact that isolated bits of a totally different system are judged from a Western value standpoint. In reality, Asian women are a strong source of stability and moral strength to the family. Even within arranged marriages, it is common practice that consent of the bride-to-be or the bridegroom-to-be is obtained beforehand by offering them an opportunity to meet the would-be spouse. Arranged marriages within Asian families have a far lower divorce rate than is common within British families. Asian culture places more emphasis on collective responsibility and family integration than on individual freedom; this is reflected in the way the work is shared and resources pooled and spent. The decision-making process within the family again reflects the values of group interest and harmony rather than competing individual freedoms within the family to earn, own and spend resources. As to religion, most Asian families in Britain rely on the practice of religion and culture as a way of preserving their ethnic identity. Hinduism is a way of life in itself.

Carers will need to examine their own attitudes to see if they are consciously or unconsciously influenced by these myths.

Ethnic issues

Training in ethnic issues in care delivery would certainly help in gaining access to culturally relevant information, but wrong attitudes whether they are racist, self-righteous or presumptuous, cannot be changed unless the carer is willing to be committed to a rigorous, open-minded self-examination. More and more literature on ethnic issues is becoming available. For example Bandana Ahmed (1990) has written about ethnically sensitive social work practice in relation to Asian clients. Rack (1982), Cox (1986), Fernando (1991), Blakemore and Boneham (1994) and many others have made contribution to understanding ethnic issues in ethnic mental health. The Confederation of Indian Organizations (UK) have published an information package (Webb-Johnson, 1991) with a view to providing guidance and practical information on developing quality mental health services. Setting up ethnic development projects with Asian service providers may bring in valuable experience for white carers. At policy level, in addition to training, aggressive anti-discriminatory practice by bringing in black perspectives, encouraging community and user consultation and promoting black user participation in developing services are likely to make significant impact on the attitudes of white carers.

Psychiatry as practised uses a 'disease model', that is the treatment follows the diagnosis based on the assessment of symptoms presented by the patient and the physical evidence gleaned through the examination of the patient and pathological tests, if necessary. As is widely recognized (Rack, 1982; Cox, 1986), this model has limited validity when applied to mental health problems for several reasons. First, mental health problems are experienced in terms of cultural categories: for example a woman who was later diagnosed as manic depressive thought that her aggressive behaviour was the result of her inability to control God's power descending into her. Secondly, Asian languages do not seem to be adequate enough (from the diagnosis point of view) to describe various states of mind. Additionally, Asian patients may use metaphors to describe their mood, even if specific words are available in their language. As Rack (1982) notes, a Pakistani woman is likely to describe her restlessness as 'Dil Pareshan hai', which is more of a poetic expression and hard to translate precisely in English. It is difficult to know whether her feelings are of anxiety or sadness, and 'yet a great deal of diagnosis heavily depends on just such a question'. Thirdly, in clinical encounters Asians are likely to present physical symptoms first and admit to the mood as an afterthought. Indeed, the mood may not be admitted at all (Rack, 1982).

Psychiatry as practised is Eurocentric because it is based on the model of symptomatology specific to European culture. The degree of universality of diagnosis as in physical diseases is not available to the psychiatrist; there is little diagnostically significant physical evidence the psychiatrist can collect and assess independently of the patient's account of what is wrong. Not surprisingly, psychiatrists find it difficult to 'fit' the ethnic patient's symptomatology to any known disease–drug model taught to them.

In an evaluation of Western and Indian psychiatry, Rao observes that in Asian culture the therapeutic emphasis is based on integrating the individual back into the family rather than isolating him or her (Rao, 1986). It is not surprising that Asian elders are likely to prefer traditional medicine, because they feel let down by the Western medicine or they have habitually used traditional medicine (Norman, 1985, p. 64). Indeed, the failure on the part of the planners of services to take into account the contrasting lifestyles of ethnic minorities owing to the Eurocentric training of general practitioners, psychiatrists and other NHS professionals has been thought to be the central feature of the lower uptake by ethnic minorities of the existing services in mental health (Doku, 1990).

To sum up, the attitudes and problems found on both sides of the care interface inevitably affect the care process itself; for example there is a high incidence of misdiagnosis. The Transcultural Psychiatry Society has estimated that at least 40,000 blacks face misdiagnosis at least once in their lives because general practitioners do not have adequate training to recognize the symptoms (Doku, 1990). Besides, mental illness is not always identified at the primary health care level. Some of the reasons relate to 'GP's failure to respond to what the patient is saying, to recognise the emotional effects of a physical condition, failure to refer the patient to other agencies and adherence to myths and stereotypes related to gender, culture and race' (Webb-Johnson, 1991, p. 68). Lower referral rates to psychotherapy and counselling are documented by Campling (1989) and Ilahi (1988), among others (studies cited in Webb-Johnson, 1991). On the other hand, over-diagnosis in Asian cases using psychotic categories is not uncommon. Cochrane (1977) and Carpenter and Brockington (1980) (cited in Webb-Johnson, 1991, p. 12) observe that members of ethnic communities who enter psychiatric services are more often diagnosed with psychotic categories than their indigenous counterparts. Similarly, a study by Shaikh (1985) (cited by Webb-Johnson, 1991) noted that among matched Asian and white groups of users of psychiatric services, the Asian sample contained a higher proportion of patients diagnosed as psychotic. Furthermore, Asians diagnosed as schizophrenic were more likely to be administered electroconvulsive therapy than the whites similarly diagnosed.

SOME OBSERVATIONS ON CARE INITIATIVES

The points relating to race and culture cover a wide ground. They have been discussed in the literature [13] pertaining to mental health of ethnic minorities and concomitant remedial actions of various kinds,[14] including the removal of racism through state action, the training of health deliverers in ethnic issues and the mobilization of ethnic community initiatives, have been suggested. Discussion of what can be done constitutes an extremely large canvas. The following examples illustrate some of the more important issues affecting the mentally ill Asian elderly.

Targeting the 50–60 age group

One of the areas that needs attention is the preventive strategy for people in the age group 50–60. This is the age group that appears to be vulnerable to mental health problems. By this age, the accumulated stress arising out of the painful process of adjusting to an entirely new environmental and social climate in this country catches up with them. Coupled with it is the trauma of coping with intergenerational conflicts of values within the family. Losses of various kinds, such as loss of homeland, loss of extended family and loss of some of their traditional roles and ways, would have become apparent and weigh heavily by this age. These are the people who will swell the ranks of the elderly in the next 5 to 10 years and create a much higher demand for care services.

There is great scope for building socially meaningful intervention strategies designed to work through ethnically sensitive instruments for this age group that would eventually reflect on service provision for a growing population of older people in the next 5 to 10 years. Some of the considerations relevant for effective service provision are discussed in the next section.

Harmonizing services with culture

In providing effective services to the mentally ill Asian elderly, some important points need to be noted. From the logistic point of view, adequate provision of outreach work needs to be made in recognition that the Asian elderly are disadvantaged in various ways when approaching services and, consequently, the services need to be taken to them rather than the other way round.

We have already seen that Asians do not find the services on offer to be relevant and acceptable, therefore a choice of therapy needs to be offered to the patients. Most Asian elders are familiar with Ayurvedic, Yunani and, on a limited scale, homeopathic medicine, and these forms of alternative medicine are quite respectable in Asian countries. Indian universities, in fact, offer university degrees in medicine in Ayurveda.

Therapy does not end with a particular medical model, whether it is allopathy or Ayurvedic. Social aspects involved in therapy are particularly culture-specific, as we have noted earlier in Rao's (1986) argument. Therefore, in the context of Asians, the role of the family needs to be recognized, valued and provided for in the project. The role of the family may be illustrated with an example from a real life situation.

An older Asian woman with a mental illness who was living in a nursing home became physically unwell and desperately needed attention to her personal hygiene but would not allow any carer to touch her. Even an Asian social worker, speaking her language, failed to persuade her. Finally, her family members (son and daughter-in-law) had to be summoned, whom she allowed to clean her. It is clear that older people from the Asian community seem to validate their existence in terms of their bonds and role in the family. Consequently, involvement of the family in the management of mental health problems is vital. This case also illustrates the plight of some of the few families who are unable to look after their older relatives due to various pressures and demands on the family's resources and time.

Similarly, the roles of religion and community need to be turned into a therapeutic resource; for example service provision for Asian elderly can be integrated within the community by creating group forums designed around temples or mosques for culturally acceptable activities. These might include luncheon clubs, religious practices, groupwork, leisure trips, entertainment videos in the client's language and other recreation activities for the mentally ill elders and facilitated by ethnically sensitive trained workers.

For those who are already in hospital, the form of care needs to be acceptable to them. Asians prefer to look after their own personal hygiene and are likely to shun the practice of nurses helping them if they can. On the other hand, the available services of recreation for the in-patients are not relevant to them and, as such, they are likely to miss out on acceptable forms of activity to occupy them, such as spending time with their friends and family members, including their grandchildren.

A successful project

Some of the factors which play a vital role in the success of ethnic mental health projects could be illustrated with an example.

One of the successful projects dealing with Asian mental health issues was the ethnic minority mental health development project set up by the Tameside and Glossop Association of MIND in 1990. It was funded by the Mental Health Foundation, London. Earlier experiences of local MIND workers had indicated that there was a clear need for support within the Asian community for dealing with mental health problems but they felt a greater understanding was needed to grasp the difficulties the Asian community seemed to experience in accessing available services. Moreover, there was also a need to understand the underlying social and cultural forces that gave rise to these difficulties. Consequently, the project was aimed at identifying the culture-related mental health needs of the Asian community living within Tameside and Glossop Metropolitan area so that appropriate services could be developed.

Over the next two years, the project used action research by offering the services of counselling, therapy, emotional support to the carers, advice, advocacy, information and training, social club services and befriending. The response to the project was overwhelming. There were more than 60 referrals, some of which were self-referrals. Very useful data was collected and analysed. As a direct result of the successful research carried out in this project, an ethno-sensitive Asian mental health team has now been set up by the Social Services Department of the Tameside Metropolitan Borough Council.

This experience illustrates some key elements of successful projects. These could be summarized as:

- use of ethnic service providers who share clients' language and culture and are trained both in therapeutic skills and cultural insights;
- adequate dissemination of translated information through carers and service providers, such as GPs, link workers, social workers, community psychiatric workers (CPNs), community-based projects and voluntary organizations, with a view to promoting the awareness and understanding of the mental health problems and services available and reducing the barriers of language and lack of understanding of mental health faced by the Asian community;
- socially meaningful interventions (e.g. counselling and other therapeutic approaches) delivered in a sensitive manner and respecting people's beliefs and traditions;
- assurance of confidentiality in providing service – vital for a community in which mental health problems carry a high social stigma;
- effective professional supervision of the project and accountability to the user group.

Ineffective projects

In contrast to some successful projects, there are many ethnic mental health projects which are not successful in achieving their objective of identifying ethnic mental health needs and providing effective service. It is also instructive to note the reasons for failure. Quite a few borough councils have now come up with new projects, usually funded by 'Section ll monies' (for short tenured posts) in the area of ethnic mental health. While the objective is laudable, the ways in which these projects are perceived, planned, managed and implemented leave much to be desired.

At the planning stages, community and service user consultations are superficial. At times they are structured in a way that does not allow freedom of expression on the part of the ethnic minorities. The aims and objectives and principles of working are not clearly spelled out. Many times the way the objectives and working principles are perceived makes them unfeasible in practice; for example in one of the projects it was naively assumed that the ethnic worker would transfer culture-related skills and insights to the white social workers within a year.

Often the funding for projects is only short term, and even a successful project may not get an extension because of the failure to plan for secure funds. Advertising of posts and recruitment takes disproportionately longer. In spite of the approval of the project and secured funds, the posts are advertised only six months later and, in some cases, even after one year. Insecure funding and the purely temporary nature of the project fail to attract qualified ethnic candidates which, in turn, becomes the alibi for the failure of the project.

At the operational level, the necessary steps are not taken to advertise services available under the project, or the project is overloaded with work of a much more extensive or intensive nature than originally planned for – a small project with limited staff may be asked to cater to the needs of a far larger area than intended. Similarly, it may be asked to provide much more intensive support, including home visits, hospital visits and counselling, while the original brief may have beeen simply to provide information and advice. When the project thus become inefficient and fails, no new project is developed, citing earlier experience as the reason.

Frequently the project is also designed in a way that it has to work in isolation from mainstream services. In some projects where ethnic workers are brought in as ethnic experts to work in coordination with other social workers in order to provide ethnic input, their ability to contribute is stifled by a number of internal factors: they are seen by their white colleagues as a threat to their power and case information is not shared. Often, in the ethnic cases, the options identified, alternatives suggested and advice offered by the ethnic workers on the basis of their expertise in the matter of assessment, crisis intervention and appropriateness of the service are not heeded. Thus, their specialist knowledge and experience are just wasted.

There is little or no support from the managerial rungs and no conscious effort to review the quality of the service. In practice, tension and conflicts arise as a result of different perspectives on the part of ethnic and white colleagues. When these problems are brought to the attention of managers, they are not dealt with in an effective manner. These projects remain mere tokens, enjoying only a peripheral priority within the department whether it is social services or health. Thus, the introduction of a project that claims to be 'ethnically sensitive', and also boasts of the use of an ethnic worker, may not be of much use *per se* unless there is a genuine commitment to the cause of ethnic sensitivity.

An understanding of the concerns of race and culture is vital, therefore, in the examination of care issues pertaining to the mental health of Asian communities. The service providers have to address these issues. The quality of the service can be greatly improved by delivering it in an anti-discriminatory and anti-racist manner. To this effect, available literature that specifically takes account of ethnic issues can be of some guidance, while the experience of both successful and failed projects is equally instructive.

NOTES

1. Figures computed from Table 1.3, in Patel, 1990 and Table 6, 'Ethnic Group', of the 1991 Census Report for Great Britain, Part 1.
2. Figures derived from Table J (p. 30) of the 1991 Census Report for Great Britain. Ethnic groups of Indians, Pakistanis and Bangladeshis constituted 1.5%, 0.9% and 0.3% respectively of the total population in Great Britain as against 94.5% white.
3. Within the general label of 'Asians', one study quoted by Norman (1985, p. 29) of Blackburn Asians has identified as many as 17 different groups: rural Indian Gujarati Muslims, rural Pakistani Punjabi Muslims, urban Indian Gujarati Muslims, rural East African Gujarati Muslims, urban East African Gujarati Muslims, urban Pakistani Punjabi Muslims, East African Gujarati Hindus, Indian Urdu-speaking Muslims, Punjabi-speaking elsewhere, Indian Gujarati Hindus, Pakistani Urdu-speaking Muslims, East African Urdu-speaking Muslims, all Marathi speakers, Punjabi Sikhs, all Bengalis, etc. Although these groups have strong individual characteristics in terms of degree of traditionalism and their relationship both to the country of origin and to life in Britain, the broad socio-cultural features are the same – food habits, styles of celebrating social events, respect for elderly, respect for education as a value, importance of family, importance of religion, etc.
4. Figures derived from Table 1.3, in Patel, 1990, p. 7.
5. Figures computed from Table 6 and Table J of the 1991 Census Report for Great Britain, Part 1.
6. Figures computed from Table 1.3, in Patel, 1990, p. 7 and from Table 6, 'Ethnic group', of the 1991 Census Report for Great Britain, Part 1.
7. Cited in Webb-Johnson, 1991, p. 11
8. Ibid., p. 11.
9. Author's experience. In addition to the people helped, a number of people who sought help could not be helped due to limited capacity.
10. Op. cit., p. 12.

11. Op. cit., p. 12.

12. Figures worked out on the basis of Section 11 application data submitted for the new projects in Bolton Social Services department and the 1991 Census County Report for Greater Manchester.

13. Some of the current literature is documented in directory form by the Nursing/Medical Library, Bradford, which issues a quarterly current awareness bulletin called *Ethnic Minorities Health*. Some documentation is also done by, among others, the National Association of MIND, the Confederation of Indian Organizations (UK) and the National Association of Health Authorities (NAHA bulletins).

14. As early as 1976, the Civil Rights Commission (CRC) had recommended provision of better information about available services, training of psychiatric interpreters, additional training to mental professionals in ethnic minority issues, recruitment of black mental professionals, special provision for diet and language in the hospital, appropriate provision to reduce isolation between hospital, day centres, social services, community psychiatric nurses, and the CRC (Ely and Denney, 1987). Bavington and Majid (1989) suggest that the delivery system needs to incorporate user perspective (e.g. hospital services need to be sensitive to the dietary needs, hygiene and religious beliefs of the ethnic patients).

REFERENCES

Ahmed, B. (1990) *Black Perspective in Social Work*, Jo Campling/Venture Press, Birmingham.

Alibhai, Y. (1988) Broken and by-passed. *New Society*, 6 May.

Barker, J. (1984) *Research Perspectives In Ageing: Black and Asian Old People In Britain*, (Manchester and London Surveys), Age Concern, London.

Bavington, J. and Majid, A. (1989) Psychiatric services for ethnic minority groups, in *Transcultural Psychiatry*, (ed. J. Cox), Croom Helm, London.

Beliappa, J. (1991) *Illness or Distress: Alternative Models of Mental Health*, Confederation of Indian Organizations, London.

Bhalla, A. and Blakemore, K. (1981) *Elders of Ethnic Minority Groups*, AFOR (All Faiths in One Race), Birmingham.

Black, J. (1987) How to do it. *British Medical Journal*, 29 August.

Blakemore, K. (1989) Does age matter? The case of old age in minority ethnic groups, in *Becoming and Being Old*, (eds W. Bytheway, T. Keil, P. Allatt and A. Bryman), Sage Publications, London.

Blakemore, K. and Boneham, M. (1994) *Age, Race and Ethnicity*, Open University Press, Buckingham.

Campling, P. (1989) Race, culture and psychotherapy. *Psychiatric Bulletin*, **13**.

Carpenter, L. and Brockington, I.F. (1980) A study of mental illness in Asians, West Indians and Africans living in Manchester. *British Journal of Psychiatry*, **137**.

Clark, S. (1993) SSDs to be investigated. *Community Care*, 21 October, p. 1.

Cochrane, R. (1977) Mental illness in immigrants in England and Wales: an analysis of mental health admissions, 1971. *Journal of Social Psychiatry*, **12**(1).

Cochrane, R. and Stopes-Roe, M. (1977) Psychological and social adjustment of Asian immigrants to Britain: a community survey. *Journal of Social Psychiatry*, **12**.

Community Care, 29.7.1993, News column, p. 5.

Cox, J.L. (ed.) (1986) *Transcultural Psychaitry*, Croom Helm, London.

Dean, G., Walsh, D., Downing, H. and Shelly, E. (1981) First admissions of native-born and immigrants to psychiatric hospitals in south-east England, 1976. *British Journal of Psychiatry*, No. 139.

Doku, J. (1990) Approaches to cultural awareness. *Nursing Times*, **86**, (39), September.

Donovan, J. (1986) *We Don't Buy Sickness, It Just Comes*, Gower, Aldershot.

Ely, P. and Denney, D. (1987) *Social Work in Multi-Racial Society*, Gower, Aldershot.

Ethnic Minorities Health: A Current Awareness Bulletin, Summer 1989 (1990) Nursing/Medical Library, School of Nursing, St Luke's Hospital, Bradford, West Yorkshire, June.

Fernando, S. (1990) *Race and Culture in Psychaitry*, Croom Helm, London.

Fernando, S. (1991) *Mental Health, Race and Culture*, MIND Publications, London.

General Synod Board for Social Responsibility (1990) *Ageing*, Church House Publishing, London.

Gray, B. and Isaac, B. (1979) *Care of the Elderly Mentally Infirm*, Tavistock Publications, London.

Hashmi, F. (1968) Community psychiatric problems among Birmingham immigrants. *British Journal of Social Psychiatry*, No. 2.

Hitch, P. (1981) The policies of intervention in Asian families. Paper presented at TCPS Workshop, Leicester, 1980. *Bulletin of Transcultural Psychiatry*.

Holland, B. and Lewando-Hundt, G. (1986) Coventry's ethnic minority elders survey: method, data and applied action. *Social Services Research*.

Ilahi, N. (1988) Psychotherapy services to the ethnic communities. Unpublished paper. Report of a study in Ealing, London.

Jadeja, S. and Sing, J. (1993) Life in a cold climate. *Community Care*, 22 April.

Jenkinson, P. (1987/1988) Opinion: minority needs. *Openmind*, **30**, December/January.

Khan, A. (1983) The mental health of the Asian community in East London health district, in *Care in the Community*. Report of MIND Annual Conference, London.

Knight, L. (1981) Racism is number one health problem. *Mind Out*, No. 49.

Kumar, A. (1992) Sanskriti: evaluation report of the Tameside Ethnic Minority Development Project, Tameside and Glossop Association of MIND, Ashton-under-Lyne.

Littlewood, R. and Lipsedge, M. (1982) *Aliens and Alienists: Ethnic Minorities and Psychiatry*, Penguin, London.

MacNaught, A. (1984) *Race and Health In United Kingdom*, Centre for Health Services Management Studies, South Bank Polytechnic, London.

MacNaught, A. (1987) *Health Action and Ethnic Minorities*, Bedford Square Press, London.

Norman, A. (1985) *Triple Jeopardy, Growing Old in Second Homeland*, Centre for Policy on Ageing, London.

Office of Population Censuses and Surveys (OPCS) (1991) *Census Reports for Great Britain, Part 1: Topical Report for People over 60 Years of Age: County Report for Greater Manchester*, HMSO, London.

Patel, N. (1990) *Race Against Time*, Runnymede Trust, London.

Pinto, R.T. (1970) A study of psychiatric illness in Cumberland area. MPhil dissertation, University of London.

Qureshi, B. (1988) Ethnic gaps to bridge in consultation. *Geriatric Medicine*, **18**(8), August.

Rack, P.H. (1982) *Race, Culture and Mental Disorder*,Tavistock, London.

Rao, A.V. (1986) Indian and Western psychiatry in transcultural psychiatry, in *Transcultural Psychiatry*, (ed. J.L. Cox), Croom Helm, London.

Shaikh, A. (1985) Cross-cultural comparison: psychiatric admissions of Asian and indigenous patients in Leicestershire. *Journal of Social Psychiatry*, **31**.

Sokolovsky, J. (ed.) (1990) *The Cultural Context of Ageing; Worldwide Perspectives*, Bergin and Garvey, London.

Tonkin, B. (1987) Black and blue. *Community Care*, 14 May.

Turnbull, J. (1985) *Greenwich's Afro-Caribbean and South Asian People*, Directorate of Social Services, Greenwich.

Webb-Johnson, A. (1991) *Cry for Change: An Asian Perspective on Developing Quality Mental Health Care*, Confederation of Indian Organizations, London.

Westwood, S. and Bhachu, P. (1988) Images and reactions. *New Society*, 6 May.

FURTHER READING

Bolton Metropolitan Borough (1987) *Viewpoints: A Survey of Minority Communities in Bolton*, Policy Research Unit, Bolton Metropolitan Borough Council.

Bould, M. (1990) Services for Asian carers. *Community Care*, 19 April.

Darrant, J. (1989) Moving forward in a multiracial society. *Community Care*, 7 February.

Dawes, T. (1986) Multicultural nursing. *International Nursing Review*, **33**(5), September/October.

Desai, M.M. and Khetani, M.D. (1979) Intervention strategies for the aged in India, in *Reaching the Aged*, (eds M.I. Teicher, D. Thursz and J.L. Vigilante), Sage Publications, Beverly Hills.

Dobson, S. (1988) Cultural identity in health care services. *Midwife, Health Visitor and Community Nurse*, 24 May.

Fenton, S. (1985) *Black Elderly in Britain* (monograph), Department of Sociology, University of Bristol.

Francis, E., David, J., Johnson, M. and Sashidharan, S. (1989) Black people and psychiatry in Britain. *Psychiatric Bulletin*, August.

Lunn, T.(1987) Sensitive to people's needs. *Community Care*, 5 November.

Mering, O. von and Kasden, L. (eds) (1979) *Anthropology and the Behavioural and Health Sciences*, University of Pittsburgh Press.

Miles, A. (1987) *The Mentally Ill in Contemporary Society*, Basil Blackwell Ltd, Oxford.

Norman, A. (1987) Down and out in Britain. *Community Care*, 12 November.

Renshaw, J.(1989) Priorities for health. *Health Service Journal*, June.

Sashidharan, S. (1989) Schizophrenia or just Black. *Community Care*, October.

Smyre, A. and Gatz, M. (1983) *Mental Health and Ageing*, Sage Publications, Beverly Hills.

Tameside Metropolitan Borough (1989) *The Provision of Services to Black Elderly People in Tameside*. Proceedings of a Conference held on 17.9.1988, Tameside Black Elderly Group.

Warren, N. (ed.) (1980) *Studies in Cross-Cultural Psychology*, Academic Press, London.

Whyte, A. (1989) The long route to hospital. *Community Care*, 28 September.

Williams, I. (1979) *The Care of the Elderly in the Community*, Croom Helm, London.

Willie, C.V., Kramer, B.M. and Brown, B.S. (eds) (1973) *Racism and Mental Health*, University of Pittsburgh Press.

<table>
<tr><td>

Flying towards Neverland

</td><td>

11

</td></tr>
</table>

John Casson

ARRIVAL AT THE DEPARTURE LOUNGE: CHECKING IN

After nine years work in adult psychiatry as a dramatherapist and psychodramatist, I was invited to work one session a week at the day hospital for older people with organic mental illness. I approached this work with some trepidation as I was not sure whether my skills were transferable and was aware of my total ignorance of the needs and difficulties of this client group. My only previous experience of people suffering from senile dementia had been nearly 20 years ago when I had been a porter in a large old 'bin' and watched with grief and horror the condition of the abandoned elderly. I wondered what I could now do that would be of use. After some weeks observing, listening to clients and staff and some reading, I began to realize I could, perhaps, make a useful contribution by coming at the work from a different angle. This chapter explores my thinking and the discoveries I made.

In introducing my special perspective it is perhaps useful to say that arts therapists value creativity as therapeutic in itself. Dr J.L. Moreno (1985), the founder of psychodrama, stressed the importance of creativity and spontaneity and stated that 'the self emerges through spontaneity' (Moreno, 1985). This suggests that if we lose spontaneity we lose our self and, conversely, if as therapists we can stimulate the spontaneity of our clients, we can encourage a greater sense of self. The potential loss of personhood in a confused elderly person is perhaps one of the most devastating aspects of dementia. Anything we can do, therefore, to rescue a sense of the unique, creative person who is struggling with the chaos of dementia is surely valuable. At the time I was also a client myself, being in therapy with a Gestalt therapist. Both Moreno and Fritz Perls stressed the value of awareness of the 'here and now'. I realized that whereas with other clients one had a hope that they would 'get better', with older people suffering the ravages of dementia there was no such hope; they were, in effect, in the departure lounge. This awareness could lead to a tragic sense of despair that could disempower workers and lead to low morale, hopelessness and lack of action: they could become listless, like people waiting in the departure lounge.

Working creatively, I began to realize, might not only be important for the patients but also for the morale of staff. In the face of the infinite horror we could find something of value, tasting the wild strawberry as we hang from the cliff – as in the Chinese fable – before the inevitable end. The dying do not have a future; they do have a past – as reminiscence therapy stresses: they also have a present and a presence. Funerals and death always enhance my sense of being alive **now** and make me see, feel and **be** more fully. If there was nothing else I could do in this work but be with these people in the 'here and now' as fully as possible, encounter them as living now and engage with them with spontaneity, joyfully, then I felt I would be doing something of value. Indeed, I began to realize that the challenge of the work was in fact a spiritual one: to contact the person and celebrate, communicate and dance together before the flight was announced. Sachs (1985, p. 38) writes:

> In ... dementia ... however great the organic damage and ... dissolution, there remains the undiminished possibility of reintegration by art, by communion, by touching the human spirit: and this can be preserved in what seems at first a hopeless state of neurological devastation.

I was also inspired by Winnicott's (1991) definition of psychotherapy in his book, *Playing and Reality*:

> Psychotherapy takes place in the overlap of two areas of playing, that of the patient and that of the therapist. The corollary of this is that where playing is not possible, then the work done by the therapist is directed towards bringing the patient from a state of not being able to play into a state of being able to play.

Departure lounges can be boring, lonely places. They are transitional spaces that can be filled with anxiety, a sense of emptiness and purposelessness due to the fact that those there have temporarily lost their usual roles in life; there is a sense of suspended animation as we wait for departure. In *Waiting for Godot* (Beckett, 1954) the two tramps, Didi and Gogo, play to relieve the emptiness. In *Waiting for God* (the TV comedy about an old people's home), the elderly couple, Tom and Diana, delight us with their mixture of fantasy and reality as they struggle to retain power against the ravages of age and the management of the home. The comedy arises from watching them playing tricks on the manager, Baynes, who seeks to domesticate them and sees them purely as sources of income/expenditure in his post-Thatcher privatized business. In a departure lounge we are often trapped – having passed through Customs we are literally locked in, like the elderly people are locked into the day hospital. As

they wait anxiously by the door for release homeward, we can choose to reinforce that anxiety and emptiness or fill the time with play, enhancing the 'here
and now' with a sense of fun, contacting their sense of self even if, like Diana, it
is a cantankerous self!

I have enjoyed my year working in the day hospital, and write this to share
some of the methods and activities I devised to stimulate awareness, maximize
spontaneity, enhance a sense of self, empower and celebrate the individuality of
the people I met.

MAKING SENSE OF NONSENSE: NEVERLAND THROUGH THE LOOKING-GLASS

Chaos theory (Gleick, 1990) has recently revealed the hidden order, the patterns
of chaos, and unveiled the breathtaking beauty of the Mandlebrot set and frac-
tural geometry. Where previously humankind had feared monstrous confusion,
we have now discovered there is a mysterious, complex, meaningful pattern.
When faced with the language of dementing patients we can, at first, be bewil-
dered by its apparent nonsense and dismiss them as talking rubbish. If we learn
to listen we may be able to discover the meaning in the meandering language.
Babies babble and a 'good enough' mother responds as if the nonsense makes
sense or joins in with playful, nonsensical sounds. The fun of making sounds,
developing communication, stimulates the child as the parent mirrors and vali-
dates the child's attempt to communicate. Gradually words emerge, and their
use is repeatedly reinforced with delight by the parent.

Little children enjoy rhymes, songs and nonsense, playing with meaning and
rhythm. Later on children and adults play with language, creating poetry, often
combining sense and nonsense: the works of Edward Lear, Lewis Carroll and
James Joyce come to mind. In *Finnegan's Wake*, Joyce exulted in the puns and
playfulness of a dream speech that sounds, when read, quite like a senile
patient's language.

> But learn from that ancient tongue to be middle old modern to the minute.
> A spitter that can be depended on. Though Wonderlawn's lost us for ever.
> Alis, alas, she broke the glass! Liddle lokker through the leafery, ours is
> mistery of pain. You may spin on youthlit's bike and multiplease your
> Mike and Nike with your kickshoes on the algebras but volve the virgil
> page and view, the O of woman is long when burly those two muters
> sequent her so from Nebob see you never stray who'll nimm you nice and
> nehm the day.
>
> *(Joyce, 1968, p. 170)*

What at first sight seems nonsense is, on closer inspection, full of meaning.
Joyce's dreamathon is a world myth of universal proportions, combining the
local, individual experience of the dreamer with the collective unconscious of

humankind. In this passage, Joyce plays with language and achieves multiple meanings, some of which are immediately visible – such as the references to Alice Liddle and the looking glass – while others are less obvious, like the references to mathematics (youthlit = Euclid) or the almost invisible reference to the marriage of HCE (Here Comes Everybody, the hero/dreamer of the book) to Anna Livia Plurabelle: 'nimm you nice and nehm (name) the day'. Joyce also refers to the fall of man and exile from Eden ('Though Wonderlawn's lost us for ever...'). In the footnote to this passage he writes, 'Dear and I trust in all frivolity I may be *pardoned* for *trespassing* but I think I may add *hell*'. The book explores the myth of the fall and redemption of mankind through love.

Senile patients have lost much, have fallen into a hell, a chaos which Tony Harrison (1993) recently likened to a snowstorm, in the television film *Black Daisies for the Bride*.

It is our responsibility as therapists to enter into our clients' chaos and make contact, to build a bridge to Neverland, to link with the patients lost in 'nonsense' and listen to what they want to say to us: to translate nonsense into known sense.

Therapists since Freud and even earlier – back to the Greeks and Egyptians – have interpreted the apparent confusion of images in dreams to make personal and cultural meaning from 'nonsense'. The non-literal, symbolic communications of the right brain have been a source of information about the client's emotional state, spiritual progress, unconscious conflicts, etc. I began to wonder if the 'nonsense' of the senile patient had within it meaning that a therapist could usefully interpret. At first, however hard I listened, it seemed the person presented me with a biological chaos. I continued to listen. It seemed that I was looking at a fractured mirror; the splinters at different angles reflecting different bits of the person's reality so that a single sentence could relate to material in the here and now, in the distant past, in the recent past, present or future; that there were elements of transference, so that the client would suddenly relate briefly to me as a father, son or other relative.

Attempting to get more into the shoes of a dementing person, I decided on an experiment (which you, too, can try if you wish). In a private place I talked utter nonsense for five minutes. As I spoke out loud in a spontaneous flow of glossolalia I also listened to the words. Allowing myself to speak uncensored, I began to notice that the nonsense held clues as to how I was feeling – unconscious material surfaced in the sudden appearance of particular words. Amidst the words were expletives that hinted at my underlying anger about certain issues in my life. Reflecting on this experience, I began to realize that perhaps if I listened to the dementing patient with an ear to symbolic and affective content I might be able to reflect back to the individual possible meanings and validate emotional states that the person was struggling to express. Senile patients present not only with chaotic language but also chaotic behaviour, so I began to observe what they were doing and try to guess at the meaning.

Laura

One day I met Laura. She was a large woman, powerfully built and angry. She was disturbed and had been violent to other patients. I offered to work with her individually, both for her and the sake of other patients and staff, many of whom were intimidated and exhausted by her. I walked with her up and down, linking arms. She accepted this physical contact, indeed she seemed to appreciate it. I have given more hugs, danced with and touched these clients (even kissed them) than I have younger people. It seems to me that many elderly people are touch-deprived and have enjoyed warm, physical encounters; it both relaxes, reassures, supports and reinforces contact with reality. Of course, I would not force such close contact on a person who did not want it, and I perform a non-verbal 'dance' to check what proximity the client can cope with. Often they would reach out directly to me; others were equally able to give very clear messages that they did not want to be touched. Sometimes, fear of her potential violence kept me a little distant from Laura, but as I got to know her, affection grew and I enjoyed meeting this very distressed woman, who also seemed to enjoy our contact.

During our peregrinations round the day hospital I responded to her questions and fed back to her my sense of her emotional state:

LAURA: Jiz nothing I can do he says Get down but help me David and sholling dinner win be in house and you tell me George! me Dat am I wrong?

JOHN: No you're not wrong but you seem worried as if you were to blame.

LAURA: Damn happy where are you? He's late and I'll be up to singsong he says out and Dad will you?

JOHN: (responding to the tone of voice and rhythm of speaking not visible in the printed word) Yes (Responding affirmatively to a transference statement of some sort) You're frightened and upset?

LAURA: Why read and chips! Blast up your house! Next her mother you you you

JOHN: You're angry ...

(This conversation is not an actual record, but it is created to give an idea of the nature of the responses.) Each time I tried to connect with Laura and reflect back to her my perception of her emotional state, which came from my sense of her language, voice timbre, rhythm, emphasis and physical tension. She seemed to benefit from this validation and acceptance of her communication. Whilst I sometimes had little or no idea what she was referring to, I tried to intuit the meaning: like a heap of broken images I caught glimpses of her past, her present anxieties and frustration.

It is possible that I was learning to listen with my right brain rather than left brain. The left hemisphere is concerned with the literal meaning of words, whereas the right brain is sensitive to the expressive quality of the voice, timbre, feeling, rhythm and symbolism. When we discuss the confusion of the elderly as nonsense, perhaps it is because we listen with the dominant left hemisphere to the literal words. If we can learn to listen with the right brain we can perhaps learn to hear, through their expressive 'poetic' language, of their feeling world. We have to be willing to step through into a looking glass world where a boat may seem to be a shoe.

I decided to invite Laura into a room where she would be contained in a private, quiet space. I took in with me some toys – miniature dolls' furniture and toy cars, boats, etc. I showed her the collection. She picked up a red and blue plastic boat. To my surprise she sat down, took off her shoe and attempted to put on the boat as if it were footwear. There seemed to be several possibilities as to what was happening:

- she had completely misperceived the nature of the boat and her action revealed her confusion;
- she was in the 'here and now' playing with me, as children play 'shop', in which case we were in a shoe shop (a memory being replayed?);
- she had made a spontaneous connection between the boat and her foot (had the colours reminded her of childhood shoes or was the connection to do with travelling – her feet were her vehicle, carrying her to different places, and we had just travelled round the day hospital);
- she was drawing my attention to her foot.

I chose a combination of the second and fourth possibilities and knelt at her foot like a shoe-shop attendant. Taking her foot I began to massage it. In doing this, I was thinking of the wisdom of reflexology and the possibility of relaxing this tense and distracted woman with massage. The toy boat had served its purpose as a transitional object, bridging the abyss of nonsense to connect us. Laura then put her hand up to her head. I took this as a signal to move and gently stroked her head. This woman, who minutes before had been bearing down on others in a menacing way, allowed me, for the next quarter of an hour, to gently stroke her head. She relaxed with this soothing contact. Thus we had gone from demanding attention in a destructive way to receiving attention that satisfied her and was safe. This was achieved by:

- making a journey together;
- finding a safe, boundaried space;
- using a transitional object to find a connecting metaphor;
- play;
- attending to her body tension through massage.

Laura had moved from hostile isolation to an emphatic contact with me in which some of her need for positive attention was met. I was reminded of how delinquent children who desperately need love and attention often only know how to attract negative attention through their violent behaviour. They cannot ask for their needs to be met directly, either because they are unconscious of those needs or due to their experience of neglect, abuse or rejection of those needs. Laura was clearly angry and frustrated, distressed and disturbed. By reflecting back to her that I witnessed her feelings, validating her experience – 'You look angry ... You're really frustrated today...' – I was able to make empathic contact, reassure her that her feelings were recognized, help her release her tension and relax. This was therapeutic for her and for the other patients and staff!

Music and dementia

I had arranged for a Chinese Ku Cheng (an ancient type of harp/zither) player to come to one of the wards for people who were severely disabled by their dementia. This visit was part of a programme of visiting musicians and followed a successful visit by a Celtic harpist who had played beautiful, relaxing music that had soothed patients. One nurse had commented to me that before the harpist had arrived the ward had been quite disturbed and the music had calmed both patients and staff. I decided to risk bringing in the Chinese music because I had heard it myself (and thought it was very beautiful) and because I wanted to offer the patients a new experience of high quality. Whilst it seems appropriate to use music that patients recognize, such as Vera Lynn, it also seems to me valuable to capture their attention and stimulate with new experience: it is in fact new experience that stimulates the brain most, as Rossi points out: 'The fact that what is novel and fascinating actually heightens brain activity is a very important, though still generally unappreciated precondition for all forms of creatively-oriented, psychotherapy' (Rossi, 1968, p. 28). Some of the old hospital wards for people with dementia become places of sensory deprivation with little or no stimulus to awaken clients from their drugged, dependent, drowsy state.

As the Chinese musician prepared to play, I looked round the day room. I was aware that patients could experience this visit as an invasion of their safe place, and concerned lest the novel stimulus of the Ku Cheng, however beautiful it seemed to my ears, might be disturbing to the older people unused to such a sound.

I noticed one woman who seemed already stressed, making movements with her arms and noises were coming from her mouth. I sat next to her and as the music started I offered her my hands. She took them and held tight. I allowed her to lead my hands, moving with her in a kind of hand-dance. I followed her tension, supporting her movement, seeing how far it extended and providing her with what I hoped was contact and an empathic response. After a while I realized that she was moving with some rhythmic response to the music: although faint, there was an expressive quality to her and she relaxed. At first she made urgent distress calls with her voice. Now she took my hand to her mouth and sucked my knuckles. I recognized this regressed behaviour as comfort seeking and I stayed with her, allowing her to do as she wished.

When ill, I notice I regress, wanting to be looked after, and I notice a childish quality in my attitudes/behaviour. Can we respond appropriately to this, or do we try to impose 'age-appropriate' standards on how we think people 'should' behave, rather than respond to how they are or what they need? Can we provide them with the holding they need, or does their regression bring up anxieties about our own regressiveness? Placing here and now contact as the prime focus, and responding in a person-centred way would allow us to be with the client in the way he/she needs. It seems important, however, not just to abandon someone to a regressive chaos but to reach them, to provide stimulus, to achieve some contact. In doing the hand-dance, I was providing some minimal structuring that enabled this disturbed woman to find some comfort and relax.

In *Black Daisies for the Bride*, Tony Harrison's poetic film, shot on the Alzheimer's ward of a large hospital near Leeds, there is a moment of great beauty. A woman who has been filmed obsessively cleaning the ward with her hands seems totally isolated, in a world of her own, out of contact with others and trapped in an endless round of dusting. A banjo player (Richard Muttonchops) approaches her, playing 'Oh you beautiful doll'. Awakened by the repeated playing of this familiar, bright tune, she responds to him and dances with a spontaneity and grace that is truly moving.

Moreno (1985) wrote that 'the self emerges through spontaneity'. Can we stimulate our clients to act spontaneously, provide them with a warm-up and then make contact with their response? What if the response seems to be nonsense?

Jim

One day I met Jim. He seemed remarkably intact and, at first, I wondered why he was there. It was explained that he had bizarre ideas about his insides and circulation. When he explained these to me I accepted them as his perception of his experience. Indeed, some of the ideas did not seem to be complete nonsense but reminded me of reflexology and Chinese ideas about 'Chi' – the energy in the body. It seemed to me that there could be a symbolic content to Jim's communication. One day, he spoke in a fluent, continuous conversation about his ideas of putting reinforcing metal rods in wheat stalks to stop them breaking. Instead of dismissing this as ridiculous I responded to the symbolism. As I listened, I free-associated in my mind with the images: wheat – harvest – autumn – being cut down – the autumn of life – the harvest as death – the vulnerability of a stalk about to be cut down – stalk as back bone – need for reinforcement when vulnerable. I began to respond to the images and gently interpret. We had a strange conversation that went something like this:

JIM   At the harvest time the wheat stalks can be broken.
JOHN   It's the end of their natural life – autumn's a bit sad.
JIM   I've got a solution.

JOHN	You've thought of a way of coping.
JIM	They could get a metal rod and put it inside the stalk.
JOHN	To support it?
JIM	To reinforce it, to stop it breaking, falling over.
JOHN	When the wind blows, it's vulnerable.
JIM	It can bend and break, then it's useless, lost.
JOHN	It's vulnerable.
JIM	Yes, and my idea is to hold it up.
JOHN	When you feel vulnerable you need some support.
JIM	Otherwise it'll break.
JOHN	Even things that are strong can break ...

Later Jim thanked me for the conversation, saying it was good to talk to someone who understood.

However we regard what older people do or say, it is our responsibility as therapists to make contact, to enter their world, to make sense of nonsense and to find the meaning that enables us to meet: just as we play with babies, we can also play with older people.

REDISCOVERING THE LOST BOYS (AND GIRLS): STORYTELLING IN NEVERLAND

Peter Pan, Wendy and the lost boys may represent the lost child within us. In order to contact them, we may need to leave the solid ground of humdrum reality and be willing to fly – to take off on flights of fancy and see what we discover, before the crocodile with the inexorable ticking clock devours us. Storytelling offers a way of providing stimulus, of nurturing and containing. It can be both adult and childlike, funny and serious, reality oriented or released from the severe limits that confine the older person, enabling them to feel some creative freedom and delight. It can help connect with feelings, memories or current concerns. It offers a safe structure to an encounter.

A storytelling session in a group

I begin with the reality of who we are, where we are and what we are doing, and saying 'Hello' and getting everyone's name, listening to how people are or what they wish to say. Some of these initial comments might be incorporated in the story.

The first aim is to recognize each individual as being present. The second is to create a group feeling. Perhaps people will say 'Hello' to each other, remember a name, give a compliment. An activity that connects the whole group together can be useful at this point: armchair football; passing an object around; passing a ball of wool whilst retaining the thread, so that a group web is created connecting people together – a statement can be made to the person you pass the ball to. All these can help create a sense of togetherness. Early in the group it is valuable to have activities to stimulate people, wake them up and warm them up to being maximally spontaneous/creative.

Props, objects, photographs, hats, fans, items to stimulate the senses (perfumes, special tasting fruits/sweets, pieces of different coloured/textured cloth, music boxes or instruments) can awaken interest. Some of these items may be things people have never experienced before – why should we not offer elderly people new experiences? Have they tasted a kiwi fruit or a mango; heard a piece of Mahler or Burmese music; seen a scarlet macaw feather or met someone from Rumania? Rossi (1968) pointed to the value of 'novel experience' to heighten brain activity: surprise can also help people focus on the here and now and, when appropriately offered, give a sense of magic and fun.

I realized the power and value of rhythm in this work, whether it was the rhythm of songs, of tapping feet to music, of clapping hands or tapping stones against each other. The sense of rhythm seems to emanate from a more basic level in the brain and to be untouched by damage to the higher centres. Tony Harrison, in *Black Daisies for the Bride*, pointed to the fact that when all else is gone, rhythm remains; that very disabled/dementing patients can still respond to the rhythm, tap their feet, sing rhythmical songs, speak in rhythm and move to rhythm. It is possible that the rhythm provides a patterned stimulus but also orders the chaos – possibly bringing structured firing to the brain's more random firing in dementia. Music therapy may prove this intuition: I can only point out here that, as a way of communicating, of working with an individual or group, rhythm can provide a way of contacting and joining together, of stimulating joy, memory, playfulness and interaction without the necessity for comprehensible language.

Once stimulated, we give people a chance to respond: what feelings are aroused, what images occur to them, what memories arise?

Out of these the group can construct a story: the therapist asks questions, gives choices, enquires how things link up, what meaning things have. This is a time when every contribution is accepted. If a song surfaces in someone's memory, we all sing it. If there are sound effects needed, we all make them (such as the sound of the sea or the voices of children in the playground). If the story is fragmentary the therapist seeks connections from the group or tentatively offers a choice, leaving the decision to a group member – 'So we're on a beach and there's a family having a picnic. We've talked about the weather – is it sunny or is there going to be a storm?' Offering people the power to make decisions is empowering when life is endlessly taking away their power. At least in the story anything can happen; here is freedom and potential.

The story is created as much as possible by group members, the therapist adding only an essential minimum and remembering the whole. At the completion of the story there are two options:

1. to elicit what the story brought up for people – feelings, memories, concerns;
2. to retell the story so it can be re-experienced as a whole, and members add or change anything.

It is essential to attend to the first, if only to listen to what people say without further investigation. The symbolism of the story may trigger memories or feelings: the sharing of these can engage the group members in a here and now conversation, bringing them into greater contact with each other as they share a concern. A series of pictures of doors elicited a story about a woman being visited by a friend. Reflections on the story brought out feelings of loneliness, fear of bogus callers and real experiences of burglars. Apart from taking the opportunity to stress the importance of using the chain on the door and reminding them to ask for identification from strangers, the therapist also supported the feelings of vulnerability, fear and anger at the situations described.

Storytelling can move between reality and fantasy, 'neverland' and 'here and now'. In closing a storytelling group, one image from the story can be chosen for people to take away as a final group experience, such as: 'Let's hold hands like they did on the beach; feel the warm relaxing sun on our faces and smile with the thought of a happy day'. The use of visualization, imagery and metaphor in therapy is now well documented (see Further reading). With this client group, imagery can be used to stimulate, to contain and to express. The senile brain continues to provide imagery that, like Joyce's apparent nonsense, we can search into and co-create with, to discover meanings and make contact. Those further interested in storytelling in therapy should read Alida Gersie's books.

Stories can provide metaphors that enable us to make our way through transitional stages, such as airport lounges, enabling us to relate and connect on many levels simultaneously and contain/hold distressing experiences at a safe distance. We can enjoy the process, just as we did as children, for storytelling is an art that works at any age. Before we said 'Goodnight' and entered the darkness, when our eyes closed, at that transitional time between waking and sleep, light and dark, known sense and nonsense – before encountering dreams and the vast void of dreamless night – we listened to stories, and the fables enabled us to relax, face the unknown and let go: to fly into Neverland.

REFERENCES

Beckett, S. (1954) *Waiting for Godot*, Grove Press, New York.
Gleick, J. (1990) *Chaos*, Cardinal/Sphere Books Ltd, London.
Harrison, T. (1993) *Black Daisies for the Bride*, Faber & Faber, London.
Joyce, J. (1968) *Finnegan's Wake*, Viking Press, New York.
Moreno, J.L. (1985) *Principles of Spontaneity: Psychodrama*, 4th edn, Vol. 1, Beacon House Inc., Ambler, PA.
Sachs, O. (1985) *The Man Who Mistook His Wife for a Hat*, Picador, London.
Winnicott, D.W. (1991) *Playing and Reality*, Tavistock/Routledge, London.

FURTHER READING

Daly, S. (1988) Dramatherapy with elderly people. *Journal of the British Association of Dramatherapists*, **11**(2), Autumn.

Gersie, A. and King, N. (1990) *Storymaking in Education and Therapy*, Jessica Kingsley Publications, London.

Glouberman, D. (1989) *Life Choices and Life Changes Through Image Work*, Aquarian, London.

Langley, D. (1987) Dramatherapy with elderly people, in *Dramatherapy Theory and Practice for Teachers and Clinicians*, (ed. S. Jennings), Croom Helm, London.

Rossi, E.L. (1986) *The Psychobiology of Mind–Body Healing*, Norton, New York.

Sandel, S. and Johnson, D.R. (1987) *Waiting at the Gate: Creativity and Hope in the Nursing Home*, Eurospan/Haworth, London.

Weiss, J.C. (1984) *Expressive Therapy with Elders and the Disabled (Touching the Heart of Life)*, Haworth Press, New York.

Abuse directed towards older people

12

Steve Pugh

INTRODUCTION

Abuse directed towards older people will present those who work with this group with perhaps the most professionally challenging area of practice development. These workers – community psychiatric nurses, social workers, home care organizers and ward-based staff – will demand information which will guide their professional response to individual situations of abuse.

These workers will also require new methods of working as they respond to complex, challenging and ethically difficult situations. The 1990s will see abuse set firmly on the agenda and it will not go away.

This chapter will explore much of the material available in order to present the range of opinion and comment which is currently being expressed with regard to abuse of older people. There is, at the moment, a considerable amount of opinion being expressed on a relatively small number of research studies, and recent studies appear to be contradictory in presenting different hypotheses. They are, however, all consistent in identifying that being abused is an everyday reality for some older people.

The chapter will concentrate on abuse directed towards older people who are not living in formal institutions. Much of the material presented can be applied to institutional abuse, with an additional element reflecting the nature of the care regime – removing walking frames and putting residents' false teeth in one large bowl represents a more extreme manifestation of this form of abuse.

More subtle expressions of institutional abuse include the denial of privacy and rights of residents. However, many older people who live in their own homes are denied privacy and rights, which further reinforces the transferability of the material presented in this chapter.

A DEVELOPING CONCEPT

The focus of research to date has been on the abuse directed towards older people, hence the framing of the concept within the terms 'elder abuse' and 'old age abuse'. The emphasis has been on victims who are defined by a socially constructed phenomenon, namely retirement. It appears that the concept has been defined by the age of the victim: an abusive activity directed toward someone who is aged 58 years would not be defined as abusive within the current understanding of the concept, but if the same activity is undertaken with someone aged over 60, then this would be regarded as elder abuse.

It seems ironic that a core element in the concept relies on an age determinant when so many other negative forces influence the lives of older people. These forces are, on the whole, based on stereotypes and negative imaging of older people, collectively known as 'ageism'. The activities which are described below are equally directed towards younger adults who share similar levels of powerlessness. Thus, younger adults who experience mental health problems and physical and learning disabilities may equally be exposed to abusive activities. To restrict the concept to age determinants repeats ageist assumptions about the vulnerability of older people and, consequently, becomes abusive in itself.

This chapter is entitled 'abuse directed towards older people'; it is not 'elder abuse' or 'old age abuse'. The material presented focuses on older people primarily because most of the research undertaken is in this area. Practitioners need to be cognizant of the wider application of the concept and not repeat ageist assumptions. The conclusion must be that through our lives we are all potentially vulnerable to abuse by others.

NATURAL HISTORY OF A SOCIAL PROBLEM

Jeffrey Burston (1977) maintained that the abuse of older people has been an element of family relationships since time began and, as such, it is not a new phenomenon. Burston's comments, whilst quite a revelation at the time, were in fact stating the obvious in that some family relationships do involve and have involved extortion, emotional pressure and physical and sexual violence.

In spite of an acceptance that abuse towards older people had existed for generations, it was not until the mid 1970s that the problem was 'discovered'. Chronologically, Burston's (1975) letter may be the earliest recording of this expression of abuse, although its discovery can be attributed to two other people, namely Baker (1975) and Butler (1975). Whilst the framework of abuse had not been applied to this form of family violence until the mid 1970s, there would appear to be some evidence to suggest that professional workers had a low level of awareness that certain types of activities were being directed towards older people, and that these activities were not in their best interest.

Isaacs comments, in a study of older people in hospital and their carers, that 'neglect by relatives played a negligible part in the need for (hospital) admission', but went on to note that 'the prolonged survival of many severely disabled and ill people into advanced old age...has created unprecedented strain on our family and social system' (Isaacs, 1971).

Peter DeCalmer and Frank Glendenning identify research that took place in the late 1950s which sought to examine the hypothesis that 'older people are less well cared for by the younger generation' (DeCalmer and Glendenning 1993). This sort of evidence confirms that there was some awareness amongst professionals prior to the 'discovery' of the problem, which begs the question why was it not discovered earlier.

This question is even more pertinent when we consider that the early 1970s saw a great deal of concern being expressed about child abuse and 'wife beating'. Erin Pizzey established the Chiswick Women's Aid Refuge in 1971 and published her work on domestic violence in 1974 (Pizzey, 1974). The Maria Colwell Child Abuse Enquiry took place in 1973, reflecting increasing anxieties about the position of children within the family. These two major but specific influences were raising awareness with regard to the amount of violence which occurs within family settings. Associated with these influences was the 1970 General Election campaign in which law and order featured prominently. Older people were thought to be especially vulnerable to violence primarily from younger strangers. The term 'granny bashing' had, in fact, been used by the media to describe the mugging of older people by much younger strangers.

It is the combination of a gradual sensitivity on the part of professionals to recognizing that families can be violent, and a more widespread concern about older people living in a violent society that gave rise to the 'discovery', or the recognition, in the mid 1970s, that older people can be subjected to activities which may be regarded as abusive.

The relatively late recognition of the problem *vis-à-vis* other expressions of abuse has a number of explanations.

- Situations which professional workers recognized as involving violence, extortion, etc. were described in pathological terms on an individual basis, with the result that those involved were viewed as failing and inadequate people – no links with other situations were made which would suggest the existence of a social problem.
- Associated with the above was the absence of a theoretical framework within which to locate specific behaviours.
- The value of older people within society, particularly in relation to children, resulted in an attitude of 'What do you expect?', 'Wouldn't you in that situation?' These comments and opinions parallel those associated with the professional response to wife beating – 'Well you asked for it', 'What do you expect, it's Friday?'.
- The ageist attitude of some professional workers showed little regard for a

devalued client group whose rights were eroded by being economically unproductive and dependent.

• The consequences of the expression of multiple chronic pathologies gave rise to physical and emotional dependence, further reducing the status of older people as citizens to that of a group of people who had things done to them, and who should be 'jolly lucky' and grateful that others are around to do these things.

Having been recognized and discovered, the diffusion of and response to the problem of abuse directed at older people took very different paths in Britain and in North America. By the end of the 1970s, a number of research studies (Renvoize, 1978; Block and Sinnott, 1979; Lau and Kosberg, 1979; O'Malley, Segars and Perez, 1979), reporting in North America, confirmed the existence of the problem. However, they were employing very different terms: 'granny bashing', 'battered elderly syndrome', 'abuse of the elderly' and 'elderly abuse'. National conferences were organized in Washington DC (1979), Tennesee (1980), Massachusetts (1981) and San Francisco (1983).

The United States legislators were also responsive, with the Select Committee on Ageing taking evidence in the late 1970s and early 1980s on the nature and scope of the problem. By 1983, 22 states had approved some form of adult protective legislation, and, by August 1988, every state had some type of legislation.

In Britain the process was very different, with the diffusion of the existence of the problem relying on a very small group of people, most notable of whom is Mervyn Eastman. However, others have played significant roles. In 1981, Olive Stevenson called for the establishment of the Non-accidental Injury system for Older People. Dr Peter DeCalmer at North Manchester General Hospital and Patricia Riley, formerly of Kent Social Services and now at Leeds, are amongst a group of people who have been prominent in their geographical areas.

Age Concern has sponsored a number of publications (Cloke, 1983; Eastman, 1984; McGreadie, 1991), and also made proposals for legislation change (Age Concern, 1986). The British Geriatrics Society (BGS) convened the first national conference on old age abuse in September 1988, and the British Association of Social Workers (BASW) held a conference in June 1990.

The pace of development in this area has quickened enormously since the late 1980s, involving the Association of Directors of Social Services (1990) and the Social Services Inspectorate (1992). However, the Government's attitude has been relatively consistent in rejecting the scale of the problem and insisting that the response, if any, should be determined by the professional bodies involved with the problem. This attitude has the result that no government department took a lead on the issue. However, local government did begin to respond, and Hildrew identified some 50 local authorities who were working on the subject. Whilst recognition and a response is being planned, as Hildrew comments: 'there is no universally accepted approach to guidelines in elder abuse' (Hildrew, 1991).

WHAT IS ABUSE?

It may appear that establishing which activities may or may not be regarded as abusive would, in fact, be somewhat straightforward. However, the only consensus which exists about defining 'elder abuse' is that there is no consensus (Valentine and Cash, 1986; Johnson, 1986; Pillemer and Sutor, 1988; Hudson, 1989).

Intrinsic and extrinsic

There are two broad mechanisms or approaches to defining abuse – intrinsic and extrinsic definitions. Johnson defines the former as those attempts to 'conceptualise the variable by targeting the linguistic meaning of the construct rather than by identifying observable events' (Johnson, 1986). Extrinsic definitions are defined by Johnson as those which 'facilitate observations by specifying concrete behaviour that relates to the conditions identified in the intrinsic definitions' (Johnson, 1986). In essence, the distinction between the two approaches is that one rests on identifying and categorizing types of behaviour (extrinsic), whereas the other attempts to compile a sentence or small paragraph which summarizes every aspect of abuse.

One of the earliest British intrinsic definitions is attributed to Dr Peter Horrocks, former Director of the Health Advisory Service, who maintains that abuse is the 'deprivation of the quality of life' (Tomlin, 1989). The most widely quoted definition of abuse is that outlined by Mervyn Eastman, which is quoted in Tomlin as 'the physical, emotional or psychological abuse of an older person by a formal or informal carer. The abuse is repeated and is the violation of a person's human and civil rights by a person or persons who have power over the life of a dependant' (Tomlin, 1989).

This definition gives cause for concern not least because it maintains that the activity must be repeated, thereby implicitly rejecting single acts of violence, theft and sexual contact as abusive. In categorizing behavioural expressions, the definition does not recognize categories identified by other researchers and commentators, such as sexual and financial abuse and the abuse which occurs within institutions. As a consequence, the breadth of the activities he regards as abusive is relatively narrow. Eastman's reliance on the abstract concept of civil and human rights raises a number of problems in defining abuse, primarily because of the lack of clarity in the understanding of what human and civil rights are. Thus the lack of clarity of a pivotal concept in the definition only serves to increase the ambiguity that is inherent in Eastman's definition.

Eastman's definition, however, does recognize the existence of the potential for abuse by professionals. In common with many other attempts to define elder abuse, Eastman's use of the term abuse to define itself is tautological. Another illustration of such self-definition comes from Chen *et al.* when they maintain that elder abuse is 'abusive action inflicted by an abuser on adults 60 years of age and older' (Chen *et al.*, 1981).

Abuse and neglect

Whilst these definitions attempt to outline what elder abuse actually represents, Hudson employs the term 'neglect', which is defined as 'carelessness in behaviours (commission) or omissions of behaviour which are reasonably warranted by elders' unmet basic needs and are implicit or explicit in the obligation of the relationship and which results in unnecessary suffering, as demonstrated by harmful, physical, psychological, financial and/ or social effects on the elder' (Hudson, 1989).

The difference between abuse and neglect would appear to rest on the intentionality of the act. Thus, if the act is deliberate and thoughtful it may be regarded as abusive, but if it is a result of carelessness, lack of knowledge or forethought, then it may be thought of as neglect. A similar distinction occurs in Fulmer and O'Malley's (1987) definition of abuse and neglect, where the former involves actions which create unmet needs, whereas neglect relates to the failure to respond adequately to the care needs of an older person.

Bennett (1990) has employed the above framework to develop an approach based on the broader concept of inadequate care. Bennett argues that such an idea is 'more relevant to the doctor's day to day work' (McGreadie, 1991) and has four main advantages:

1. It is easier to reach a consensus on what constitutes inadequate care than it is to agree upon what is acceptable or unacceptable behaviour within families or caring professionals.
2. It is easier to operationalize definition of inadequate care because it is easier to identify.
3. There is much less reluctance on the part of health care professionals to identify inadequate care than there is to evoke the labels of abuse or neglect.
4. It helps to focus interventions on the care needs of all elderly persons. We are able to respond to cases of abuse and neglect with only minor modification in the approach that we use with any other inadequately cared for elder.

(McGreadie, 1991)

Extrinsic definitions, as previously mentioned, rely on grouping together behaviour into categories or typologies. McGreadie (1991) has identified the generally accepted categories of abuse: physical, psychological, financial, sexual, sociological abuse and neglect.

However, there remains a degree of inconsistency amongst researchers in locating some behaviours within these broad categories; Lau and Kosberg (1979) recognize withholding personal care as physical abuse, whilst Douglas *et al.* (1980) place such activities with active neglect. In contrast, Sengstock and Laing (1982) locate the same behaviour within the category of psychological neglect.

MEASURING THE PROBLEM

One of the most important difficulties associated with defining the subject is that of establishing how much of it exists. Without a clear understanding of what is being measured, the results of studies will be variable. The House of Representatives Select Committee on Ageing estimates that 1 million older people in America are being abused by relatives, but this recognizes that only one case in six comes to the attention of the authorities. Pillemer and Sutor (1988) identify two studies which have examined the prevalence of elder abuse by employing population surveys. Block and Sinnott (1979) surveyed three groups by post – community agencies, a random sample of elderly people living in the community and health and human service professionals. Whilst the response rate was low, their findings have been extrapolated to the total elderly population in the United States, giving rise to an estimate of 1 million cases nationwide. The other survey was conducted by Gioglio and Blakemore (1986) which estimates a 1% incidence.

Strauss and Gelles (1986) undertook a survey of family violence and concluded that 3.3% of the elderly respondents reported that husband to wife violence had occurred in their marriage in the previous years. Other surveys have produced incidences of 4% (Crouse *et al.*, 1981) and Lau and Kosberg (1979) 9.6%. McGreadie (1991) maintains that the most reliable study of incidence is the Three Models Project undertaken in Boston, Massachusetts, which reports an incidence of 32 per 1000 (3.2%) who have been subject to maltreatment, but it is thought that only one in 14 cases come to public attention. Glendenning comments that there has been no major study of the prevalence or incidence of elder abuse in Britain (DeCalmer and Glendenning, 1993).

Eastman (Tomlin, 1989) has estimated that 500,000 older people in Britain are subject to abuse. The widely varying reports of incidents clearly indicate that the acts being measured were the subject of very different definition. The Three Models Project, for example, was only measuring physical abuse, neglect and psychological abuse.

WHO IS THE ABUSER AND WHO THE ABUSED?

In identifying characteristics of the perpetrator and the victim, care should be observed that this information is not employed mechanistically, in that people who maintain the stereotype are not automatically assumed to be the abuser or the victim and conversely that people who do not have such characteristics are not regarded as potentially at risk. With this caveat in mind, the research studies do, on the whole, agree that both the abuser and the abused do have particular characteristics.

Tomlin identified the stereotypical victim as a woman aged over 80 years, experiencing dementia, Parkinson's disease or cerebrovascular disease and perhaps regarded as roleless; she is functionally impaired, lonely, fearful and living at home with an adult child (Tomlin, 1989). Horrocks (1988) identified the victim as also heavy and experiencing incontinence.

In Canada, Shell (1988) found that two thirds of victims were women, aged over 80 years and had lived with relatives for 10 years or more. However, the Ryerson study concluded by Podnieks (1990), found that gender, marital status and living arrangements did not assist in distinguishing between those older people who were abused and those who were not. McGreadie (1991), commenting on the research, found that those who were subjected to 'material abuse' were more likely to be living at home. Those who were physically or verbally abused were more likely to be married or married and living with an adult child – a definite correlation between the abusive act and the availability of the victim.

This idea of availability appears to be reflected in the stereotype of the perpetrator. Homer and Gilleard (1990), for example, comment that all carers who undertake some expression of abuse were living with the person they abused. There would also appear to be an interaction between alcohol consumption, depression and the abuse which has taken place. There was also little effective communication within the caring relationship and the perpetrator had given up work in order to care.

PHYSICAL INDICATIONS OF ABUSE

Peter DeCalmer (DeCalmer and Glendenning, 1993) has produced an excellent check-list (reproduced below) of the physical consequences of abusive activities.

1. Unexplained bruises and welts
   (a) on face, lips, mouth, on torso, back, buttocks, thighs
   (b) human bite marks in various stages of healing
   (c) clustered, e.g. forming regular patterns
   (d) reflections of shape of article used to inflict abuse (e.g. electric cord, belt, buckle)

    (e) different surface areas noted

    (f) regularly appear after weekend or vacation.

2. Unexplained burns
    (a) cigar, cigarette burns, especially on soles, palms, back or buttocks
    (b) immersion burns, sock-like, glove-like, doughnut shaped on buttock or genitalia
    (c) patterned like electric burner, iron, etc.
    (d) rope burns on arms, legs, neck or torso.

3. Unexplained fractures
    (a) to skull, nose, ear (cauliflower ear), facial structure
    (b) in various stages of healing
    (c) multiple or spinal fractures.

4. Unexplained lacerations or abrasions
    (a) to mouth, lips, gums, eyes, ears
    (b) to external genitalia.

5. Unexplained hair loss
    (a) haemorrhaging beneath scalp
    (b) possible hair pulling, by self or other
    (c) possible evidence of underlying severe head injury (subdural haematoma).

6. Evidence of past injuries
    (a) deformities – skull, nose and ears, cauliflower ears, hands (twisting reflex)
    (b) contractures resulting from restraint and delay in seeking treatment
    (c) dislocation, pain, tenderness and swelling.

7. Physical neglect
    1. consistent hunger, poor hygiene, inappropriate dress including soiled clothing, unexplained weight loss, dehydration
    2. consistent lack of supervision, especially in dangerous activities or over long periods
    3. constant fatigue or listlessness, unexplained or increasing confusion
    4. unattended physical problems or medical needs, including urine burns or pressure sores
    5. lost or non-functioning aids, e.g. glasses, dentures, hearing-aids, walking-aids and wheelchairs
    6. over-/under-medication
    7. abandonment, immobility, hypothermia; indicates possible isolation.

8. Sexual abuse
    1. difficulty in walking or sitting
    2. torn, stained or bloody underclothing
    3. pain or itching in genital area

4. bruises or bleeding in external genitalia, vaginal or anal areas
5. unexpected and unreported reluctance to cooperate with toileting and physical examination of genitalia.

9. Emotional mistreatment
   1. habit disorder (sucking, biting, rocking, etc.)
   2. conduct disorders (antisocial, destructive of self and others)
   3. neurotic traits (sleep disorders, speech disorders, compulsion, phobias, hypochondria).

(DeCalmer and Glendenning, 1993, pp. 39–41)

DIAGNOSING ABUSE

The identification or 'diagnosis' of some forms of abuse is undoubtedly much more straightforward than with other expressions of abuse. This is particularly the case with physical abuse and neglect abuse where, on the whole, physical manifestations are present in the form of bruising, scalding, welt marks, etc. However, this is further complicated with the presence of multiple chronic pathologies which can result in some older people consuming a large quantity of medication some of which impair the clotting potential of the blood, i.e. anticoagulants, so the bruising potential increases sharply. As a result, everyday activities can produce bruising which has nothing to do with abusive activities.

Thinning of the skin – natural or as a consequence of the use of steroids – and senile purpura due to the ageing process also complicate the identification of physical abuse, not least because the markings may be caused by rough handling and disguised or dismissed as part of the ageing process.

With regard to psychological abuse, DeCalmer notes that there is an apparent lack of interest in psychology literature, although researchers looking at elderly abuse have identified the existence of what may be called psychological abuse and some clinical indicators. Tomlin (1989) noticed that the abused person feels lonely, fearful and roleless. Taler and Ansello (1985) noted a more generalized fear and a cowering when approached. It is much more difficult to conclude that psychological abuse has given rise to specific behaviours because there is not an agreed direct causal link between actions and consequential behaviour, giving rise to the prospect that many other processes may result in such behavioural manifestations.

Somewhat more specific and identifiable is the area of financial abuse, where indications would include large debts related to apparently inappropriate expenditure, inability to pay bills, reassignment of assets, no control of income, i.e. carer holding pension book, and the unexplained disappearance of furniture and other personal possessions. The key element here is the ability of the abused person to give informed consent and the circumstances in which that consent is obtained.

The area of sex abuse of older people is particularly difficult, not least because it requires practitioners to overcome ageist assumptions about the sexuality of older people and the sexual activity they may be or have been engaged in. All too often older people are viewed as asexual and, if sexuality is recognized, it tends to be within the narrow parameters of heterosexual penetrative sex, where the woman is viewed as a passive somewhat disinterested participant.

Eastman specified that 'Infirmity of age can be sexually provocative and is a form of sexual perversion' (Eastman, 1984), and goes on to identify 'ageing dependency sexuality'. DeCalmer and Glendenning (1993) place sexual abuse within the confines of cross-generational abuse located within an incestuous framework. The permutations of relationships are wide and include paid carers from the health and social services as well as volunteers from the voluntary organizations, although this does not mean that all such people are involved in these activities.

Taking the parallel of child sexual abuse, we may assume that most sexual abuse is undertaken by heterosexual men and, on the whole, their victims would be women. Of crucial importance in the area of sexual abuse is the ability of the person who is regarded as the victim to give informed consent, and the environment in which the consent was obtained, i.e. whether the consent was obtained in a threatening manner. Processes such as dementia do not automatically preclude the obtaining of informed consent. Having ascertained whether consent was obtained and the validity of that consent, practitioners need to have regard to the previous practice of sexual activity within that relationship. In a relationship in which penetrative heterosexual sex has been the norm, and in which one partner has dementia, how should practitioners view a change in sexual practice which may involve 'golden showers', where one partner urinates over the other?

Consent and what had been the norm form essential elements in determining whether abuse has taken place; the opinion of the abused person is obviously very important, how they were feeling, how they regard the relationship and the activities, all inform as to the perception of the events.

Through all of these areas of difficulty cuts the law which is somewhat emphatic about proscribing certain activities and relationships, consensual or otherwise. Practitioners need to distinguish between those activities which are illegal or criminal and those which are abusive, because they are not always the same. Should we regard a mother–son sexual relationship, where the former is in her eighties and the latter in his fifties and where sexual activity has been taking place for over 30 years, as abusive because it is a criminal act?

It is, therefore, very important for practitioners to exercise caution and to examine a range of possible indicators before concluding that abuse has or has not taken place.

SITUATIONAL INDICATORS OF ABUSE

The problem with situational indicators is that they may be employed mechanistically by practitioners who use them to determine that abuse is present, perhaps without any other sign of abuse. Therefore, in identifying a range of indices caution must be an element in how they are used. The presence of an indicator, either singularly or in combination with others, does **not** mean that abuse **is** taking place.

In looking at the relationship which exists between an identified potential abuser and an abused person, a number of factors stand out as significant, not least how the relationship came about. A 'caring relationship' does not emerge out of thin air and is not without context: perhaps the carer has foregone a career to look after a loved one; possibly the person being looked after is not and never has been a loved one; other family members may have abandoned the relationship; or perhaps role expectations have left one family member – usually a woman – in the position of caring.

The person being cared for may have been an abuser or an authoritarian figure and a centre of considerable restraint on the carer's life when younger. Each of these elements is brought to a caring relationship and may give rise to a considerable amount of resentment on the part of the person offering care.

The General Household Survey (1985) identified that around 6 million people had some responsibility for caring for another person: 1.7 million carers lived with the person they are caring for; 20% of carers look after more than one person; and 66% of carers receive no assistance from the health and social services. These figures highlight the amount of caring that is undertaken, a significant proportion of which is intense and isolated.

Coping is a very individual response. As practitioners, we have seen people cope with the most difficult of situations, whilst others say they do not wish to carry on coping with the slightest of problems. Consequently, it is difficult to know how people will and do respond to very demanding situations, and so we must not be mechanistic in employing situational indicators in determining whether or not abuse is taking place or has taken place.

THEORETICAL APPROACHES TO ABUSE

All too often practitioners root their responses to situations within the parameters of common sense, otherwise known as practice wisdom. However, little understanding or regard is given to the theoretical influences which are exerted on such common sense or practice wisdom. In responding to abuse, an understanding is required of the influences which are being brought to bear, together with the associated values implicit in their work. Practitioners who exercise a victim-blaming approach will too quickly collude with the perpetrator; those who emphasize the value of self-determination to the furthest possible extent will fail to respond to statutory and organizational requirements.

Situational stress model

Perhaps the most widely employed theoretical model applied to abuse of older people is the **situational stress model**. Many of the factors which indicate the potential for abuse (as outlined above) are all consistent with the stress model. Practitioners employing these indicators are engaging with the stress model. The premise of this model rests with 'the stress associated with certain situational and/or structural factors [which] increase for the abuser the likelihood of abusive acts directed at a vulnerable individual who is seen as being associated with the stress' (Phillips, 1986). Phillips comments that the victim is presented by the perpetrator as the source of the stress in a particular relationship. Block and Sinnott (1979), Lau and Kosberg (1979) and Rathbone-McCuan (1980) all indicate a relationship between elder abuse and the presence of mental or physical impairments of the victim. Giordano and Giordano (1983) found that a victim's physical illness was a significant element in the physical abuse of two comparative samples of older people.

Phillips (1986), however, found no significant difference in the abilities of older people to perform activities of daily living between those who have or have not been abused. If there is not a particular fit between individual characteristics of the victim and the perpetrator, then perhaps external elements may represent considerable stress within particular relationships.

O'Malley, Segars and Perez (1979), Block and Sinnott (1979) and Douglas *et al.* (1980) found unemployment, medical problems and life stress to be important in relationships with abuse as an element.

Phillips (1986) identifies what she refers to as four sources of support for the situational stress model, namely:

- model makes sense, being based on conventional wisdom related to the position of carers *vis-à-vis* a group of people who represent a burden on them (and reflecting many ageist attributes which present older people as burdens in an emotional and economic sense);
- child abuse and intra-family violence literature also place considerable emphasis on stress, both situational and structural;
- model has proved effective in explaining child abuse and intra-family violence;
- model presupposes a relatively simple interventionist and preventative tool.

Psychopathological model

A second theoretical framework which is receiving increasing support within the United States is the **psychopathological model**. Quinn and Tomita comment that the abusers have 'profound disabling conditions; addicted to alcohol or other drugs; dementia, mental retardation or chronic inability to make appropriate judgements where the care of a dependent elder is concerned' (Quinn and Tomita, 1986).

Wolf, Straell and Godkin (1982), in their research, identified that 31% of abusers had a psychiatric history and 43% had problems associated with substance abuse. The abuser is further portrayed as being unable to respond to the needs of an older person; they fail to see the connection between their actions and the injuries they cause, giving elaborate and preposterous explanations for the abusive behaviour.

The situational stress and psychopathological models are not mutually exclusive. The stresses identified by the situational model can, in themselves, give rise to specific psychiatric illness or misuse of substances as well as exacerbating previously held problems. Of course the presence of mental ill-health, cognitive impairment and/or substance abuse may, in themselves, add to the stress which is being experienced in particular relationships.

Social exchange theory

The third theoretical explanation for abuse directed towards older people is **social exchange theory**, the basis of which involves the exchange and associated rewards and punishment that take place between at least two people. The principle behind the theory is that everybody seeks to minimize punishment and maximize rewards. The mechanisms by which such punishment and rewards are transmitted are those of sentiment, resources, specific behaviours or instrumental services. Thus rewards can be conveyed by statements of love, money or gifts and punishment by displeasure, dislike or by specific behaviours such as violence.

Phillips comments that social exchange theory can be easily applied to an abuse framework if assumptions are made that the abused older people are 'more powerless, dependent and vulnerable than their care giver and have fewer alternatives to continued interaction' (Phillips, 1986). The abusive activity arises from the rewards not equating to the costs involved in maintaining the relationship.

Symbolic interactionism

The final theoretical explanation for abuse directed towards older people examines the process of social interaction and is referred to as **symbolic interactionism**. McColl and Simmons (1966) identified that the process takes place between at least two people, occurs over time, has identifiable phases and requires constant negotiation and renegotiation in order to establish a working consensus with regard to the symbolic meaning of each encounter. The phases of social interaction include the cognitive process, the expressive process and the evaluative process. The former involves the mental activities which are used to organize understanding of what is happening and, therefore, the definition of the situation.

In any given interaction, the individual will plan actions based upon their perception of self and others rather than true reality, with the consequences that characteristics, motives and goals are imputed to the other person.

During this phase, improvised roles and identities are assumed which are, in turn, based on separate and negotiated definitions of the situation. A store or repertoire of roles is developed and used in accordance with the principles of the situation in which the person is placed. Associated with the store or repertoire is, as Goffman (1962) identifies, a constantly evolving dossier of the other person, containing a history of events, impressions and evaluations. The expressive process involves the display of behaviours that are consistent with the roles being adopted, and which are consistent with moral and social obligations employed to support the role. Role synchrony will occur when each person employs a similar definition of the situation and the roles used work together, thus ensuring the continuation of the interaction. Role asynchrony will occur when there is a mismatch in either the definition of the situation or the roles adopted, and will usually have the result that the interaction will be terminated. When the interaction cannot be terminated, negative attributes will be associated with each person.

The final process involves 'the basis for consensus negotiation as the actors alter their own behaviours and their expectations of the others in response to their independent assessments of the situation' (Phillips, 1986). Abuse directed towards older people employing a symbolic interactionist perspective can be viewed as an inappropriate or inadequate role enactment. The events set in motion begin with negative behavioural expressions created, perpetrated and located within the family, thus images are developed about who the person is and was thought to be, which, in turn, can be defined, normalized or stigmatized. The discrepancy which exists between past and present roles influences the symbolic meaning of present encounters by affecting motives, characteristics and goals. Relationships in which abuse occurs are those which give rise to negative attributes and stigmatize the older person, attributing ulterior motives and a perception that the older person was deliberately difficult or uncooperative. These images of the person, past and present, are divergent and problematic to resolve.

Other theories

The applicability of theories related to other expressions of abuse – most notably child abuse and wife beating – depends on the association of abuse directed towards older people and those other forms of domestic violence. Finklehor and Pillemer maintain that abuse directed towards older people should be regarded as a distinct and separate category of abuse. Their argument is based on 'the special characteristics of the elderly which affect their vulnerability to abuse and the nature of the abuse they suffer and also by the nature of society's relationship to older people' (Finklehor and Pillemer, 1988). They maintain that older people:

- share characteristics related to psychological and cognitive processes which place limitations on their functioning, with particular reference to the skills associated with daily living;
- have a devalued social status which is a consequence of the attitudes maintained by younger people which are, in turn, reinforced by such features as retirement; and
- have a special relationship with society which informs the need for special service provision, such as elderly persons homes.

It would seem somewhat ironic when discussing abuse to locate the rationale for a separate category which is based on stereotyped images of older people and the organizational arrangements that have been established based on these stereotypes to meet their needs. The stereotypes of older people are maintained in a society that is youth orientated and dominated by a youth culture.

The stereotypes are sustained by negative images of old age and as Stevenson notes, 'arises from the existence of deeply ingrained antagonisms even revulsion towards old people' (Stevenson, 1989).

Such attitudes have become collectively known as 'ageism', reflecting a system of oppression related to age as racism is to culture, sexism to gender and homophobia and heterosexism is to sexual orientation. Finklehor and Pillemer's (1988) assertion that abuse should be a separate category because of society's relationship to older people is based, as we have seen, on negative stereotypes and myths. If the criteria for a separate category are not met, are there criteria which identify similarities between abuse directed at older people and other expressions of abuse? The experience of being abused, irrespective of age, has the result of lowering self-esteem and coping skills, giving rise to stigma and self-blame.

Available approaches

The theoretical approaches which are available include the following.

- Sociobiology (Storr, 1970) – maintains that aggression is a basic human instinct in which men require periodic discharge of the pent up aggression and that aggressive competition ensures that the fittest survive to breed. (Domestic violence is viewed within the context of the discharge of aggression.)
- Victim precipitated violence (Gayford, 1976; Pizzey and Shapiro, 1982) – states that women themselves, some of whom may be addicted to violence, are responsible for the violence directed at them because of their behaviour.
- Aggression as a learned response (Bandura, 1973) – also known as social

learning theory, explains that aggression on the whole is learnt and not biologically determined.

- Disease model associated with child abuse – 'a single identifiable organism...can be isolated and understood in the laboratory, populations...can be identified as being at risk of attack from the organism, preventative strategies...are developed on the basis of knowledge about the organism, a disease with a predictive course and duration and one with sufficiently uniform manifestations that it can be diagnosed with great accuracy (Giovannoni, 1982, p. 24); child abuse is seen as an illness which can be diagnosed, where 'the pathology resides primarily in the parents but manifests itself in the relationship with the child' (Parton, 1985, p. 132).
- Material deprivation approach (Garborino and Gilliam, 1980) – argues that child abuse is an expression of the poor quality of life of some families.
- Cycle of violence – maintains that people who have been abused go on to abuse.

One particular theoretical approach has been applied successfully to both wife beating and child abuse, namely **patriarchy**. Feminist commentators have identified the influence of the social structure in which such violence takes place. The concept of patriarchy reflects an understanding of the differential distribution of power based on gender differences. Thus it is men who hold and exercise power and ensure that other men inherit it. As an adjunct to this, it is men who define property status and value and, until relatively recently, it was only men who could own and inherit such property.

In regard to domestic violence, Jan Pahl (1985) maintains that violence directed towards wives is legitimized and interwoven into our culture at every level and has been so throughout history. Wife abuse has been traditionally accepted and applauded and, until the nineteenth century, British law gave a husband the right to beat his wife for lawful correction.

The explanation of wife beating must be placed into the context of the structural and ideological forces shaping relationships between men and women, both within marriage and in the wider society. Thus not only is wife beating legitimized, it becomes one of the symbols of masculinity and male dominance.

Pahl (1985) identifies a division between the public and the private spheres of life. Men, on the whole, function and relate to the public spheres while women at home are located within the private aspects of life. Domestic violence is differentiated from stranger violence because it is set in a location which is perceived as a haven of safety, and within a set of social relationships which are regarded as essentially private.

Men's structural power over women is paralleled in their power *vis-à-vis* children. Thus children experience similar expressions of powerlessness to women: child abuse occurs within the privacy of the home, and state intervention, whilst slightly more positive, has had an emphasis on maintaining the integrity of the family unit.

The parallels between wife beating and child abuse can be applied to the abuse of older people, in that a similar distinction is made between the public and private spheres, and with the recognition that older people are more vulnerable to stranger danger than to similar activities taking place within the home and undertaken by family members.

The exercise of male power enforces this distinction but is also directly responsible for the acts themselves and it is not unreasonable to account for the abuse undertaken by women within the realms of the exercise of this power. If we assume that male violence (in its broadest sense) is the socially accepted and legitimized mode of the exercise of power, then those who have been victims and witnessed the application of this power may, in turn, internalize such mechanisms and employ them on others who are more vulnerable than themselves (Albert Bandura (1973) comments that aggression is learnt).

The stress model would suggest that practitioners need to examine an abusive situation for stresses and attempt to relieve such pressure, either by assisting the perpetrator to redefine the perception of the activities regarded as stressful, by adopting different coping mechanisms or by service provision directed at the stressful components of the relationship.

Social exchange theory and symbolic interactionism would require practitioners to work with both parties in order to redefine the perception of the interaction involved. However, where the abused person experiences a dementing-type illness, or other processes which give rise to behavioural changes, advice, support and reassurance may assist in the redefinition of activities away from the purposeful and malevolent interpretation to one which reflects previous patterns of behaviour affected by an additional component such as dementia.

Whilst this has been a very brief exploration of the theoretical approaches that can be employed in examining and understanding the dynamics within relationships which may give rise to abuse, their relevance should not be understated.

INTERVENING IN ABUSIVE RELATIONSHIPS

A statutory duty to intervene in relationships where an older person is being abused, as presently exists with children who are abused, does not exist in Britain. The police have a remit where criminal activities have taken place, but this is mitigated by the nature of the witness, whether a complaint is made, the reliability of the evidence obtained and whether a prosecution is likely to be successful. However, a moral and professional duty may exist which directs medical and nursing staff and those employed by social services departments not to ignore such incidents but to work with other professionals, particularly with the abused person and, if possible, with the perpetrator.

A number of health authority and social services departments have compiled, or are in the process of compiling procedural guides which aim to advise and support staff working in potentially complex and difficult situations. Tameside Metropolitan Borough Council's Social Services Committee approved a notes of guidance and procedural guide in August 1992. This guide forms the basis of the work that social services staff will undertake with reported incidents of abuse. Tameside and Glossop Health Authority are also working to this document, and wide consultation has taken place with a range of voluntary organizations working within the Tameside area.

The Tameside document, in common with many similar approaches, is based on a number of principles which aim to inform the intervention and establish minimum standards of response to abusive or potentially abusive situations. Phillipson (1993) advises that four principles should guide the response.

1. Workers should be encouraged to be vigilant about the possibility of abuse/neglect, while being aware of the fact that there are no clear criteria for identifying abused elders and no good interventions that are totally acceptable to all parties involved.
2. Shared decision making is essential. Sharing should be conducted by involving a range of professional workers in developing a strategy for tackling abuse, and by ensuring that workers are supported in the decisions they make about protecting vulnerable elders.
3. Departments will need to develop policies which empower older people in situations where they are leading marginal lives. Policies for tackling abuse must, therefore, be concerned with advocacy and strengthening self-care abilities in old age.
4. The emphasis in work with all older people in private households and residential settings should be how to develop lives free of mistreatment. This means focusing on a variety of areas, of which activities with informal carers, the primary focus of the Department of Health Report, may be a relatively small part.

Eastman (1984) identifies six principles which he feels should guide intervention:

- abused person's right of self-determination;
- intervention should be as appropriate and as intensive as required;
- important to keep the family together;
- resources employed should be community based rather than relying on residential care;
- an avoidance of blame;
- adequate or inappropriate intervention wiser than none at all.

Tameside's approach recognizes some ten principles which should guide and inform the response to abusive situations. There is also a recognition that many of the principles may, in fact, conflict with other principles, and the guide attempts to assist staff in working through these.

1. Service user self-determination – reflects the essential aspects of working with adults, in that they are, on the whole, able to make their own decisions and should accept the repercussions of these decisions. There is, however, a need for practitioners to provide information about all the options which are available to that person in order that decision making can be as informed as possible.

2. Protection – may conflict with self-determination in that workers may require statutory intervention through the Mental Health Act (1983) or the police in order to stop abusive activities taking place, and thereby offer some protection to an abused person. In the case of physical assault, workers will have to address the need to stop someone abusing another person rather than maintain strict adherence to the principle of self-determination.

3. Joint-working – is a key aspect of Tameside's approach to many areas of service provision and forms an important aspect of the guidelines, not least because various professionals bring with them a body of professional knowledge which assists in checking out and interpreting the information being presented.

4. Shared decision making – should be associated with joint-working to ensure that decisions are owned by the various professionals who may be involved with a particular service user and carer. However, shared decision making should not exclude service users and carers who should be involved in the process from the start. The normal forum for sharing decisions is the case conference or care planning meeting.

5. An open and honest approach to service users and carers – involves not compounding abuse with further abuses, therefore it is important that workers are open with service users about why they are there, what their conclusions are and what they are going to do.

6. Accountability via line managers – is important when workers are engaging in difficult areas.

7. Staff support – is associated with accountability in that staff need to feel supported and be supported by their line management.

8. Managing conflicting principles – accountability and staff support should be able to assist workers in working through the difficult areas, such as self-determination and responsibility to the organization in which they are placed and protected.

9. Least disruptive alternative – should be used when planning intervention, which does not mean that residential care is not appropriate, but that it should not be used as a first reaction unless it is wholly appropriate to do so.

10. Whistle blowing – staff who report incidents of abuse by fellow workers should be supported.

These principles are reflected in the more detailed procedure which provides advice to workers about how to proceed through an investigation. Of central importance is the assessment process which seeks to gather information, analyse it and present conclusions upon which care planning and evaluative exercises may be based.

Assessments require practitioners to examine a range of areas of a person's life and situation. Michael Davies (1993) has suggested one such tool for nurses. An assessment should contain basic elements – details of physical and mental health and how they interact; the scope of a person's daily living skills and what assistance they require; social history, providing details of how the relationship has come together and pertinent events during the history; how the situation is perceived and the wishes of the service user and carer.

The National Health Service and Community Care Act (1990) places emphasis on the assessment process and in particular the needs of older people and their carers. The needs-led focus of the assessment requires that needs are addressed with specific attention to detail, and from this basis care planning can be approached.

Employing the stress model, attention should be given to those needs which are regarded as stressful, with care planning addressing these needs as a priority. In line with the principle of the least disruptive alternative, it is not good enough to flood an abusive situation with services, not least because, without careful analysis, such services may not address the specific stressors in any given situation and may, in fact, add to the general level of stress being experienced, as home-care workers, district nurses, etc. undertake tasks, and may disrupt an existing routine where the presence of others may, in fact, represent more stress.

THE LAW

It is not my purpose here to give a detailed outline of the legal remedies available to those working with abuse. This has been covered by Griffiths, Roberts and Williams (1993), but I will briefly examine some of the difficulties that workers dealing with abusive situations may find when engaging the law.

Many practitioners who have been involved with abusive situations have bemoaned the apparent lack of legal response open to them. In essence, much of this reflects the lack of availability of measures which are available to those working with child abuse, namely the Emergency Protective Order. Age Concern has proposed legislative change which would include an Emergency Intervention Order (Age Concern, 1986). The availability of such an order may not, in fact, assist workers in responding to abuse, and may complicate further an already complex area which is fraught with its own ethical and moral dilemmas.

In an excellent review of the legal situation in Britain, Griffiths, Roberts and Williams (1993) pose the question why 'little use is made of legal and/or quasi-legal processes as a means of protection and redress'. These processes already exist but are not widely employed, they argue, because of the:

- reluctance of victims to initiate legal process;
- presence of mental incapacity;
- fear of retaliation;
- way perpetrators are viewed;
- attitudes of professionals to legal procedures.

Associated with this minimal use of legal procedure is the manner in which abuse is conceptualized and categorized by professionals whose background rests either with a positivist medical model or with social welfare models. As a consequence, the language employed does not parallel that of the legal profession; in many instances the categories are broader than legal definitions and the burden of proof is less than for a criminal prosecution.

Some professionals have had difficulty getting to grips with the concept of abuse *per se*, and those that have may find it easier discussing sexual abuse rather than indecent assault, rape or incest. This mismatch of language does not assist medical and social welfare professionals engaging with the police. Add to this the prevalence of the situational stress model where perpetrators are perceived as victims, then engaging the law is a very low priority.

If professionals are to offer protection and/or redress to older people who have been abused, then there is a need for all concerned to work together side by side, developing a common language and minimizing the barriers which do exist between various professionals.

CONCLUSION

An enormously wide range of material has been presented in this chapter, some of which is contradictory. As more interest is generated in the subject, greater clarity will be applied, hopefully, to the main themes, which will further assist practitioners working with abuse. It is clear that the abuse directed towards any adult places practitioners in very stressful and complex situations. Employing all the available material and support should assist practitioners through this difficult but vitally important area, because the reality is that our service users, or patients, are living through intolerable events and should expect our full attention and complete professionalism.

REFERENCES

Age Concern (1986) *The Law and Vulnerable People*, Mitcham, Surrey.
Baker, A.A. (1975) Grannybattering. *Modern Geriatrics*, August, 20-24.

Bandura, A. (1973) *Aggression: A Social Leaning Analysis*, Prentice Hall, Englewood Cliffs, NJ.

Bennett, G. (1990) Report of interviews, in *Elder Abuse: An Exploratory Study*, (ed. G. McGreadie), Age Concern Institute of Gerontology, King's College, University of London, London.

Block, M.R. and Sinnott, J.D. (1979) The battered elderly syndrome: an explanatory study, in *Annual Review of Gerontology and Geriatrics*, (ed. C. Eisdorfer), Springer, New York, pp. 81–133.

Burston, G. (1975) Grannybattering. Letter to *British Medical Journal*, 6 September, 592.

Burston, G.R. (1977) Do your elderly patients live in fear of being battered? *Modern Geriatrics*, **7**(5), 54–5.

Butler, R.N. (1975) *Why Survive? Being Old in America*, Harper and Row, New York.

Chen, P.N., Bell, S., Dolinsky D. *et al.* (1981) Elderly abuse in domestic settings: a pilot study. *Journal of Gerontological Social Work*, **4**, 3–17.

Cloke, C. (1983) *Old Age Abuse in the Domestic Setting*, Age Concern, Mitcham, Surrey.

Crouse, J.S., Cobb, D.C., Harris, B.B. *et al.* (1981) *Abuse and Neglect of the Elderly in Illinois: Incidence and Characteristics, Legislation and Policy Recommendations*, University of Illinois.

Davies, M. (1993) Recognising abuse: an assessment tool for nurses, in *The Mis-Treatment of Elderly People*, (eds P. DeCalmer and F. Glendenning), Sage, London.

DeCalmer, P. and Glendenning, F. (1993) *The Mis-Treatment of Elderly People*, Sage, London.

Douglas, R.I., Hickey, T. and Noel, C. (1980) *A Study of Maltreatment of the Elderly and Other Vulnerable Adults*, Institute of Gerontology, University of Michigan.

Eastman, M. (1984) *Old Age Abuse*, Age Concern, Mitcham, Surrey.

Finklehor, D. and Pillemer, K.A. (1988) Elder abuse: its relation to other forms of domestic violence, in *Family Abuse and Its Consequences; New Directions in Research*, (ed. G.T. Hotaling), Sage, Beverly Hills, CA.

Fulmer, T. and O'Malley, T.A. (1987) *Inadequate Care of the Elderly*, Springer, New York.

Garborino, J. and Gilliam, G. (1980) *Understanding Abusive Families*, Lexington MA.

Gayford, J.J. (1976) Ten types of battered wives. *Welfare Officer*, **25**(1), 5–9.

General Household Survey (1985) HMSO, London.

Gioglio, G.R. and Blakemore, P. (1986) *Elder Abuse in New Jersey: The Knowledge and Experience of Abuse Among Older Jerseyans*, Department of Human Services, Tronton, NJ.

Giordano, N.H. and Giordano, J.H. (1983) Individual and family correlates of elder abuse. Paper presented to the American Sociological Association, Washington DC, quoted in Phillips (1986).

Giovannoni, J.M. (1982) Prevention of child abuse and neglect: research and policy issues. *Social Work Research and Abstracts*, **18** (3), pp. 23–31.

Goffman, E. (1962) *Stigma*, Prentice-Hall, Englewood Cliffs, New Jersey.

Griffiths, D., Roberts, G. and Williams, J. (1993) Elder abuse and the law, in *The Mis-Treatment of Elderly People*, (eds P. DeCalmer and F. Glendenning), Sage, London.

Hildrew, M.A. (1991) *Guidelines in Elder Abuse: Which Social Services Departments have Them?*, British Association of Social Workers, London.

Homer, A.C. and Gilleard, C. (1990) Abuse of elderly people by their carers. *British Medical Journal*, **301**, 1359–62.

Horrocks, P. (1988) Elderly people: abused and forgotten. *Health Service Journal*, 22 September, **1085**.

Hudson, M.F. (1989) Analysis of the concepts of elder mistreatment: abuse and neglect. *Journal of Elder Abuse and Neglect*, **1**, 1.

Isaacs, B. (1971) Geriatric families: do their families care? *British Medical Journal*, 30 October, 282–6.

Johnson, T.F. (1986) Critical issues in the definition of elder mistreatment, in *Elder Abuse: Conflict in the Family*, (eds K.A. Pillemer and R.S. Wolf), Auburn House Publishing Co., Dover, Mass.

Lau, E. and Kosberg, J.I. (1979) Abuse of the elderly by informal care providers. *Ageing*, **11**, 299–301.

McColl, G.J. and Simmons, J.L. (1966) *Identities and Interactions*, Free Press, New York.

McGreadie, C. (1991) *Elder Abuse: An Exploratory Study*, Age Concern Institute of Gerontology, King's College, University of London, London.

O'Malley, H.C., Segars, H.D. and Perez, R. (1979) *Elder Abuse in Massachusetts: Survey of Professionals and Paraprofessionals*, Boston Legal Research and Services to the Elderly.

Pahl, J. (1985) *Private Violence and Public Policy: The Needs of Battered Women and Response to the Public Sector*, Routledge and Kegan Paul, London.

Parton, N. (1985) *The Politics of Child Abuse*, Macmillan, London.

Phillips, L.R. (1986) Theoretical explanations of elder abuse: competing hypotheses and unresolved issues, in *Elder Abuse: Conflict in the Family*, (eds K.A. Pillemer and R.S. Wolf), Auburn House Publishing Co., Dover, Mass.

Phillipson, C. (1993) Abuse of older people: sociological perspectives, in *The Mis-treatment of Elderly People*, (eds P. DeCalmer and F. Glendenning), Sage, London.

Pillemer, K.A. and Sutor, J. (1988) Elder abuse, in *Handbook of Family Violence*, (eds V. Van Hassett *et al.*), Plenum, New York.

Pizzey, E. (1974) *Scream Quietly or the Neighbours Will Hear*, Penguin, Harmondsworth.

Pizzey, E. and Shapiro, J. (1982) *Prone to Violence*, Hamlyn, Rushton.

Podnieks, E. (1990) *National Survey on Abuse of the Elderly in Canada: The Ryerson Study*, Ryerson Polytechnical Institute, Toronto.

Quinn, M.J. and Tomita, S.K. (1986) *Elder Abuse and Neglect: Causes Diagnosis and Intervention Strategies*, Springer, New York.

Rathbone-McCuan,E. (1980) Elderly victims of family violence and neglect: social casework. *Journal of Contemporary Social Work*, May, 296–304.

Renvoize, J. (1978) Grannybashing, in *Web of Violence*, (ed. J. Renvoize), Routledge and Kegan Paul, London.

Sengstock, M.C. and Laing, J. (1982) Identifying and characterizing elder abuse. Unpublished manuscript, in *Neglect and Abuse: A Review of Literature*, (eds M.F. Hudson and F.F. Johnson).

Shell, D.J. (1988) Elder abuse: summary of results – Manitoba, in *Abuse of the Elderly: Issues and Annotated Bibliography*, (eds B. Schlesinger and R. Schlesinger), University of Toronto Press, Toronto.

Stevenson, O. (1989) *Age and Vulnerability,* Edward Arnold, London.

Storr, A. (1970) *Human Aggression*, Penguin, Harmondsworth.

Strauss, M.A. and Gelles, R.J. (1986) Societal change and changes in family violence from 1975 to 1985 as revealed by two national surveys. *Journal of Marriage and The Family*, **48**, 465–79.

Taler, G. and Ansello, E.F. (1985) Elder abuse. *Association of Family Physicians*, **32**(2), 107–14.

Tomlin, S. (1989) *Abuse of Elderly People: An Unnecessary and Preventable Problem*, British Geriatrics Society, London.

Valentine, D. and Cash, T. (1986) A definitional discussion of elder mistreatment. *Journal of Gerontological Social Work*, **9**(3), 17–28.

Wolf, R.S., Strugnell, C.P. and Godkin, M.A. (1982) *Preliminary Findings From Three Models Project on Elder Abuse*, University Center of Ageing, University of Massachussets.

FURTHER READING

Callahan, J. (1986) Guest editor's perspective. *Pride Institute Journal of Long Term Health Care*, **5**, 3.

Cicirelli, V.G. (1986) The helping relationship and family neglect in later life, in *Elder Abuse: Conflict in the Family*, (eds K.A. Pillemer and R.S. Wolf), Auburn House Publishing Co., Dover, Mass.

Pedrick Connell, C. and Gelles, R.G. (1985) *Intimate Violence in Families*, Sage, Beverly Hills.

Shell, D.J. (1982) *Protection of the Elderly: A Study of Elder Abuse*, Manitoba Association of Gerontology, Winnipeg.

13

Shaping the cutting edge: strategy development for nurse managers

Liz Matthew

SHARPENING THE SAW

Every nurse should have a vision. In my case it may be a world where health services always have enough money to spend, where the recognition of meeting needs with appropriate resources is top of the agenda. I have a vision of a world where being old is revered and where society has a positive view of mental health.

In reality the world is not like that, as life is turbulent and uncertain. All the time we are expected to take immediate action, but to do this we all must have an understanding of what we are trying to achieve. It is the very essence of leadership to have a vision. As Tom Peters points out: 'Effective visions are controls when all else is up for grabs' (Peters, 1987).

If you are a nurse who manages – whether a newly trained staff nurse or a nurse manager – you will need a clear view of the service in its broadest context. Not only will it give you guidance for leading and inspiring your own staff, it will give you a clear view of where you fit into the order of things.

No one says that putting a vision into practice is easy. There are a variety of complex influences which affect our life and work. There are those of the Government, the Minister of Health, society, the nurse, the client, the carer, the trust. All have varying degrees of power.

It is easy to explain away these influences as reasons for inaction – the Government's attitude, lack of money or an unsympathetic line manager. The most common reason given by nurses is that they do not have the time to take a strategic overview of their service. Their commitment is to the client first, and the pressure around the demands of front-line service allows no time for such luxuries.

Stephen Covey, an American management consultant, illustrates this attitude by an analogy to a woodcutter:

> Suppose you were to come upon someone in the woods working feverishly to saw down a tree.
>
> 'What are you doing?' you ask.
>
> 'Can't you see?' comes the impatient reply. 'I'm sawing down this tree.'
>
> 'You look exhausted!' you exclaim. 'How long have you been at it?'
>
> 'Over five hours,' he returns, 'and I'm beat! This is hard work.'
>
> 'Well, why don't you take a break for a few minutes and sharpen that saw?' you inquire. 'I'm sure it would go a lot faster.'
>
> 'I don't have time to sharpen the saw,' the man says emphatically. 'I'm too busy sawing!'
>
> *(Covey, 1992, p. 287)*

It is not uncommon to hear the view that most issues are beyond our control and that the major part of our time should be spent on providing high quality care. I would not disagree with the last part of this statement, but we all need to sit back and give ourselves time to think. Only then will we have some influence over the situation. We need to be able to recognize the influences of the world around us, and match them to our vision the best way we can.

George Bernard Shaw suggested that all progress depends on the unreasonable man. Whereas the reasonable man will adapt to the world, the unreasonable man expects the world to adapt to him. To progress we need to be unreasonable, we need to adapt the world to our vision.

In this chapter I will propose some practical ways of doing just that. I will suggest how to record the vision in a format that provides some practical guidance and that will be understood by line management, peers and staff. I will also be concerned with how to deal with change, since, as we progress, we are unable to avoid it.

STRATEGIC MANAGEMENT?

The first step will be to create a framework for the process. A recommended tool for such a framework is the strategic management model. Strategic management is concerned with how an organization goes about meeting its objectives. Its key elements are having an overview of the organization and a process which allows us to review and monitor what we are doing. The concept can and should be applied to a whole organization, such as a health authority or trust, or the same principles can be applied to a ward, day hospital or community mental health team.

To make the process easier to understand, it can be broken down into three logical steps. We need an overview of our present position, a knowledge of what options are open to us and finally how to implement the options we choose. The process can be summarized as in Figure 13.1.

Where are we now?
This will require a close look at services being provided, by asking key questions, such as: How successfully are we providing our service? If we are doing something well or badly, what are the reasons for this? What direction do we want our service to move in? How prepared are we to do this? What are our strengths and weaknesses, what opportunities do we have and what threats are there to our progress or even survival?

Where do we want to go?
This follows on by asking how realistic are our ideas for the future. How do we ensure that we have all relevant information from staff, clients and carers? What are our alternatives and how do we make the right choices, and, probably most importantly, how do we change these ideas into reality?

How will we make things work?
This examines how to introduce functional policies and relevant structures, and how to provide staff and systems which operate through a process of change.

WHERE ARE WE NOW? AN OVERVIEW OF OUR PRESENT POSITION

To make this process easier, we can break the examination down into three areas. The first is the context in which we work (social environment); the second is the resources that we have available; and the third is our own ways of working (our culture).

Environment

Nursing operates in a broad social context. There has been criticism in the past that nurses are 'locked into' a medical model of care, and that the social aspects of health care have generally been ignored. This has been less true in mental health, but it still needs stressing that the social aspects of care should be clearly understood. With the growth in partnership with other agencies and Care in the Community, care has changed from the health service being sole provider to being part of a mixed economy.

Government legislation has moved the focus on to the rights of the client and our accountability to them through initiatives such as the Patient's Charter. This

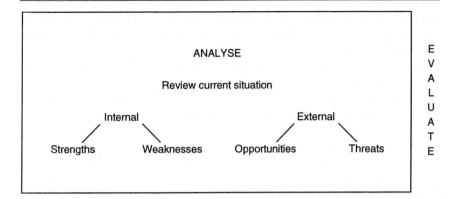

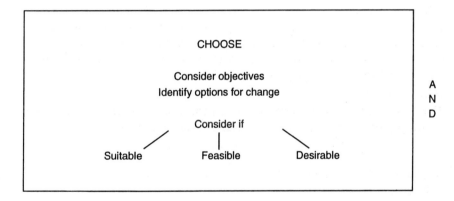

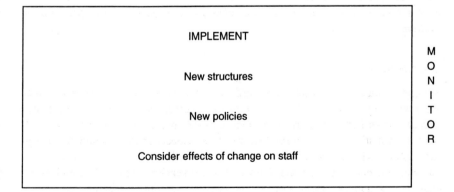

Figure 13.1 Process of strategic management

has resulted in an emphasis on the quality of services we are providing, and is particularly important for older people with mental health problems because, first, they often do not have the opportunity to articulate their view, and, secondly, the culture in which they were born and brought up may be in conflict with the culture of the care situation they find themselves in now.

It is clear that nurses do not work in isolation. They will need to take into account the views of a variety of individuals and groups with an interest in their particular area of service delivery. These people are commonly know as stakeholders (Freeman, 1984). Stakeholders will have varying levels of influence and power which may or may not be proportionate to the needs of the services or the nurses, organizational objectives.

It is of particular importance that we recognize the stakeholders in our service and are aware of the level of power and interest they have in the service. Figure 13.2 illustrates a method of recording stakeholders. A continuing care ward is used as an example.

First, think of everyone who has an interest in the service, then try and place them on a grid designed like the one opposite. In doing so we will need to recognize the level of power and interest they have. We may wish to change this position in future; for example I, myself, feel that it would be desirable for carers to have more power in future, so I have added an arrow to show the direction I would like them to move.

Not only will this exercise give an overview of the context of the service at the time, but it will identify areas where changes can be made. This will be useful when related to SWOT (strengths, weaknesses, opportunities and threats) analysis (see below), providing a visual guide to any changes required to achieve a chosen strategy.

Resources

Resources are bound to have a major effect on our service. There is increasing pressure to provide a more efficient service, so the appropriate use of resources deserves a closer look.

Operations

All operations should relate to standards, as standards are the basis of our working philosophy. They are the guidelines to define parameters of responsibility, and people should be clear about what is expected of them and what they are accountable for. They will range from drug procedures to key-worker responsibilities.

Look at the service standards in use. Who put them together? Were the staff involved? However they were created we need to check that everyone uses them as a working tool. This means everyone: day staff, night staff, ward clerks, consultants, carers and clients.

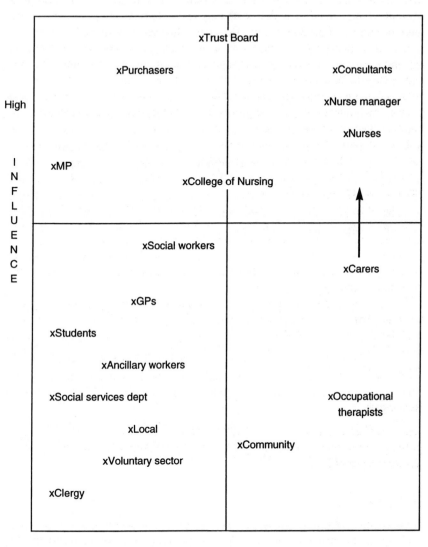

Figure 13.2 Influence and interest of service stakeholders

An effective and objective way of looking at how we measure up is to get someone else to do a mini-audit, someone who understands the context but is far enough away to be objective – the ward opposite, for example. There are pitfalls to this, however – your staff may feel defensive and perceive the exercise as being critical of their work (it is likely that you will find a lot of areas for improvement). The key to success is to develop a culture of openness and communication: an audit is not meant to be punitive but a bench mark for advancing good practice.

Professional standards also need scrutiny. Supervision sessions, both clinical and managerial, are ideal for checking how clear the lines of accountability are, and provide an opportunity to be sure that everyone is aware of where their own responsibilities and accountability lie. We need to assess how committed our staff are to their own development and how aware they are of current issues; for example, in acute medicine nurses would be expected to keep up to date with current drugs. Are your staff aware of the same issues in the care of older people, current thoughts on therapeutic interventions as well as current drugs and treatments, which still relate to their job?

People

Nursing staff are the most important (and most expensive) resource that we have. For this reason it is essential to evaluate their effectiveness across our whole area of responsibility.

Our first task should be to list the skills required in our service – again, make this an opportunity for staff involvement as this will make the process easier. It is tempting to look at the skills our staff already possess, but try instead to take the client point of view. What are their needs, and what skills do we have to meet them?

Now we can do an audit of our own staff skills, but we should not be surprised if they do not match. What will have been achieved is an overview, maybe for the first time, of where training and development are required.

Finance

Finance is an important driving force behind the service, but, at this point, the key question to ask is what areas of finance we have control over. We will find that these areas neatly fall into three categories: areas where we have no control; those where we need to make a case; and those where we have responsibility for budgets. Do not waste time worrying about those areas where we cannot influence the situation (although when the objectives exercise below is completed, there will probably be fewer than expected).

In areas where it is necessary to make a case, examine past experience. It is difficult to give guidelines on obtaining finance as methods vary and local conditions and opportunities are so different. Were the right people approached? Was this done in the appropriate way? What were the areas of success?

With budgets for which we have responsibility, again look at past experience. Have we adequate control over spending? In what areas were we overspent/ underspent and why?

Information

People do not usually think of information as a resource since the processes of information collection and dissemination are usually taken for granted.

The more information we have about what is going on in the organization, the more prepared will be our own planning. Information provides the context in which we work, the right information in the right place at the right time is bound to affect decision making, and it allows the generation and evaluation of alternative courses of action.

Look around at our own information systems. How do we communicate? Is a lot of information passed formally, through team briefing and memos? How do these relate to formal communication, such as meetings? How important is informal discussion? How is adequate communication from the bottom up ensured?

Culture

The culture of an organization is illustrated in the way people perform tasks, the way they think and feel at work, and even what kind of people are recruited to the job. We will need a clear idea of the culture of an organization to understand the level of initiative people will take or how they will react to change.

Nursing has been very much a role-based profession. It is a job built around defined rules and procedures. People fit into jobs and are recruited for that purpose; it is meant to be rational, stable and predictable. This is not a criticism; for it to function properly, it is important that people are clear about their role and parameters of decision making. It is a system designed to be efficient in a stable environment.

Charles Handy (1976), a professor in Management Studies, defined this type of culture as being like a Greek temple. He used this analogy because he felt that the strength of the organization lay in its pillars which are joined managerially at the top, this being where the power lies.

Things are changing, however. New ways of working are making it more important to use a variety of methods. Now, we not only deliver directly but through partnerships. Our core staff work in other environments, we in turn have people working with us. We expect people to more involved in setting agendas rather than simply working to them.

This means that we will have to look more closely at the boundaries of people's jobs and, to get the best out of them, consider what they have to do and what they can and cannot do. This gives the parameters needed for flexibility within a job. There will always be an outer boundary which people cannot pass, and within that there will be certain areas which are strictly defined in great detail. On the other hand, there are areas which are 'softer' within these boundaries and allow for some flexibility.

Imagine an analogy with a box of chocolates, with the chocolate covering marking the boundaries of the job and the fillings representing the hard core elements and the softer flexible areas of the job.

- The caramel
  The caramel job would be almost all core work, bounded by the parameters of its chocolate cover. Nearly all of the work would be directed by strict adherence to very specific guidelines and there would be limited room for manoeuvre. Typical caramel jobs might be ward manager, nursing assistant or ward clerk.
- The cherry cup
  The cherry cup job has a hard centre, perhaps not as hard as the caramel but certainly distinguishable from the fluidity of the 'liquid' around it. It, too, has a clear, hard chocolate boundary. Typical cherry cup jobs might be the community psychiatric nurse or the social worker.
- The coffee cream
  The coffee cream job is almost all soft centre, but still with a hard chocolate boundary. A typical coffee cream job might be arts/creative therapist.

We need to look closely at our own 'chocolate box' of staff mix to see how it matches up to the challenges of the new culture. Remember that boundaries between soft, hard and the parameters are negotiable. We cannot assume, however, that everyone will share the same perception of their boundaries. Joint-working will bring in different cultures, for example from social services departments or volunteers, so we must spend time exploring the culture which people bring with them.

The strategic mix

A clear strategy will rely on planning which takes into account the balance between the areas of environment, resources and values.

Thompson (1993, p. 15) suggests that the greater the areas in which these three overlap (the E-V-R congruence), the more effective will be the organization.

It is also important, therefore, that the values of the organization match the needs of the environment and the key success factors. It is the values and culture which determine whether the environment and resources are currently matched, and whether they stay congruent in changing circumstances.

The SWOT analysis

A more structured method of examining these areas, particularly the resources and environment elements, is the SWOT analysis. SWOT stands for 'strengths, weaknesses, opportunities and threats'. Strengths and weaknesses should relate to the resources of the ward, day hospital, etc., whilst the opportunities and threats relate to the environment.

Under these headings, we list everything relating to our service in the area of work for which we are responsible, taking into account the pointers listed above.

As this is a brainstorming exercise, it will be useful to involve others, because the broader the input and views, the better the quality of the insight gained. For example, a day hospital brainstorm might come up with the following:

FACTORS RELATING TO INTERNAL INFLUENCES (RESOURCES)

Strengths

- offers wide range of service/skill mix
- base for broad staff mix in one building
- building specially adapted to meet client needs
- services cater for both individual and group needs
- provides treatment without hospitalization
- allows client to stay within home environment.

Weaknesses

- limited opening times
- opening times are service- not client-led
- underutilized as a resource
- often too big
- not always locally based within client's own community
- clients rely on transport to get there.

FACTORS RELATING TO EXTERNAL INFLUENCES (ENVIRONMENT)

Opportunities

- promotion of building for complementary use
- use of facilities at weekends.
- use of facilities for short stay for carers' special events (e.g. hairdresser, wedding)
- use on a sessional basis

- increase community 'ownership' (visits from schools, etc.) to avoid stereotyping.

Threats

- could be provided by others (more cheaply?)
- cost implications (lack of funding)
- boundaries not clear between day hospital and day care
- staff skills/professionalism not defined clearly enough (other people being
asked to do the job)
- ageist view of society (who should/should not care for its older people).

Having got so far, we should now have a clear overview of the position of
our service. The next question to ask is where do we want to go?

WHERE DO WE WANT TO GO? STRATEGIC CHOICE

It almost goes without saying that an organization should know exactly what
business it is in and ensure that all its activities are concentrated to this end. It
could also be said that the activities of nursing are obvious. Despite this, there is
still a need for a clarity which is tangible and can be measured. Generalizations,
such as 'we are in the business of patient care', need some elaboration. What
kind of patient care? Who is it aimed at? How is it delivered? It is this logical
movement from the general to the particular which characterizes the objective-
setting process.

The objective-setting process starts with a mission statement which is
concerned with a broad general overview of the direction of the service. From
this, we will need to identify particular ways in which this general principle is
put into practice. This is the function of the objectives.

As an illustration, I have used the Mission Statement and Objectives of
Tameside Community and Priority Services Trust, my employer.

Mission Statement

The Community and Priority Services Trust will provide high quality and
cost effective services in a reassuring environment to the people of
Tameside and Glossop. It will concentrate on preventing illness, promoting good health and providing treatment and care which meet the unique
health care needs of the local population.

Objectives

- ensuring that the NHS and the Community Care Act 1990 and the
Children Act 1989 are smoothly implemented and evaluated;

- working closely with all purchasing agencies, in order to meet local health needs and achieve the goals of the *Health of the Nation* and the *Patient's Charter*;
- developing further the integration of primary and secondary care.

Care in the community will remain the guiding principle of the Trust.

(Tameside and Glossop Community and Priority Services, 1993)

There are other objectives than those above, but they are enough for the purposes of illustration. A mission statement provides the opportunity to talk about the values of an organization; for example, the illustration above uses words like 'quality', 'cost-effectiveness', 'preventing' [illness], 'reassuring', 'unique' and 'local'.

The mission statement, however, will not tell you how things will be done; that is the role of objectives. An objective should be easily recognizable from the fact that it can be measured; for example, it would be easy to recognize if you had achieved the last objective (see above), i.e. 'developing further the integration of primary and secondary care'. We need only measure progress from one particular point to another.

This brings us to the next element of objective setting, and that is monitoring performance. If something can be measured, then targets can be set for achieving it, and these can be very specific. Let us look at another example. A joint care planning team for elderly services in the community has set itself the following objectives:

- to help maintain older people in their own homes;
- to recognize personal choice in meeting client needs;
- to facilitate access to appropriate services for the individual;
- to develop more effective joint planning.

All these objectives are measurable. They should cover the scope of the work of the team, but if they do not, there are two explanations: either the team is wasting its time in areas it should not be involved in, or a key element of work is missing from the objectives. This process of refining, then, focuses the mind. As an exercise it has practical implications. Sometimes it can raise questions about the fundamental nature of the work schedule, which will have to be addressed.

Objectives, although more practical, do not give us the degree of detail we require for an individual work plan. But we can break them down further. Taking the last objective above – to develop more effective joint planning – imagine that a meeting was held to focus on how this could be done. Some suggestions might be:

- a more formal means of communication is required, e.g. individual planning and review meetings;
- appropriate people to involve in the team;
- provision of training sessions;

- informal methods of communication;
- working with other agencies with similar aims to ourselves.

The results of this meeting might highlight two things: first, a logical order of doing things is appearing, i.e. some things should be done before others; and, secondly, some things are too general to be identified as tasks.

This leads on to defining specific projects within these objectives – known as targets. In our example, these might be:

Objective: to develop more effective joint planning

Targets:

(i)   to carry out an audit of potential partners for joint-working and assess the relevance to the team's work;
(ii) to set up and implement an effective process of planning and review;
(iii) to set up and implement an effective method of communication;
(iv) to introduce a relevant training and development plan for the team.

These targets cover all the areas mentioned in the brainstorm, but they are now more specific – we are not suggesting just training, but a **relevant** training and a **development plan**.

Now that we have a more detailed 'feel' of the objectives, we should be able to come up with some way of measuring them. Having used the word 'effective', we would expect to see some effect, a change to the current situation, hopefully for the better. This is because the interest should be in outcomes rather than process. We may set up an efficient system of weekly meetings with all the relevant partners, but we will only have been successful if the planning is actually better.

Finally, the degree of detail teased out can be expanded further – the logic progression talked about earlier, to look at milestones (measures along the way), who will be involved and what costs there are, if any. To illustrate this, consider the following example:

Target	To introduce a relevant training and development plan for the team
Milestones	Identify relevant training needs
	Discuss support and availability with training officer
	Write paper on strategy
	Implement training sessions
	Review training
Staff	Jim Jones, social work (lead); June Jackson (CPN); others as appropriate
	Laura Lee (training officer)
Resources	Jim Jones, June Jackson (2-weekly meeting)
	£1000 training course fees, room booking, etc. (estimated)
Timescale	January–October 1995

It is clear that the detail of the exercise has led us into a detailed work plan of who does what, where, when and how. It has also brought us to the area of accountability. If work does not progress (or progresses well), it is clear who is responsible.

Making the right choice

What constitutes a good choice on the right way forward? As one might expect, there is no right answer. What is appropriate depends very much on the circumstances at the time. There are, however, some guidelines to follow when making a choice. Three areas are generally agreed to be important, although they are not mutually exclusive – suitability, feasibility and acceptability.

Suitability

The clue to the suitability of a particular course of action will be in the SWOT analysis. How far will it overcome the problem areas (weaknesses and threats)? What advantages does it exploit (opportunities and strengths)?

Do not forget to check it against your objectives, and be sure it actually improves things. Change for change's sake might give the impression of moving on, but is unlikely to be of value unless it has a positive impact. Check as well that the skill mix will be adequate for the intended proposal. Will there be the right combination of 'hard' and 'soft' jobs?

Most importantly, is the plan clear enough to be communicated for people to understand it and, hopefully, be supportive of it?

Feasibility

How feasible a project is depends on a variety of factors, the most important being the availability of finance. Additionally, it can only be successful if it reaches the standards required around quality. These again will depend upon the situation, but may include Patient's Charter standards, operational policies and quality assurance programmes.

Is the time right for this particular initiative? Some times are obviously better than others. Finally, it is also important to recognize that strategies for change do not have to be 'one off', large-scale initiatives. In many cases incremental change is much more effective.

Desirability

Stakeholders and staff will need to understand and, hopefully, be supportive of any change. This is where we need to consider our stakeholder chart (Fig. 13.2) and test out whether there are likely to be any changes in relationships with them.

Internally, we will need to consider whether or not existing systems will need to be altered to accommodate our new structures and, most importantly of all, we need to ensure that the change is capable of being implemented smoothly.

IMPLEMENTING CHANGE

Unless we already have an almost perfect strategy in operation, we are bound to be involved in examining new ways of working. It is impossible to avoid the effects of change. The important issue is whether we are prepared for change or try to ignore it.

Effects of change

Charles Handy, in his book *The Age of Unreason*, relates two stories about change.

> I like the story of the Peruvian Indians who, seeing the sails of their Spanish invaders on the horizon put it down to a freak of the weather and went on about their business, having no concept of sailing ships in their limited experience. Assuming continuity, they screened out what did not fit and let disaster in. I like less the story that a frog, if put in cold water, will not bestir itself if that water is heated up slowly and gradually and will in the end let itself be boiled alive, too comfortable with continuity to realize that continuous change at some point becomes discontinuous and demands a change in behaviour.
>
> *(Handy, 1989, pp. 7–8)*

There are lessons for nurses here. When the Griffiths Report (1983) was published, it aimed to limit public responsibilities for the provision of care services and to encourage the growth of the mixed economy of care, particularly the provision by commercial and voluntary services. This was not surprising in view of Government philosophy of the time, which identified its mission as moving from bureaucratic centralism to regulated pluralism.

But, like Peruvian Indians, most nurses on the front line of care dismissed these 'sails of Spanish invaders', because they failed to recognize the influence that this would have on them. This probably overstates the case. Perhaps they did recognize the new environment which would be created but felt powerless to influence, react or use positively the opportunities provided. Like frogs, they continue delivering front-line patient care and are in danger of being boiled into irrelevance.

This does not have to be the case. Nurses have a place in being part of the solution, by being able to influence the agenda into moving towards a positive model of patient care. Although it should be recognized that the external environment often initiates change, the individual within the organization has the ability to affect its implication. This is brought about by two factors. First, by creating an environment of acceptable challenge to the *status quo* and, secondly, by having the power to influence decisions.

Implementing change can be particularly traumatic, and it is worth some discussion around the best ways of achieving this. These strategies are relevant to all situations in which change is necessary. First, it is worth considering the responses of different levels of staff. Let us assume the nursing management has decided to implement a change of ward sister.

Figure 13.3 Levels of staff

Figure 13.3 illustrates who will feel the most pressure. The staff nurse will be under pressure from management to implement something practical. Front-line staff are likely to be resistant to change and their resentment will be targeted towards their manager. Remember, then, that the sandwich we create will put pressure on our own 'middle management'.

This illustrates the value of one basic principle of change, i.e. involve people.

Involve people

It is apparent that people who are involved in planning a change are less likely to be resistant to it. This is why it is crucial to involve people from the earliest possible moment. It is quite easy to fall into the trap of a 'need to know' model, where colleagues whose opinions or ideas you value are the only ones involved in planning. Although this is a move in the right direction, unless you communicate with everyone they will not be inclined to 'own' any changes you make. This does not mean you have to take on board everyone's ideas – it is quite acceptable to state what is open to negotiation.

Train for new values and work methods

It is easy to assume, especially if we have been personally involved in introducing new ideas, that everyone has as clear an idea as ourselves about the value system behind the change. It is also likely that new systems and procedures will be introduced, and training should be given for these.

When setting out a new strategy for change, it is quite common not to have thought everything through in detail. A common criticism from front-line workers is that what to them are core tasks have been overlooked. This does little for a manager's credibility, but it can be put to positive use. Of course, one cannot think of everything, but by creating an environment where people can contribute to the change in a context of openness we will be using people's skills appropriately. It is important also not to be too defensive: it is not our job to think of everything, but to ensure that everything is covered and taken on by those who have the most appropriate skills. These strategies will have a much broader pay-off; they will encourage teamwork, and that in itself will increase commitment.

Establish symbols of change

If lucky enough to be involved in major upgrades of service, such as refurbishments or opening a new ward, it will be quite clear that something different is happening. This is the ideal time for implementing new strategies, as staff will be in a mental 'change' mode.

In most cases the change will not be so visibly obvious, so it may be necessary to introduce some symbols of change – new styles and formats for new paperwork routines, for example. A more detailed description of the practical implementation of change in a clinical setting is included elsewhere in this book.

Whatever else change requires, it should be stressed that the most important factor in achieving practical success is strong leadership. Change requires someone to be its champion. They must keep things moving when all others are immersed in practicalities, and ensure a continuous enthusiasm for the change itself.

This brings us full circle by recognizing the importance of a strong and all-embracing vision.

SOME CONCLUSIONS

Working on behalf of older people with mental health problems is not an easy task. If the situation is analysed carefully, it will be recognized that many of the factors affecting this area of work relate to broad perceptions, that the specific cannot be tackled without a clear understanding of the general.

We can advise nurses how to deal with a client through the guidance of a specific procedure, but, if they have not a broader understanding of the factors surrounding that client, the factors which make up that person and the standard of care to which they are entitled, then they will be unable to provide a service of an acceptable quality.

This process of standing back is particularly important in dealing with older people and their mental health problems, as it is becoming clear that there are increased options of care available, options that vary in the quality of their delivery, standards and resources.

Standing back is not easy; it is a discipline to be learnt, but, like the analogy of the woodcutter sharpening his saw at the beginning of this chapter, it is well worth the investment.

As nurses we have more control over events than we think. It is easy to react but not very effective; reacting is accepting someone else's agenda. If we take time to consider the situation, there is always more than one option open.

Although the context in which we work is complex, it is still possible to influence where our service is going and to introduce some practical methods of ensuring that it gets there. Strategic management is a useful tool in developing this process. It is certainly more complex than can be examined here, but it is intended as a framework with a logical progression for analysis, consideration, implementation and review.

It also has the advantage of not necessarily being a cyclic process. A SWOT analysis can be done any time. We can develop different areas at different speeds in different contexts; after all that is how things work in real life. However, it is vital to have a vision, a clear overview, which can be communicated to others.

As a last exercise, imagine that the service we provide is 'up for grabs'. Let us assume it is to be put out to tender to a whole host of other agencies and organizations. Can we sell it now? Can we provide a strategic view of the services? Do we know its strengths, weaknesses, opportunities and threats? Do we know its major stakeholders and how influential they are? Do we know what options for development we could or could not pursue? Do we know what performance measures purchasers would be looking for? How would we measure a good service?

If we can do all that, then we are in a strong position to develop a high quality service for our clients. We have found a way of putting our vision into practice!

Good luck!

REFERENCES

Covey, S.R. (1992) *The Seven Habits of Highly Effective People,* Simon & Schuster, London, p. 287.
Freeman, R.E. (1984) *Strategic Management: A Stakeholder Approach*, Pitman, London.
Griffiths, R. (1983) *NHS Management Enquiry*, Department of Health, London.
Handy, C.B. (1976) *Understanding Organizations*, Penguin, London.
Handy, C.B. (1989) *The Age of Unreason*, Business Books, London.
Peters, T. (1987) *Thriving on Chaos*, Pan, London, p. 403.

Tameside and Glossop Community and Priority Services (1993) An application for NHS Trust status. Tameside and Glossop Community and Priority Services, Ashton-under-Lyne.

Thompson, J.L. (1993) *Strategic Management: Awareness and Change*, 2nd edn, Chapman & Hall, London.

Index